FACILITATING INTERGROUP DIALOGUES

FACILITATING

INTERGROUP DIALOGUES

Bridging Differences, Catalyzing Change

Edited by
Kelly E. Maxwell,
Biren (Ratnesh) A. Nagda,
and Monita C. Thompson

Foreword by Patricia Gurin

STERLING, VIRGINIA

COPYRIGHT © 2011 BY
STYLUS PUBLISHING, LLC.

Published by Stylus Publishing, LLC
22883 Quicksilver Drive
Sterling, Virginia 20166-2102

Library of Congress Cataloging-in-Publication Data

Facilitating intergroup dialogues : bridging differences,
catalyzing change / edited by Kelly E. Maxwell,
Biren (Ratnesh) A. Nagda, and Monita C. Thompson ;
foreword by Patricia Gurin.
       p.   cm.
    Includes bibliographical references and index.
    ISBN 978-1-57922-290-1 (cloth : alk. paper) –
ISBN 978-1-57922-291-8 (pbk. : alk. paper)
    1. Communication in education.   2. Interpersonal
communication.   3. Intercultural communication.
4. Group facilitation.   5. Group relations training.
6. Educational change.   I. Maxwell, Kelly E., 1970–
II. Nagda, Biren (Ratnesh) A., 1965–   III. Thompson,
Monita C., 1960–   IV. Gurin, Patricia.
    LB1033.5.F33 2011
    378′.017–dc22   2010022468

13-digit ISBN: 978-1-57922-290-1 (cloth)
13-digit ISBN: 978-1-57922-291-8 (paper)

Printed in the United States of America

All first editions printed on acid free paper
that meets the American National Standards Institute
Z39-48 Standard.

Bulk Purchases

Quantity discounts are available for use in workshops
and for staff development.
Call 1-800-232-0223

First Edition, 2011

to all teachers who came before us and planted the seeds for our learning;
to our students past and present from whom we continue to learn;
to teachers-learners still to come who will give birth to newer ideas and practices.

for my son, Jackson, who inspires me to work for a world where dialogue, not war, is
the catalyst for social change.

—Kelly

for all my relations—parents, sisters, spiritual guides, and beloved friends—with
whom I celebrate our lessons of *satyagraha, harambee, ubuntu,* and *social healing.*

—Ratnesh

for my parents, William and Corinne, and my nieces and nephews, Jermall, Shanna,
Kadija, Ibrahim, and Jonathan—you are my teachers.

—Monita

CONTENTS

ACKNOWLEDGMENTS

The period of racial tensions at the University of Michigan campus and other campuses nationwide in the mid-1980s brought home the need for higher education institutions to openly and honestly grapple with the issues of identity, difference, and inequality. From the 1954 *Brown v. Board of Education of Topeka, Kansas* to the 1965 Civil Rights legislation, the issues of access, opportunities, and rights for all peoples are responsibilities that we have all inherited. The intergroup tensions on campus in the 1980s brought forth the reality of dreams and promises not yet fulfilled. Rather than seeing these as passing trends and tensions located simply among some individuals or in small pockets of campus, administrators at the University of Michigan saw this as a wake-up call to think deeply about the role of higher education in constructively addressing the issues of diversity and democracy. At Michigan, specifically, student activism and administrative vision led the then-President James Duderstadt to craft the *Michigan Mandate* that recognized diversity as an institutional value. It was a catalyst for faculty, staff, and students to actualize this value through the daily work of academic and student affairs.

Our work on intergroup dialogue and formalizing intergroup dialogue facilitation was borne out of this vision and responsibility. Based on commitments to dialogic and empowering education, student leadership, and multicultural communities, progressive faculty and staff conceived of ideas to engage students to learn about intergroup conflicts in constructive ways and to develop capacities to be responsible participants in building socially just communities. The founding of the Program on Conflict Management Alternatives (PCMA) with funding from the William and Flora Hewlett Foundation, and its affiliate, The Program on Intergroup Relations and Conflict (IGRC; now The Program on Intergroup Relations), provided vehicles for interdisciplinary faculty collaborations on scholarship and teaching about intergroup conflict and social change.

We pay tribute to the seven founders of The Program on Intergroup Relations (IGR) at the University of Michigan: Mark Chesler, Patricia Gurin, Ratnesh Nagda, David Schoem, Todd Sevig, Luis Sfeir-Younis, and Ximena Zúñiga. We are indebted to their foresight and honored that they continue to be part of our professional and personal lives. Over the last two decades, many alumni and admirers of IGR have started their own programs at different universities and colleges across the United States. We are thankful to be part of a larger movement that seeks to honor, not erase, differences; build bridges, not divides; and catalyze change and responsibility for the greater good, not just individual benefit.

Our deep gratitude to colleagues and associates of the Intergroup Dialogue, Education and Action (IDEA) Center at the University of Washington. Professors Mary Lou Balassone, Stan de Mello, and Sue Sohng, Associate Dean Margaret Spearmon, and Dean Edwina Uehara were all key in initiating intergroup dialogue efforts at Washington. Akua Campanella, Amelia Seraphia Derr, Scott Harding, Dominique Moise-Swanson and Norma Timbang are among graduate students who have worked long term with the IDEA Center. Through what we sometimes refer to as action teaching, their collaboration has strengthened the work of intergroup dialogue facilitation. Many of our undergraduate and graduate facilitators are now social justice workers who are translating intergroup dialogue principles to social work practices in their own spheres of responsibilities. Their visions and creativity inspire the work we do in the academy. Our South African partners Clem Van Wyk and Glenda Wildschut, formerly of the Desmond Tutu Peace Center, and now with the Global Development for Peace and Leadership and Collective Leadership Institute, have expanded intergroup dialogue work with youth in South Africa and other countries. Their dedication and perseverance remind us of the importance of sustained dialogue in places where conflict is as much a part of the daily social fabric as community, and how young people as emerging leaders are crucial to actualizing justice and democracy.

Our sincere appreciation and thanks to the faculty and staff of the IGR at the University of Michigan for their support of this project: Mark Chesler, Adrienne Dessel, Rebecca Grekin, Patricia Gurin, Josephine Li, Xinyan Mitchell, Joseph Person, Taryn Petryk, Robin (Robbie) Routenberg, Nita Shah, Toshia Watkins and Jennifer Yim, all of whom supported this project unconditionally and contribute to students' learning and growth each and every day. All of the IGR staff create the solid foundation for intergroup and social justice education work. They have enriched our work and our personal lives immeasurably. We have special appreciation for Charles Behling, who led IGR for many years and remains committed and involved, even in retirement. Special thanks also to Roger Fisher for his untiring efforts to expand our knowledge and reach beyond higher education. We are also so thankful for our intergroup dialogue facilitators who were transformed through the facilitation process and, in turn, changed our lives for the better.

We are grateful to our dear colleagues across the world who are engaged in facilitation, dialogue, and deliberation. We continue to be inspired by their dedication to promote peace and justice in higher education, communities, and social institutions locally and globally. We are fortunate to have some of them as chapter authors, without whom this book would not have been possible. They have provided us with valuable knowledge and insight through their work and many consultations.

We owe profound thanks to administrators who have believed in and supported intergroup dialogue over the many years. At the University of Michigan, we especially thank E. Royster Harper, Vice President for Student Affairs, and Evans Young, Assistant Dean for Undergraduate Education. At the University of Washington, we thank Edwina Uehara, Dean of the School of Social Work; Nancy Hooyman, former Dean of the School of Social Work; and Debra Friedman, former Associate Vice Provost. They have all supported our programs in many ways and made it possible for us to continue providing students with transformative intergroup dialogue experiences.

To our copy editor, Bridget Laundra, many, many thanks for her suggestions and expedient work, especially with the tight deadlines.

Finally, to John von Knorring and the staff at Stylus Publishing, who exhibited much patience throughout the process. Thanks ever so much for believing in this book.

The Supreme Court ruled in *Grutter v. Bollinger* (2003) that educational benefits of racial diversity provide a compelling governmental interest that justifies the use of race as one of many factors in student admission to higher education institutions. A critical question that emerged from the Court's 2003 majority opinion supporting the University of Michigan's claim about the value of diversity is: What kind of education leverages the potential of diversity to produce educational benefits for all students? Evidence presented to the Court and research conducted since have made clear that if diversity is to have educational benefits, colleges and universities need to make full use of it as an institutional resource (Gurin, Dey, Hurtado, & Gurin, 2002; Milem, Chang, & Antonio, 2005). Colleges and universities have to create academic initiatives that engage students in learning from each other, considering multiple perspectives, and collaborating across differences. Intergroup dialogues (IGD), which have been offered at some institutions since the early 1990s and have increased in number and vitality in recent years, are one such initiative.

Intergroup dialogues aim to help students gain intergroup understanding, increase positive intergroup relationships, and promote intergroup collaboration (Nagda, Gurin, Sorensen, & Zúñiga, 2009). They do that by utilizing an explicit pedagogy that involves three important features: content learning, structured interaction, and facilitative guidance. *Content learning* refers to ways in which students are intellectually involved in learning course material. Intergroup dialogues use readings and written assignments to engage students in active learning. *Structured interaction* is the intentional creation of group learning across differences. Interaction is structured so that each dialogue comprises equal numbers of students from each identity group, thereby encouraging equal status that Allport (1954) considered crucial for positive intergroup contact. It is also structured with active learning activities that integrate readings with sharing, listening, and reflection. The third feature, the focus of this book, is *facilitative guidance.* Because students may replicate the dynamics that often exist in the wider society between high- and low-power groups when they interact in courses and in campus organizations, facilitators have to recognize those dynamics and guide students to recognize and alter them as well (Nagda, Gurin, Sorensen, & Coombes, 2009).

As is evident in the chapters of this book, facilitative guidance is crucial to the success of intergroup dialogue, whatever model of facilitation a program adopts. Some models utilize peer facilitators, others professional staff and faculty. Training of facilitators is carried out differently across the models described in the book. Yet, across these models there are remarkable commonalities in what facilitators are supposed to accomplish. They help create an inclusive space for dialogue. They model dialogic communication and an equal relationship between themselves as a team. They pay keen attention to the dialogue group's dynamics, making sure that all students participate. They normalize conflicts and disagreements as expected aspects of intergroup life, and they stress that students will learn more from each other when they leave what students call "their comfort zones." They help students cope with complex emotions and motivations for intergroup interaction. They contextualize thoughts and feelings that are expressed in the dialogue within the context of power dynamics that the readings and in-class interactions both illustrate.

During the past five years, collaborators from nine universities carried out a rigorous evaluation of intergroup dialogue in which the importance of facilitation was repeatedly demonstrated. This study included 52 experiments pairing either a race or gender intergroup dialogue with a wait-list control group. Students were assigned randomly from applicants either to a race or gender dialogue course or to a race or gender control group, thereby ensuring that any effects that were demonstrated by greater change among students in the dialogue courses could actually be attributed to the dialogue experience. This feature of the design controls the possibility that students motivated to engage in intergroup dialogue might change over the course of the semester *even without being in a dialogue course.* The results are impressive. Students in both race and gender dialogue courses increased in intergroup understanding, positive intergroup relationships, and commitment to intergroup action significantly more than the students in the control groups. Moreover, change was still significantly greater among dialogue than control group students a year later (Gurin, Nagda, & Zúñiga, in press; Nagda et al., 2009; Sorensen, Nagda, Gurin, & Maxwell, 2009).

What is most important for this book on facilitation is the role that facilitators played in that study in explaining the positive impact of intergroup dialogue. Evidence of the importance of facilitators was demonstrated both in quantitative analyses of the survey data that provided measures of change and in qualitative analyses of the final papers that the students in the dialogue courses wrote. Facilitators and structured interaction were connected, as predicted, to four communication processes: (1) engaging self, (2) critical reflection, (3) appreciating difference, and (4) building alliances (see Nagda, 2006, and chapter 1 in this book for a discussion of the communication processes). Together, facilitators, structured interaction, and the communication processes were related to three sets of psychological processes: (1) increased cognitive openness (active thinking and consideration of multiple perspectives), (2) increased positivity in intergroup interactions (positive emotions and more personal and positive interactions), and (3) greater centrality and involvement in group identity. These psychological processes then helped explain the impact of dialogue on intergroup understanding, intergroup empathy, and intergroup action (Gurin et al., forthcoming).

Students also wrote in their final papers about the importance of facilitators in their learning. They especially stressed how facilitators reminded them to speak from personal experience without generalizing to groups of people, how facilitators encouraged them to take ownership of their own learning, how facilitators helped them take risks by revealing their fears and ignorance about the lives of people who had grown up in different economic and social situations, and how they supported the expression of opinions that might or might not conform to those of other students so everyone learned to understand each other and *why* students might hold different perspectives. Students also noted that facilitators made group dynamics transparent by naming what they observed happening in the dialogue and intervening when dominance and inequalities that often characterize intergroup relationships in the wider society became evident in the dialogue as well.

Throughout this book the authors describe these kinds of facilitator behaviors and delineate how training prepares facilitators to help ensure that intergroup dialogue achieves its aims. The role of facilitators could not be more important in light of recent research in social psychology that has revealed both positive and negative outcomes of intergroup contact. Intergroup dialogue, which in the most basic sense is a particular kind of intergroup contact, will benefit greatly by focusing on what this research implies for the training of facilitators. To be sure, there is a major difference between intergroup dialogue and most of the contact situations on which this research is based. Intergroup dialogue involves *sustained and guided contact*, whereas the typical intergroup contact intervention lasts only during one experimental session and is not facilitated.

What should educators interested in intergroup dialogue heed from past and new research on interaction across difference? One caveat is important in considering the relevance of this body of research. It is nearly exclusively focused on cross-racial interaction, whereas intergroup dialogue courses cover a much broader set of groups and social divides. Still, everyone can learn from this body of work, all of which supports the importance of the chapters in this book.

First, a large body of research, both from experimental studies (Pettigrew & Tropp, 2006) and from higher education field studies, now supports that cross-racial/ethnic interaction is associated positively with a host of measures of cognitive, sociocognitive, diversity attitudes, democratic sentiments, and voting behavior (Gottfredson et al., 2008; Gurin et al., 2002; Hu & Kuh, 2003; Hurtado, 2005; Milem et al., 2005). A longitudinal study of students at the University of California, Los Angeles (UCLA) also shows that interaction across race and ethnicity had numerous positive consequences, including reduction in prejudice and an increase in egalitarian values (Sidanius, Levin, van Laar, & Sears, 2008). Studies of college roommates who were randomly assigned to live the first year in college with a student from either the same or a different race/ethnicity as their own also demonstrate some positive effects, namely, more positive attitudes toward various ethnic groups, less symbolic racism, more heterogeneous friendship groups (Sidanius et al., 2008; Van Laar, Levin, Sinclair, & Sidanius, 2005), a reduction in intergroup anxiety and in automatically activated (implicit) prejudice (Shook & Fazio, 2008), and more positive attitudes toward affirmative action and greater comfort with minorities several years later (Boisjoly, Duncan, Kremer, Levy, & Eccles, 2006).

Second, research also reveals challenges that arise in cross-racial/ethnic interactions that facilitators must be trained to address. One of the most robust findings from social psychological research on intergroup contact is that both majority and minority group members experience anxiety (Stephan & Stephan, 1985); both may find such interaction stressful, and they often expect prejudice to emerge in difficult ways, affecting White students who worry about appearing prejudiced and students of color who dread yet another experience of overt or subtle prejudice being expressed against their group (Richeson & Shelton, 2007; Richeson & Trawalter, 2005; Vorauer, 2006). Members of groups that historically (and/or currently) differ in power often come into intergroup contact situations with different motivations for the interaction that is to take place. Those from high-power groups more often want to talk about commonalities and to get to know members of the other group in personal ways, whereas those from lower-power groups prefer to address power differences directly and discuss how they can be changed both within the immediate interaction and in the broader society (Saguy, Dovidio, & Pratto, 2008). The studies of roommates of the same or different racial/ethnic backgrounds also demonstrate that even with many positive consequences, the cross-racial roommate situation involves some emotional challenges. For both White and non-White students there are fewer positive emotions, less intimacy, and fewer such positive behaviors as smiling, talking, and appearing engaged in the cross-race situation than in the homogeneous roommate situation (Trail, Shelton, & West, 2009). A few studies that focused specifically on the experiences of minorities in interracial living situations reveal greater concerns about being the target of prejudice and more negative emotions in the interracial than in the same-race roommate situation (Shelton, Richeson, & Salvatore, 2005).

What do these studies mean for educators in promoting positive intergroup relationships and through those relationships helping students develop the cultural competencies they will need in the 21st century? Sorensen et al. (2009) summarize, "Taken together, laboratory and roommate research on interracial interactions suggests that both positive and negative outcomes are possible and that these interactions must be negotiated. Thus, efforts to promote effective interactions must address these challenges by helping students find ways to overcome their fears and anxiety about interracial interactions, and refocus the goal of these encounters from preventing bad outcomes to promoting good ones—intergroup understanding, relationships, and effective communication" (p. 11).

Diversity and intergroup contact initiatives need to use guided facilitation to help students learn how to communicate effectively; to deal with the psychological issues that may arise for members of all groups that are interacting with each other; and, specifically, to provide exposure to how power, group-based inequalities, and need for social change can address the motivations of both high- and lower-power groups. Saguy et al. (2008), who have discerned the different motivations of these groups in a series of studies, also have shown that members of advantaged groups are more willing to engage in communication about group-based power differences when they are helped to perceive that their advantaged status is relatively illegitimate. Thus, facilitators in intergroup dialogue have a huge task in helping students from different identity groups cope with their anxieties and with their complicated motivations while applying a critical lens to societal power structures. It is in how facilitators are trained and supervised that they are prepared to accomplish this task. That is what this book, the first to focus on intergroup dialogue facilitation, addresses with examples from multiple institutions, using different models of training and supervision, and in varied educational curricular and cocurricular settings.

This book is a treasure trove of theory, research, and personal narratives of both successes and challenges. Anyone interested in developing an intergroup dialogue program, or using the intergroup dialogue method in other courses, campus organizations, research labs, or other educational settings composed of people from diverse backgrounds, will find this book their most important resource. So, too, will practitioners who work with diverse groups of people in communities and in state, national, and international organizations.

—Patricia Gurin

References

Allport, G. W. (1954). *The nature of prejudice*. Oxford, England: Addison-Wesley.

Boisjoly, J., Duncan, G. J., Kremer, M., Levy, D. M., & Eccles, J. (2006). Empathy or antipathy? The impact of diversity. *The American Economic Review, 96*, 1890–1905.

Gottfredson, N. C., Panter, A. T., Daye, C. E., Wightman, L. F., Allen, W. A., & Deo, M. E. (2008). Does diversity at undergraduate institutions influence student outcomes? *Journal of Diversity in Higher Education, 1*, 80–94.

Grutter v. Bollinger, 539 U.S. 306 (2003).

Gurin, P., Dey, E. L., Hurtado, S., & Gurin, G. (2002). Diversity and higher education: Theory and impact on educational outcomes. *Harvard Educational Review, 72*(3), 330–366.

Gurin, P., Nagda, B. A., & Zúñiga, X. (in press). *Talking and collaborating across differences and inequalities: The impact of intergroup dialogue*.

Hu, S., & Kuh, G. D. (2003). Diversity experiences and college student learning and personal development. *Journal of College Student Development, 44*, 320–334.

Hurtado, S. (2005). The next generation of diversity and intergroup relations research. *Journal of Social Issues, 61*, 595–610.

Milem, J. F., Chang, M. J., & Antonio, A. L. (2005). *Making diversity work on campus: A research-based perspective*. Washington, DC. Association of American Colleges and Universities.

Nagda, B. A. (2006). Breaking barriers, crossing boundaries, building bridges: Communication processes in intergroup dialogues. *Journal of Social Issues, 62*, 553–576.

Nagda, B. A., Gurin, P., Sorensen, N., & Coombes, A. (2009). *Not just a dialogue but a just dialogue*. Unpublished manuscript. University of Washington, Seattle, WA.

Nagda, B. A., Gurin, P., Sorensen, N., & Zúñiga, X. (2009). Evaluating intergroup dialogues: Engaging diversity for personal and social responsibility. *Diversity & Democracy, 12*, 3–6.

Pettigrew, T. F., & Tropp, L. R. (2006). A meta-analytic test of intergroup contact theory. *Journal of Personality and Social Psychology, 90*, 751–783.

Richeson, J. A., & Shelton, J. N. (2007). Negotiating interracial interactions: Costs, consequences, and possibilities. *Current Directions in Psychological Science, 16*, 316–320.

Richeson, J. A., & Trawalter, S. (2005). Why do interracial interactions impair executive function? A resource depletion account. *Journal of Personality and Social Psychology, 88*, 934–947.

Saguy, T., Dovidio, J. F., & Pratto, F. (2008). Beyond contact: Intergroup contact in the context of power relations. *Personality and Social Psychology Bulletin, 34*, 432–445.

Shelton, J. N., Richeson, J. A., & Salvatore, J. (2005). Expecting to be the target of prejudice: Implications for interethnic interactions. *Personality and Social Psychology Bulletin, 31*, 1189–1202.

Shook, N. J., & Fazio, R. H. (2008). Interracial roommate relationships: An experimental field test of the contact hypothesis. *Psychological Science, 19*, 717–723.

Sidanius, J., Levin, S., van Laar, C., & Sears, D. O. (2008). *The diversity challenge: Social identity and intergroup relations on the college campus.* New York: Russell Sage Foundation.

Sorensen, N., Nagda, B. A., Gurin, P., & Maxwell, K. (2009). Taking a "hands on" approach to diversity in higher education: A critical-dialogic model for effective intergroup interaction. *Analyses of Social Issues and Public Policy, 9*(1), 3–35.

Stephan, W. G., & Stephan, C. W. (1985). Intergroup anxiety. *Journal of Social Issues, 41,* 157–175.

Trail, T. E., Shelton, J. N., & West, T. V. (2009). Interracial roommate relationships: Negotiating daily interactions. *Personality and Social Psychology Bulletin, 35*(6), 671–684.

Van Laar, C., Levin, S., Sinclair, S., & Sidanius, J. (2005). The effect of university roommate contact on ethnic attitudes and behavior. *Journal of Experimental Social Psychology, 41,* 329–345.

Vorauer, J. D. (2006). An information search model of evaluative concerns in intergroup interaction. *Psychological Review, 113,* 862–886.

1

DEEPENING THE LAYERS OF UNDERSTANDING AND CONNECTION

A Critical-Dialogic Approach to
Facilitating Intergroup Dialogues

Biren (Ratnesh) A. Nagda and Kelly E. Maxwell

I ntergroup dialogue has emerged as an educational and community-
building approach that brings together members of diverse social and
cultural identities to engage in learning together—sharing and listening
to each other's perspectives and stories and exploring inequalities and community issues that affect them all, albeit differently—so that they may work
collectively and individually to promote greater diversity, equality, and justice
(McCoy & Scully, 2002; Schoem & Hurtado, 2001; Walsh, 2007; Zúñiga,
Nagda, Chesler, & Cytron-Walker, 2007). Be it involving middle or high
school students, college students or community constituents, intergroup dialogue provides a structured, supportive, and sustained environment in which
participants can grapple with issues and questions that may otherwise remain
taboo and divisive (Tatum, 1997). Issues as broad and intractable as racism,
sexism, and classism or as specific as racial health disparities, violence against
women, immigration, abortion, gay marriage, and racial profiling may remain
silent because of fear and a lack of structured opportunities for people to engage across lines of differences in perspectives, experiences, and identities.
Discussing these issues may also be taboo for questioning and challenging
established norms and practices, for maintaining a social order that privileges
some groups over others, or for the personal shame and guilt that the issues

evoke. Not only may we feel constrained in saying what we may be thinking, but also we often do not hear others clearly because of what we are thinking (Warner, 2009). With increasing social diversity in workplaces, communities, and educational institutions, some advocate for ignoring social identities and differences, while others advocate for embracing a multicultural perspective that recognizes differences in power and privilege. Both sides may be emboldened by their concerns for fairness and equality, yet they seem oppositional in the ways that they actualize the paths and means to justice.

But these differing perspectives and the parties holding these perspectives do not engage authentically in a public setting. Personal concerns remain separated from group-based analyses and private deliberations remain disconnected from public discourse. Intergroup dialogue intervenes in these spaces of estrangement that both reinforce and are reinforced by the ignorance, silence, or cautious discourse. It seeks to be a medium for transformative engagement that can change contentious arguments into productive dialogues. It engages participants to create ways of understanding, living, and working together that are more equal and just. It seeks to unearth barriers in thinking, feeling, and relating so that there is both a better understanding of inequalities, differences, and conflicts that divide and a stronger foundation for building bridges that may help members of different groups across separations and disconnections. Even when intergroup dialogue may not lead directly to change, it can help create the conditions to catalyze greater community collaboration among previously estranged groups.

Focus of This Book

This book, therefore, seeks to extend our understanding and knowledge of intergroup dialogue practice with a focus on intergroup dialogue facilitation. Intergroup dialogue is a co-facilitated learning endeavor that brings together members of two or more social identity groups to build relationships across cultural and power differences, to raise consciousness of inequalities, to explore the similarities and differences in experiences across identity groups, and to strengthen individual and collective capacities to promote social justice. With guidance from trained co-facilitators, dialogue groups of about 12–16 participants, meet weekly over a period of 10–14 weeks. Co-facilitators, representing the groups that are in dialogue, provide balanced leadership for the learning process. They use an educational curriculum that integrates multiple dimensions of learning: content and process learning; intellectual and affective engagement; individual reflection and group dialogue; individual, intergroup, and institutional analyses; and individual and collective actions (see Zúñiga et al., 2007, for a detailed description).

Despite a growing number of books and articles in professional journals and magazines focusing on intergroup dialogue, there remains a dearth of writing and in-depth understanding of intergroup dialogue facilitation. Other than chapters in books or a brief mention within other chapters, little has been written specifically about intergroup dialogue facilitation (see Beale, Thompson, & Chesler, 2001; Nagda, Zúñiga, & Sevig, 1995; Zúñiga et al., 2007) or facilitating social justice education courses or workshops (see Burke, Geronimo, Martin, Thomas, & Wall, 2002; and Griffin & Ouellett, 2007, for exceptions). In this book, the first dedicated entirely to intergroup dialogue facilitation, we draw on our joint practice and research knowledge to define the facilitation role in greater detail, articulate the broad and specific foci of training and supporting facilitators, and share emerging research on intergroup dialogue facilitators with implications for practice. Many of the contributing authors have worked in higher education settings as well as collaborated with community organizations and youth in K–12 schools. We bring insights gained from these experiences to contribute to the overall knowledge and practice base of dialogue in a variety of contexts.

In this introductory chapter, we focus on our experiences with a particular kind of intergroup dialogue—the critical-dialogic model of intergroup dialogue that is now being used at many different U.S. colleges and universities. Rather than only discussing facilitation training and multicultural competencies, as others have done previously (see Beale et al., 2001; and Zúñiga et al., 2007), we seek to connect intergroup dialogue facilitation to the unique, transformative potential of intergroup dialogue and the underlying processes of change in intergroup dialogue.

Intergroup Dialogue: Critical-Dialogic Engagement and Facilitation

We lay a foundation here for understanding the importance and uniqueness of intergroup dialogue facilitation. We elaborate on facilitation within a critical-dialogic model of intergroup dialogue, an interdisciplinary model informed by the fields of multicultural and social justice education, intergroup contact and intergroup relations, and communication and conflict studies.

Discursive Engagement With and Across Differences

Table 1.1 shows a critical-dialogic model of intergroup dialogue in the context of other models of discursive engagement such as debate and discussion that are also concerned with teaching and learning about differences and diversity. The framework shows the unique ways in which intergroup dialogue works

TABLE 1.1
Approaches to discursive engagement with and across differences
(Nagda & Gurin, 2007)

	Debate	*Discussion*	*Intergroup Dialogue*
Understanding Difference and Dominance	• Differences as diversity—differences seen as individual differences, the result of individual prejudices and stereotypes • Differences in the context of sociocultural and power relations—differences seen to represent/emerge from cultural differences and unequal power (dominant-subordinated) relationships; analyses of structural and institutional systems of oppression and privilege; and consideration of differential social identity development processes for participants		
Goals of Discursive Engagement	• To clarify pros and cons of issues • To develop critical thinking skills	• To generate different perspectives on issues • To increase perspective taking and critical thinking skills • To weigh or make decisions among different options	• To increase critical self- and societal awareness • To increase intergroup communication, understanding, and collaborative actions
Modes of Discursive Engagement	• A back-and-forth of arguments • Perseverance and advocacy of perspective • One right answer, determined by force of argument, identifying flaws in others' logic	• Openness to different perspectives • Disparate or connected knowing • Varies in personalization and contextualization • Cognitive inquiry	• Emphasis on connected knowing (discerning similarities and differences) • Personalization, affective expression and empathic relations • Contextualization in larger systems • Self- and other inquiry
Role of Community and Conflict	• Community not considered • Fight to convince other • Conflict defined by positions	• Community as group of individuals,- emphasis on similarities • Recognition of conflict of ideas without critical exploration • Compromise ("agree to disagree")	• Diverse community, acknowledges differences as well as similarities • Conflicts surfaced and normalized; treated as opportunities for learning • Search for collaborative possibilities and social justice

Note: Nagda & Gurin, 2007, used with permission.

with the dimensions of participatory learning about and across differences and sets the stage for understanding intergroup dialogue facilitation within this model (see also Nagda & Gurin, 2007). We refer to our model of intergroup dialogue as a critical-dialogic approach to differentiate it from approaches that only build relationships among participants without an explicit recognition of differences, and models that focus on raising consciousness to lead to action but do not deal fully with the complexity of relationships among the participants.

The *dialogic* goals of intergroup dialogue are aimed at building affective self–other relationships through personal storytelling and sharing, empathic listening, and interpersonal inquiry (Kim & Kim, 2008; Young, 1997). Dialogue seeks understanding across differences through connected knowing rather than an imposition of a singular perspective (as in debate) or serial monologues (as in discussion) (see chapter 8 for further distinction between debate and deliberation). Dialogue, in a critical-dialogic approach, seeks not only an understanding of one's own and others' perspectives on issues, but also an appreciation of life experiences that inform those perspectives. Participants learn to listen to others, share their own perspectives and experiences, reflect on their learning, and ask questions to more fully explore differences and commonalities within and across social identity groups.

The *critical* goals of intergroup dialogue are centered on understanding how power, privilege, and group-based inequalities structure individual and group life as well as on fostering individual and collective responsibilities for redressing inequalities and promoting social justice (Delgado & Stefancic, 2000; Freire, 1970). Dialogues across differences do not happen in a vacuum; intergroup dialogue is centrally concerned with issues of power and privilege and their effects on personal and social identities. Intergroup dialogue takes a critical understanding of difference, one that conceptualizes difference in the context of dominant-subordinated relationships and not simply as diversity (McMahon, 2003). In the intergroup context with participants from privileged and less-advantaged groups (such as people of color and White people, or women and men), participants usually hold different understandings and experiences of identities and inequalities (Tatum, 1997). Thus, we extend the basis of dialogue to *intergroup* dialogue; that is, we bring a critical perspective to dialogue.

Jointly, the *critical-dialogic* goals seek to mobilize the power of cross-group relationships not only as a focal point of analysis of structural inequalities and the consequences on group and individual lives, but also as sites for relating in ways that advance individual and collective agency for transformative social change (Nagda, 2006; Saunders, 1999). Through sharing, listening, and inquiry, we aim to explore the commonalities and differences in experiences. Oftentimes, these narratives are grounded in identities, privilege, and/or social exclusion. We aim to gain a deeper understanding not only of our personal biographies but also of the contextual situations and structures that affect us similarly and differentially. Within such a critical-dialogic approach, community building and conflict exploration are not oppositional; rather, they are important processes toward greater social justice through acknowledging and recognizing inequalities, structuring opportunities for greater access and participation in social institutions, reforming relationships, and exploring sustainable redistribution of power.

Emerging research on intergroup dialogue, directly on facilitation and indirectly on what the facilitators create, leads to three conclusions. First, simply, facilitation matters! Facilitation and structured interaction in intergroup dialogue has been found to be more favorably effective in learning compared to traditional lecture/discussion methods (Nagda, Gurin, Sorensen, & Coombes, 2009). Second, psychological processes fostered in intergroup dialogues are important because people's individual experiences and internal change, both cognitive and affective, are related to positive outcomes (Nagda, Kim, & Truelove, 2004; Stephan, 2008). Third, four communication processes characterize intergroup dialogue (Nagda, 2006):

1. *Appreciating difference* involves an openness to learn from others through intentional listening, asking questions, and appreciating life experiences and perspectives different from one's own.
2. *Engaging self* speaks to active involvement of participants in intergroup interactions characterized by personal sharing, voicing disagreements, and addressing difficult issues.
3. *Critical reflection* involves students examining and understanding their own perspectives and experiences, and those of other students in the dialogue, through the lenses of privilege and inequality.
4. *Alliance building* is defined as a process that involves both talking about ways to collaborate on action to work against injustices and bring about change, and strengthening the relationship by working through disagreements and conflicts (Nagda, 2006).

Psychological and communication processes are intimately related to the work of the facilitators. We discuss the facilitation principles involved in dialogue across differences with facilitators as guides who themselves are intimately connected to the learning process and who are committed to fostering critical-dialogic communication processes among participants.

Facilitation Principles in Discursive Engagement With and Across Difference

Like intergroup dialogue itself, intergroup dialogue facilitation is a distinct and principled approach to guiding engagement with issues of social justice that bridges the personal and the political, connects reflection and dialogue, and mobilizes relationships for collaborative action. Table 1.2 expands on Table 1.1 with an explicit focus on facilitation. In the following sections we discuss three major principles that inform intergroup dialogue facilitation.

Principle 1: Guiding, Not Just Teaching

Intergroup dialogue facilitation is mindful, responsive, and responsible guidance, not formalized teaching or instruction. Participants in dialogue are not passive receptacles to be filled with the facilitators' knowledge, but are themselves educators of their own experiences and understandings of social reality. Whereas in debates or discussions the facilitator referees or directs the instruction and interactions, intergroup dialogue facilitators pay keen attention to the conjoint learner–educator roles that every participant plays. A mode of facilitators as guides rather than facilitators as teachers allows them to partner with students to create a joint learning experience (see chapter 6). The emphasis on guiding learning through reflection, dialogue, and action does not mean laissez-faire facilitation, but an intentionality to create an inclusive learning environment that can foster meaningful engagement.

Creating an Inclusive Space for Differences and Dialogue

Because intergroup dialogues bring together equal numbers of participants from the different groups in dialogue—usually groups situated in dominant-subordinated power relations—facilitators work to create an inclusive learning space that can hold divergent *and* convergent experiences and perspectives. Intergroup dialogues use intentional pedagogy that builds appreciation for and understanding of differences that are often connected to participants' identities and positionalities. In discussions or debates, the group composition is not necessarily structured with social identities in mind, nor is there explicit attention to engaging with identities. Differences may be conceived of as simply about perspectives and information that are open to being challenged. Or, they may be acknowledged as related to group-based experiences in the larger society but engaged with only abstractly or theoretically. Views and perspectives may or may not be personalized by individual participants. Within the ground rules for dialogue, particular attention is paid to how

TABLE 1.2
Facilitator roles in discursive engagement with and across differences

	Multicultural, Anti-oppression and Social Justice Learning Environments		
	Debate	*Discussion*	*Intergroup Dialogue*
Group Membership in Learning Community	• As is in the classroom • Open invitation without intentional structuring • Small groups formed without attention to identities	• As is in the classroom • Open invitation without intentional structuring • Some attention to mix of small-group and large-group settings	• Intentional structuring of groups with as equal a number of members of different groups as possible • Members of both subordinated and dominant groups • Meetings in both heterogeneous and homogeneous (caucus) groups
Instructor/ Facilitator Role	• Facilitator and teaching directed and centered • Instructor/facilitator as moderator/referee sets tone, agenda for group, and norms of discourse • Procedural (rules of debate)	• Facilitator and teaching directed and centered • Instructor/facilitator as "neutral" and director • Procedural to maximize participation but limited processual in terms of attention to communication dynamics	• Co-facilitator guided, student and learning centered • Focused on fostering an intergroup learning community • Procedural *and* processual
Self and Power	• "Self" as objective and not part of engagement • "Self" conceptualized in context of role	• "Self" as objective and not part of engagement • "Self" conceptualized as individual	• Use of "self" to deepen dialogue among participants • "Self" conceptualized in context of individual, social identity, and social positionality
Processes of Engagement	• Clarity of argument • Convincing-oriented • Dynamic of critique-defense • Close-ended	• Serial monologues • Heavy emphasis on talking participation • Idea oriented, not inclusive of experiences	• Narrative oriented • Asking questions and sharing • Grounded in experience, combined with intellectual ideas to coconstruct meaning

Note: Nagda (2007) used with permission.

participants and facilitators work to hold the differences and see them as enriching and not undermining the learning. Yeakley (chapter 2) provides helpful suggestions on how to create a foundation for an inclusive climate.

Co-facilitation

Intergroup dialogue uses a co-facilitation approach, not solo facilitation, and embraces alliance building at the heart of its relationship. Intergroup dialogue facilitators share power with each other and with members of the dialogue group in ways that make the best use of everyone's aspirations, skills, and abilities. For group participants, the co-facilitation model ensures, as much as possible, representation and support in the facilitative leadership. Co-facilitators are not neutral or impartial but multipartial and balanced as a team in supporting all group members (see chapter 3). Co-facilitators can support and challenge participants from their own identity groups empathically and, at the same time, model for participants ways of connecting across social boundaries. The co-facilitation alliance provides facilitators a site for enacting and modeling their commitments to intergroup collaboration, mutually beneficial learning, and a shared project to advance the learning of others (see chapters 4, 5, and 12).

Integrating Content and Process

Obviously, facilitators bring immense commitment and passion to their work in addition to the knowledge, awareness, and skills they develop in training. While they do not lecture or formally teach as part of instruction, facilitators work with both content and process to stimulate the dialogue. They draw on content by using reading materials and cognitive organizers that provide informational and conceptual foundations to guide participants to reflect on their own lives and pertinent social issues (Adams, Bell, & Griffin, 2007). They generate content for dialogue by engaging participants in structured exercises and experiential activities and then guide them in connecting their individual in-exercise experiences to their lived experiences and to those of others in the dialogue. They also use the group process and group dynamics as *in vivo* content for a dialogue about dialogue whereby students are asked for their own reflections about the dialogue process and the intergroup dynamics (see Zúñiga et al., 2007). None of these sources of content are mutually exclusive and the most engaging facilitators integrate all three. Facilitators use content from readings, experiences of activities, or the group dynamics as a foundation to stimulate dialogue or a reference point for examining emergent issues and deepening the dialogue.

Principle 2: Empowering, Not Just Being Empowered

Intergroup dialogue facilitation, in seeking to promote a joint learning environment for both participants and facilitators, recognizes that learning about identities, inequalities, and social justice is a continual process. The leadership role of facilitators does not mean that they have achieved some ultimate outcome of social justice learning; rather, it often means that facilitators are committed to a process of continued learning through *praxis,* a cyclical process of action and reflection in dialogue. Specifically, facilitators focus on developing greater critical reflexivity that connects their understanding of power inequalities and their positionalities with their work—with participants and with each other—to promote constructive uses of power and empowerment (see chapters 6, 11, and 12). Thus, while being a part of the group and not apart from the group, facilitators must also be aware of the different levels of learning for themselves and participants. They must honor the learning trajectory of individual participants and attend to the dynamics of group development while promoting individual skills development and group ownership.

Embracing a Productive Use of Self

Perhaps the most distinctive dimension of intergroup dialogue facilitation from other modes of discursive facilitation is the use of self. By productive, we refer to how facilitators can purposefully use themselves and their experiences as a way to guide and deepen the dialogue while being mindful not to reproduce the unequal hierarchical power dynamics that the intergroup dialogues seek to challenge. Rather than seeing the self as an autonomous individual, the self is grounded in social group memberships, identities, and social relationships (dominant and/or subordinated) that influence the individual experience (see chapter 11). The facilitators model how to speak from a self standpoint grounded in identity and status. Not only does this normalize the conversation about identities and positionalities, it also gives participants examples of experiences that connect to their own in some ways. In intergroup dialogue, the subjectivity enriches the conversation. In discussion or debate, the facilitator "self" is seen as objective and facilitator subjectivity is considered to be a distraction, or worse, a weakness. There is a considerable boundary maintained between the facilitator/instructor and participants and an emphasis on being neutral. A productive use of self also means that power dynamics in the group—between co-facilitators, among group members, and between co-facilitators and group members—are surfaced to serve as opportunities for learning for all, including the facilitators.

Framing and Naming

Learning about privilege and power, and especially how students are themselves affected by systems of inequalities and the conscious and unconscious roles they play in those systems, is not easy by any means. Facilitators, drawing on their own learning and training, are also active in normalizing the personal and group dynamics that accompany the learning process. Cognitive learning is not the only desired educational outcome; so is affective learning, as it enables a deeper and more complex understanding of the person-structure connection of inequalities (Khuri, 2004; see also chapter 3). Emotions such as ambivalence, dissonance, discomfort, anger, and guilt, among others, are very much a part of the learning process. When facilitators help students name these emotions, normalize them, and dialogue about them, students are less likely to feel isolated or shameful about these emergent feelings. Normalizing does not mean colluding with participants or with inequalities, but empathizing and affirming the learning as a process that moves through different phases, emotions, and relationship dynamics. In a way, it enables facilitators to partner with and guide students through newer explorations about themselves, their relations with others, and how they are situated in the world.

Facilitators also use intergroup dynamics that occur in the intergroup dialogue as learning moments. Whether it is a reversion to debate or discussion-oriented engagement, an imbalance of who is talking and who is listening, an asymmetry in cognitive and affective engagement, or a pattern of who connects with or diverts from whom, facilitators surface the dynamics in order to deepen the dialogue. Oftentimes, facilitators may pause the dialogue process and ask the group for their in-the-moment observations or feelings. They may then name what they saw and invite students to examine it through the frame of dynamics of inequalities, internalized oppression, and internalized dominance that may be playing out in the dialogue. Facilitators are intentional in not calling out or blaming individuals but contextualizing their observations in systems of socialization and inviting participants to dialogue from their own standpoints. Facilitators also reinforce the opportunity to learn from such moments or conflicts in the group such that it enables students from diverse backgrounds to build authentic understanding and collaborations.

Cultivating Facilitative Engagement and Skills

As much as facilitators are a part of the group and the learning process, their primary responsibility is to advance the learning of others. They do so not only by performing particular facilitator behaviors and techniques, but also by guiding students to develop facilitative mind-sets and behaviors that contribute to relational learning (see chapter 8). For example, not only should the facilitators ask for elaboration or more questions to engage participants but they should also encourage participants to do the same with each other. Or, not only should the facilitators respond to participants' questions seeking the "expert answer" to an issue, but they should also redirect the question to the participants by opening the floor for everyone's thoughts on the issue or engaging the participants in reflecting on the origin of and assumptions in the question. Or, facilitators should support participants' own naming of issues and dynamics in the dialogue. Instead of seeing this as a criticism or failure on their part in equalizing power in the group, facilitators can encourage participants to own that responsibility and help facilitate a constructive dialogue. Interactions in the dialogue group then become less facilitator centered or facilitator directed and more participant centered and guided jointly by participants and facilitators.

Principle 3: Attending to Processes, Not Just Procedures

Procedural issues in any form of discursive engagement have to do with following the rules of engagement, while processes refer to the collective sense making and learning derived from the engagement. Of the three discursive modes, debate is likely to be the most procedural with a clear set of rules to follow in terms of presentation of arguments, rebuttals, and more. Discussion may vary in terms of following the procedures of maximizing participation and the processes of deepening the discussion. The power of intergroup dialogue is in deepening the reflection and dialogue process through interaction and inquiry. As much as procedures are important in getting participants involved in structured activities, the subsequent debriefing process deepens and expands the learning through reflection, dialogue, and probing inquiry. Many intergroup dialogue facilitators are enamored by the power of structured activities. The active involvement and the affective and experiential learning sparked by the activities is a strong memory for facilitators from their time as dialogue participants. Such learning is often contrasted with their educational experiences in other courses and workshops. They are reminded of the critical lessons they learned in those activities. Furthermore, new intergroup dialogue facilitators may depend more on structure and activities as a semblance of certainty and safety rather than be comfortable with the ambiguity of the organic process that unfolds through open dialogue. The dilemma here is in getting caught on the procedures for the dialogue activities versus using the activity to generate a process of dialogue.

As discussed earlier, recent research and practice in intergroup dialogue has centered on the important role of communication processes—engaging self, appreciating difference, critical reflection, and alliance building—to promote learning (Nagda, 2006; Nagda, Gurin, Sorensen, Gurin-Sands, & Osuna, 2009). By integrating content and structured interactions in intergroup dialogues, facilitators are responsible for cultivating these communication processes geared toward equalizing exchanges and interrupting unequal power dynamics in intergroup interactions. In many ways, facilitating intergroup dialogues is social justice in action. Facilitators see their work with students in intergroup dialogue as a way of acting on their social justice commitments, and students see their own work with each other and the work of facilitators with them as examples of working toward social justice. The critical-dialogic framework of intergroup dialogue helps facilitators focus their attention on fostering specific communication processes.

Dialogic Facilitation to Build Self–Other Relationships Within and Across Differences

With the potentially contentious and emotional issues raised in intergroup dialogues, building relationships across differences brings forth the challenge of creating reciprocal and mutual self–other relations. In many intergroup dialogue situations, participants are coming together carrying histories of separation, estrangement, and ignorance of each other. For disadvantaged groups, the coming together may represent an opportunity to talk about the social inequalities, while privileged groups may want to talk more about commonalities (Abu-Nimer, 1999; Dovidio, Saguy, & Schnabel, 2009; Walsh, 2007). For the former, intergroup contact entails acknowledgment of social identities and statuses and a desire to be respected for each other's opinions. For the latter, such contact may be defined more interpersonally with the desire to be liked as a motivator in engagement (Shelton, Richeson, & Vorauer, 2006). Be it due to inexperience in intergroup situations and the real fears of appearing prejudiced or being the target of prejudice (Shelton, Richeson, & Salvatore, 2005), the conversation can also become stilted with the predominant participation of members of just certain groups depending on the content or process of the conversation.

Facilitators focus on instilling a practice of *engaging self* and *appreciating difference* as the important communicative actions to build relationships across differences. Such an emphasis necessitates not only clear communication but also a connected speaking and listening among participants. Narayan (1988) details the emotional cost of disconnected conversations across differences.

Oftentimes, in sensitive conversations among people with diverse experiences, certain stories may not be acknowledged due to a lack of understanding or, at worst, due to overt marginalization. Even when acknowledged, the stories may not be reciprocated with how they were received by other participants, or met with interest or curiosity. Facilitators work to ensure that there is acknowledgment of what someone says, perhaps encouraging more sharing by the original participant or opening up the floor to others who may have had similar experiences. In essence, there needs to be a validation that the contribution was heard. It is also important that facilitators work to balance the processes of engaging self and appreciating difference. Examples of facilitator phrases and questions to encourage engaging self are *Please say more,* or *Can you help me understand your thinking here?* or *Seems like that really affected you. Can you share some about how you felt and the impact of that experience on you?* Examples of cultivating appreciation of differences may be *What is something that each of us appreciates about what others have been sharing?* or *What is something new or different that each of us has learned from all the perspectives in our dialogue?* or *What are some questions that you would like to ask each other based on what you all have heard?* Furthermore, some questions to bridge appreciating difference *and* engaging self may include the following:

- How is everyone affected by what has been said?
- How does that resonate with something of your own experience?
- As you all listen and take in what everyone has shared, what are the commonalities and differences you see emerging?

Critical Facilitation to Connect Personal Experiences and Structural Inequalities

Not only does intergroup dialogue bring people of diverse identities together but also the participants themselves hold different perspectives and ideologies related to difference and equality. Members of disadvantaged and advantaged groups usually differ in their endorsement of multicultural or color-blind ideologies (Richeson & Nussbaum, 2004), construction of self-identity through social identities or personal attributes (Tajfel, 1974), and understanding of intergroup conflict situations through structural and/or individual analyses (Jones, Engelman, Turner, & Campbell, 2009). Because intergroup dialogues are situated within dynamics of inequalities and seek to surface these differences, facilitators pay particular attention to the communication processes of *critical reflection* and *alliance building.* Facilitators encourage participants to both personalize and contextualize experiences and issues vis-à-vis systems of power, privilege, and resistance/empowerment. Personalization refers to examining the issues of social identities and inequalities and the affective and cognitive impact on participants, individually and collectively. Contextualization involves questioning personal biases and misinformation, and understanding differences in experiences that flow from differential societal locations (see chapters 5 and 12 for examples). Facilitators support and challenge participants to step beyond simply appreciating diversity from a distanced perspective to examining how social inequalities impact groups differently, and how they too are a part of the larger social structure (Nagda, 2007). Facilitative inquiry may involve asking

- What feelings come up as we examine the systematic nature of inequality?
- Some people are expressing ideas that seem to be very different from others. What do you think accounts for the different experiences and perspectives?
- What insights and new questions emerge as we listen to all the different perspectives in the group?

Within the dialogue group setting, participants can be encouraged to engage in actions that counter the cycles of socialization or oppression. Facilitator responsiveness, such as affirmation or empathy, may be critical when participants exercise agency by voicing their experiences and feelings in a mixed group. In other cases, when some participants may exhibit privileged or dominating behaviors, facilitator intervention can challenge them to listen more to other group members as a way of enacting social justice. When interactions in the group reflect larger sociopolitical processes (e.g., members of privileged social groups dominating the dialogue session or members of oppressed groups retreating into silence or erupting in anger), the facilitators may guide the group in a "dialogue about the dialogue" (Nagda, 2006):

- What is facilitating and hindering participation for each of us?
- How are the dynamics of inequalities that are the content of learning being manifested and/or challenged here?
- How can our dialogues be deepened in more socially just ways?

In addition, facilitators may also remark on changes in the group dynamics that show how the group itself has broken through the barriers and restrictions of dominating and oppressive behaviors to more inclusive and equalizing ways of engagement.

Critical-Dialogic Facilitation to Bridge Dialogue and Action

For many, engaging in dialogic relationship building and critical analysis may be enough in itself as a sign of improved intergroup relationships. The critical-dialogic approach, however, is geared toward redressing inequalities and promoting social change, not just building friendships across social identity groups (Nagda, 2006; Wright & Lubensky, 2009). Thus, facilitators in intergroup dialogue push to connect critical analysis to actions that promote diversity and social justice. *Alliance building* as a communication process helps bridge dialogue to action and bridge learning in the dialogue group to applying learning outside the group. Facilitators often have to demystify actions simply as social protest or civil disobedience and have participants appreciate the range of actions from reducing individual prejudice and interrupting misinformation and derogatory comments to educating others and engaging in collective organizing for wider and more sustained impact. Examples of facilitative inquiry may include the following:

- Based on what we have learned about inequalities and the different spheres of influence in our lives, what actions can we take to bring about change?
- As members of disadvantaged or privileged groups, what are our responsibilities to connect the dialogue to actions both within our own group and across groups?
- What are the personal risks and rewards of challenging inequalities?

As a communication process, alliance building involves more than just taking action; it also involves working through conflicts and deepening trust by intentionally examining individual and group issues related to collaboration (Nagda, 2006). Facilitators can further alliance building by integrating dialogic relations and critical analysis and action. Facilitators can foster a deeper dialogue about how participants bring their different conceptions for change and self-assessed abilities to a collective mix as well as examine the relational impact of action. There exists a tension, also informed by status relations, between change as prejudice reduction and change as collective action to redress inequalities (Wright & Lubensky, 2009). From a relationship perspective, this tension parallels that of being friends and being allies (Nagda, 2006; Tatum, 2007). Thus, dialogue about the relational impact means understanding how actions of one group (or its members) affect another group (or its members), the nature of relationships that engender or hinder individual and collective capacity for change, and the participation and leadership opportunities that can sustain commitments to action and learning. For example, facilitators may create opportunities where participants can dialogue in intragroup settings about the impact of internalized oppression and internalized dominance on working across differences. Participants from disadvantaged and privileged groups can each dialogue about the following:

- What is the impact of internalized oppression [dominance and superiority] on our relationships with each other and with members of privileged groups?
- How does internalized oppression [dominance and superiority] affect our approaches to collaborative social change?

Reflections and insights from these intragroup conversations can be brought to the intergroup setting so that participants can negotiate collaborative relations that are mutually empowering and also attend to the unequal power relations, and thus the different and common responsibilities each group has to advance justice. Honest dialogues stimulated by these questions are important in deepening the relations between groups and developing understanding about the important individual and collective needs in collaborative efforts.

Facilitators also encourage students to talk about actions they have taken outside the dialogue setting. Talking about actions allows participants to inspire and be inspired by each other, to appreciate their own and others' efficacy in applying their learning from the dialogues through actions, to be honest about the risks of interrupting or intervening in incidents of power abuses, and perhaps even to challenge each other to reflect on their own complicity or collusion in injustices. Facilitators continue to encourage critical reflection on actions and alliance building through questions such as the following:

- How do our individual actions toward interrupting injustices affect our collective efforts?
- How can we work together so that we are *all* empowered to act?
- How do we work together for sustained social justice (as allies) and build strong relationships (be friends)?

Intentional dialogues about actions and continued learning can help participants negotiate what is important to them in collaborative efforts to advance social justice and not reproduce the dynamics that they are seeking to challenge.

In summary, intergroup dialogue facilitators bring their learned expertise to guide the critical-dialogic process but do not reproduce a hierarchy of expert teachers and passive learners. As facilitator–participants, they foreground their roles as facilitators but use their selves and their own life standpoints as appropriate and, in strategic ways, to generate the learning in the group. Allowance for such subjectivity carries an ethical responsibility to maintain the focus of learning on participants, and not simply for the sake of the facilitators' own learning process. The power of facilitation lies in the processual work of intergroup dialogue, that is, fostering communicative exchanges that bridge self and others, person and structure, and dialogue and action. Facilitative inquiry related to the communication process enables participants to take active responsibility and approach learning in intergroup dialogues with a spirit of openness, curiosity, and commitment to collective learning. Furthermore, because intergroup dialogue facilitators usually work in partnership, the co-facilitator relationship models for participants the promises, possibilities, and challenges of collaborative social justice action. Intergroup dialogue facilitation training, the focus of this book, includes attention to the facilitation principles and inquiry skills highlighted in this chapter as well as other specific facilitator roles and techniques necessary in social justice–based group work on campus (chapter 7) and in the community (chapters 9, 10, and 13) (Burke et al., 2002; Griffin & Ouellett, 2007; Zúñiga et al., 2007). As a whole, the contributions in this book help paint a fuller picture of facilitation roles, skills, and training.

Organization of This Book

This book is organized into three sections. The introductory chapters (1 and 2) seek to provide foundational, conceptual, and practical considerations about intergroup dialogue facilitation that directly influence facilitator training. Yeakley, in "In the Hands of Facilitators: Student Experiences in Dialogue and Implications for Facilitator Training," draws on her qualitative study of positive and negative experiences in intergroup dialogue as well as her practical experiences to provide guiding implications for facilitation training.

Section one elucidates some of the critical issues raised in training intergroup dialogue facilitators, bringing together the breadth and depth of intergroup dialogue facilitation in college classroom settings. Intergroup dialogue facilitators can be undergraduate peers, graduate students, and even professional staff and faculty. Chapters 3 and 4 in this section describe undergraduate peer facilitation training models at two very different institutions: a large public university and a small liberal arts college. In "Training Peer Facilitators as Social Justice Educators: Integrating Cognitive and Affective Learning," Maxwell, Fisher, Thompson, and Behling highlight a focus on undergraduate peer facilitation training at the Program on Intergroup Relations at the University of Michigan. Rodríguez, Rodríguez-Scheel, Lindsey, and Kirkland, in "Facilitator Training in Diverse, Progressive Residential Communities: Occidental College as a Case Study," distinctively examine three classic training themes: setting the context; guiding inclusive, reflective practice; and nurturing constructive co-facilitation relationships. Chapter 5, "Preparing Critically Reflective Intergroup Dialogue Facilitators: A Pedagogical Model and Illustrative Example," describes a graduate training course in education. Zúñiga, Kachwaha, DeJong, and Pacheco provide an in-depth case study of co-facilitation to illustrate their core training method of critically reflective practice. Finally, Wong(Lau), Landrum-Brown, and Walker, in "(Re)Training Ourselves: Professionals Who Facilitate Intergroup Dialogue," write in first-person narrative about the tacit theoretical and practical knowledge that faculty and practitioners in social justice–related disciplines bring to intergroup dialogue work, as well as the distinctive challenges these same professionals face when conducting intergroup dialogues in a classroom setting.

Section two includes facilitation training for contexts that have adapted intergroup dialogue pedagogy to wider campus and community settings. "Training Students to Change Their Own Campus Culture Through Sustained Dialogue," by Parker, Nemeroff, and Kelleher, focuses on training student moderators for a student-initiated and student-run deliberative dialogue program on college campuses. Knauer's "Democracy Lab: Online Facilitation Training for Dialogic Teaching and Learning" speaks to a unique program of online deliberation and self-facilitation training that connects classroom experiences with community deliberation. Chapter 9, "Intergroup Dialogue Facilitation for Youth Empowerment and Community Change," by Fisher and Checkoway, emphasizes a community adaptation of intergroup dialogue where undergraduate facilitators act as community organizers working with youth to break down barriers created by residential segregation. Spencer, Martineau, and warren's "Extending Intergroup Dialogue Facilitation to Multicultural Social Work Practice" describes their adaptation of intergroup dialogue facilitation training in graduate-level social work education for clinical, community-based, and policy settings.

The final section of the book presents lessons from research studies highlighting learning through the experiences of facilitators. For many facilitators, especially undergraduate students, intergroup dialogue facilitation is perhaps one of the few opportunities they have had to exercise leadership in a classroom for a sustained period of time, to work across difference intensively, and to learn with fellow facilitators. In "Identity Matters: Facilitators' Struggles and Empowered Use of Social Identities in Intergroup Dialogue,"

Maxwell, Chesler, and Nagda examine the role of social identities at the intersection of intergroup dialogue facilitation and implications for consultative
support. In "Not *for* Others, but *With* Others for *All of Us:* Weaving Relationships, Co-creating Spaces of Justice," Nagda, Timbang, Fulmer, and
Tran combine poetry, prose, and narrative to understand how facilitators
conceive of being in alliance and how they deepen both their co-facilitation
relationship and their facilitation practice. Finally, Vasques-Scalera's "Changing Facilitators, Facilitating Change: The Lives of Intergroup Dialogue Facilitators Post-College" discusses the impact of facilitation on facilitators'
postgraduate lives and considers training implications that can sustain them
long term.

Intergroup dialogue facilitation can be a transformative, democratic approach to teaching and learning about social identities, social inequalities,
and social change. For former participants, becoming an intergroup dialogue
facilitator provides one pathway for building on their learning in intergroup
dialogues and for exercising their passion and commitments for social justice.
Themselves committed to lifelong learning, intergroup dialogue facilitators—
undergraduate students, graduate students, staff, faculty, and/or community
members—foster learning for others that necessarily involves support and
challenge, safety and discomfort, triumphs and tribulations. Facilitating intergroup dialogues is a form of learning that goes beyond the dichotomies of
learner–student and educator–teacher, self–other, and privileged–oppressed
to the hopeful and integrative possibilities of alliances where we are interconnected in learning, cognizant of the personal and social impact of structured
inequalities, courageous in pushing the boundaries of relating across differences, and regenerative in pursuit of justice.

References

Abu-Nimer, M. (1999). *Dialogue, conflict resolution, and change: Arab-Jewish encounters in Israel*.
    Albany, NY: State University of New York Press.
Adams, M., Bell, L. A., & Griffin, P. (Eds.). (2007). *Teaching for diversity and social justice* (2nd
    ed.). New York: Routledge.
Beale, R., Thompson, M., & Chesler, M. (2001). Training peer facilitators for intergroup
    dialogue leadership. In D. Schoem, & S. Hurtado (Eds.). *Intergroup Dialogue: Deliberative
    democracy in school, college, community, and workplace* (pp. 227–246). Ann Arbor: University
    of Michigan Press.
Burke, B., Geronimo, J., Martin, D., Thomas, B., & Wall, C. (2002). *Education for changing
    unions*. Toronto, ON: Between the Lines.
Delgado, R., & Stefancic, J. (2000). *Critical race theory: The cutting edge*. Philadelphia: Temple
    University Press.

Dovidio, J., Saguy, T., & Schnabel, N. (2009). Cooperation and conflict within groups: Bridging intragroup and intergroup processes. *Journal of Social Issues, 65*(2), 429–449.

Freire, P. (1970). *Pedagogy of the oppressed*. New York: Continuum.

Griffin, P., & Ouellett, M. (2007). Facilitating social justice education courses. In M. Adams, L. A. Bell, & P. Griffin (Eds.), *Teaching for diversity and social justice* (2nd ed., pp. 89–113). New York: Routledge.

Jones, J. M., Engelman, S., Turner, C. E., Jr., & Campbell, S. (2009). Worlds apart: The universality of racism leads to divergent social realities. In S. Demoulin, J. P. Leyes, & J. F. Dovidio (Eds.), *Intergroup Misunderstandings: Impact of divergent social realities* (pp. 117–133). Psychology Press.

Khuri, M. L. (2004). Working with emotion in educational intergroup dialogue. *International Journal of Intercultural Relations, 28*(6), 595–612.

Kim, J., & Kim, E. J. (2008). Theorizing dialogic deliberation: Everyday political talk as communicative action and dialogue. *Communication Theory, 18*, 51–70.

McCoy, M., & Scully, P. (2002). Deliberative dialogue to expand civic engagement: What kind of talk does democracy need? *National Civic Review, 91*(2), 117–135.

McMahon, B. J. (2003). Putting the elephant in the refrigerator: Student engagement, critical pedagogy and anti-racist education. *McGill Journal of Education, 38*(2), 257–273.

Nagda, B. A. (2006). Breaking barriers, crossing boundaries, building bridges: Communication processes in intergroup dialogues. *Journal of Social Issues, 62*(3), 553–576.

Nagda, B. A. (2007). *Weaving a tapestry of courage and justice: A resource guide for intergroup dialogue facilitation*. Seattle, WA: IDEA Center.

Nagda, B. A., & Gurin, P. (2007). Intergroup Dialogue: A critical-dialogic approach to learning about difference, inequality and social justice. *New Directions for Teaching and Learning, 111*, 35–45.

Nagda, B. A., Gurin, P., Sorensen, N., & Coombes, A. (2009). *Communicative actions: Not just a dialogue but a just dialogue*. Unpublished manuscript, University of Washington, Seattle.

Nagda, B. A., Gurin, P., Sorensen, N., Gurin-Sands, C., & Osuna, S. M. (2009). From separate corners to dialogue and action. *Race and Social Problems, 1*(1), 45–55.

Nagda, B. A., Kim, C. W., & Truelove, Y. (2004). Learning about difference, learning with others, learning to transgress. *Journal of Social Issues, 60*(1), 195–214.

Nagda, B. A., Zúñiga, X., & Sevig, T. D. (1995). Bridging differences through peer-facilitated intergroup dialogues. In S. Hatcher (Ed.), *Peer programs on the college campus: Theory, training, and 'voice of the peers'* (pp. 378–414). San Jose, CA: Resource Publications.

Narayan, U. (1988). Working together across difference: Some considerations on emotions and political practice. *Hypatia, 3*(2), 31–47.

Richeson, J. A., & Nussbaum, R. J. (2004). The impact of multiculturalism versus color-blindness on racial bias. *Journal of Experimental Social Psychology, 40*(3), 417–423.

Saunders, H. H. (1999). *A public peace process: Sustained dialogue to transform racial and ethnic conflicts*. New York: St. Martin's Press.

Schoem, D., & Hurtado, S. (Eds.). (2001). *Intergroup Dialogue: Deliberative democracy in school, college, community, and workplace*. Ann Arbor: University of Michigan Press.

Shelton, J. N., Richeson, J., & Vorauer, J. (2006). Threatened identities and interethnic interactions. *European Review of Social Psychology*, *17*(1), 321–358.

Shelton, N., Richeson, J., & Salvatore, J. (2005). Expecting to be the target of prejudice: Implications for interethnic interactions. *Personality and Social Psychology Bulletin*, *31*, 1189–1202.

Stephan, W. (2008). Psychological and communication processes associated with intergroup conflict resolution. *Small Group Research*, *39*(1), 28–41.

Tajfel, H. (1974). Social identity and intergroup behavior. *Social Science Information*, *13*, 69–89.

Tatum, B. D. (2003). *"Why are all the Black kids sitting together in the cafeteria?" And other conversations about race*. New York: Basic Books.

Tatum, B. D. (2007). *Can we talk about race?* Boston: Beacon Press.

Walsh, K. C. (2007). *Talking about race: Community dialogues and the politics of difference*. Chicago: University of Chicago Press.

Warner, J. (2009). A lot said, and unsaid, about race. *New York Times*. Retrieved July 27, 2009, from http://warner.blogs.nytimes.com/2009/07/26/a-lot-said-and-unsaid-about-race/.

Wright, S. C., & Lubensky, M. E. (2009). The struggle for social equality: Collective action versus prejudice reduction. In S. Demoulin, J. P. Leyes, & J. F. Dovidio (Eds.), *Intergroup Misunderstandings: Impact of divergent social realities* (pp. 291–310). New York: Psychology Press.

Young, I. M. (1997). *Intersecting voices: Dilemmas of gender, political philosophy, and policy*. Princeton, NJ: Princeton University Press.

Zúñiga, X., Nagda, B. A., Chesler, M., & Cytron-Walker, A. (2007). *Intergroup Dialogues in higher education: Meaningful learning about social justice*. ASHE Higher Education Report Series, *32*(4). San Francisco: Jossey-Bass.

2

IN THE HANDS OF FACILITATORS

Student Experiences in Dialogue and Implications for Facilitator Training

Anna M. Yeakley

Intergroup dialogues have been found to promote positive educational outcomes in understanding issues of diversity and social justice (Alimo, Kelly, & Clark, 2002; Gurin, Dey, Hurtado, & Gurin, 2002; Gurin, Nagda, & Lopez, 2004; Hurtado, 2003; Nagda, Kim, & Truelove, 2004). The learning process in intergroup dialogues is unique because much of the learning comes from the dialogue participants themselves, as they share their personal experiences and diverse perspectives along their different social identities. While readings and other educational materials also form a foundation for dialogue[1] learning, participants report that hearing the personal experiences of their peers in dialogue is what most influenced their growth in understanding intergroup relations and social justice issues (Yeakley, 1998). Thus, it is the quality of engagement among the dialogue participants—the extent to which they share honestly, actively listen, challenge each other's assumptions, and seek to understand each other's perspectives—that influences their learning in the dialogue. Dialogue facilitators support the quality of engagement among the participants, so having well-trained facilitators is critical to the success of the dialogue experience.

This chapter describes the findings from my dissertation research on intergroup dialogue *processes* and how they shape dialogue outcomes (Yeakley, 1998). The study found that the process of "connecting through a depth of personal sharing" played a significant role in positive outcomes, while the process of "disconnecting in response to hurtful intergroup conflicts" was common for those who described having negative outcomes. I end the chapter with a discussion of implications for facilitation skills development emerging from these findings: (1) creating a safe space, (2) recognizing warning signs of negative processes, (3) supporting a depth of personal sharing, (4) working with conflict, and (5) attending to (identity) group dynamics that reflect differences in power and privilege.

Research Study on Intergroup Dialogue Processes

I conducted a qualitative interview study with students who had completed an intergroup dialogue course to better understand the *processes* that shape the learning outcomes for intergroup dialogue participants (Yeakley, 1998). The impetus for this study originated from the questions that came up for me when I was facilitating an intergroup dialogue for the first time, and I realized that the range of outcomes I observed among the participants could not be explained by the intergroup contact theories I had learned about in graduate school. My previous training in intergroup relations and intergroup contact had taught me that when certain intergroup contact conditions are met (e.g., having equal status in the group, working toward a common goal, having the approval of authority figures) positive intergroup attitudes would result (Allport, 1954 /1979; Cook, 1978; Pettigrew, 1998; Pettigrew & Tropp, 2006; Sherif, Harvey, White, Hood, & Sherif, 1961).

Because the participants in an intergroup dialogue go through the same experience together, with the same set of conditions (e.g., having the same set of readings, experiential activities, and dialogue discussions led by the same pair of co-facilitators), I expected everyone would emerge from the experience with the same (positive) outcomes. This was not the case, however. Most participants had experienced a high degree of positive learning and intergroup attitude change, but some had negligible growth in learning and, most disconcerting, one or two students appeared to have had negative experiences.

To help answer my questions on how different participants could experience different outcomes in the same dialogue group, I conducted an interview study with 14 students who had completed an intergroup dialogue course and had expressed a range of different outcomes and evaluations of their experience. I also interviewed a comparison group of 12 psychology students who never participated in an intergroup dialogue but reported a change in their intergroup attitudes over time, to see which change processes are unique to the dialogue experience and which are part of intergroup experiences more generally. In interviews that ranged from one to two hours, I asked the 26 participants to go into great detail about the types of changes they experienced (positive, negative, or none), to what they attributed their changes, and how the process of change unfolded for them over time.

Using a grounded theory approach (Glaser & Strauss, 1967), I looked for patterns in the interview transcripts for processes that differentiated positive versus negative outcomes. The patterns that emerged formed two categories: *Positive Change Processes* and *Negative Change Processes*. A summary of the research findings below details which processes were found to support positive versus negative outcomes for the dialogue participants.

Positive Change Processes: What Produces Intergroup Connection

Four levels of Positive Change were found in this study, with increasing levels of intergroup connection and understanding. The outcomes varied from a small-level change (e.g., increased comfort) to greater empathy and understanding of other identities' experiences and feelings (e.g., intergroup understanding). The process common to all of the positive change outcomes was *increased connection through depth of personal sharing*, with greater depth of personal sharing corresponding to stronger positive outcomes. In order of increasing connection, Positive Change outcomes included the following:

<u>Positive Change</u>

<u>Level of Connection—Resulting From (depth of personal sharing)</u>

1. **Increased Comfort**—sharing small talk or time together
2. **Increased Connection/Friendship**—sharing common interests or hobbies
3. **Increased Understanding of Different Perspectives**—sharing different perspectives on controversial issues (e.g., affirmative action, gay marriage), including the feelings and reasons behind the differences in perspectives
4. **Intergroup Understanding, or Increased Understanding of Identity Experiences**—sharing personal experiences related to one's social identity, such as experiences with prejudice or discrimination

Increased Comfort, the lowest level of connection, has no personal information shared; only small talk or time together. For example, a White man from the comparison group reported feeling very uncomfortable around

African Americans, having never interacted with them before college. His comfort level increased only after meeting two African American students he felt comfortable joking around with. He did not share anything beyond jokes with them, so his comfort did not progress to friendship.

In this study, Increased Connection/Friendship depended on sharing personal information, particularly similarities or shared interests. A heterosexual student from a sexual orientation dialogue, for example, developed her first friendships with lesbians, and two White students from the comparison group developed their first friendships with students of color after they discovered common interests in music, sports, or hobbies. These interests provided a basis for spending time together and developing friendships.

Increased Understanding of Different Perspectives and Intergroup Understanding involved the most intimate sharing of the self: personal perspectives and personal experiences. For example, a White man described how his understanding of different perspectives on affirmative action had a dramatic shift after taking a race/ethnicity dialogue. He had been strongly against affirmative action, but then became much more supportive after hearing an African American student he really respected and considered "brilliant" explain how affirmative action addresses educational inequities and makes it possible for students like him, who did not go to the best high schools, to still go to college. A man from a gender dialogue also explained that he had more respect for perspectives he did not agree with, because he was able to hear and understand where those beliefs came from.

Intergroup Understanding, or Increased Understanding of Identity Experiences, developed through the sharing of identity-related experiences, such as experiences with prejudice and discrimination. A student from a sexual orientation dialogue described an example of Intergroup Understanding, sharing how she gained a deep understanding of the coming-out process and how hard it is to be gay, by listening to the personal experiences of the lesbian, gay, and bisexual students. Hearing their experiences also made her realize that she never struggled with her sexual identity in the same way, making her aware of her heterosexual privilege.

Two target group members from the sexual orientation dialogue also experienced Intergroup Understanding. A bisexual man reported an increased understanding of the experiences of lesbians and how those differ from the experiences of gay men. A gay man also gained a better understanding of the diversity among gay people by listening to the diverse experiences of the gay men in his dialogue. This helped him to work through some internalized homophobia and gain more acceptance of his gay identity because he realized he did not have to fit the stereotypes to identify as a gay man.

Negative Change Processes: What Produces Intergroup Disconnection

Four Negative Change outcomes were found in this study, each with negative intergroup experiences or conflicts creating increasing degrees of intergroup division. The outcomes ranged from Increased Stereotyping/Prejudice, where intergroup distancing took place without hurt feelings or conflict, to Increased Disconnection, where multiple intergroup conflicts produced the greatest intergroup distancing and enduring negative feelings. The process shared by all the Negative Change outcomes was *increased disconnection in reaction to hurtful intergroup conflicts*. Depending on how the conflicts were experienced and processed, the conflicts may have been resolved or left unresolved, and the negative feelings associated with the conflict may have dissipated or persisted. In order of increasing disconnection, the Negative Change outcomes were as follows:

Negative Change

Level of Disconnection—Resulting from (type of conflict)

1. **Increased Stereotyping/Prejudice**—No conflict (observing patterns only)
2. **Increased Separation**—Resolved (temporary) conflict
3. **Increased Resentment**— Unresolved conflict, from single experience
4. **Increased Disconnection**—Unresolved conflict, multiple experiences

Increased Stereotyping/Prejudice does not involve conflict or hurt feelings, but it does entail intergroup distancing because differences between the self and others are exaggerated. Increased Stereotyping/Prejudice occurred when patterns of unlikable traits or behaviors were observed among those of a different identity, without the direct communication needed to break down stereotypes. This outcome was found only in the comparison group of psychology students; the personal sharing among the dialogue participants allowed for the breaking down of stereotypes.

The remaining types of Negative Change—Increased Separation, Increased Resentment, and Increased Disconnection—involved direct intergroup conflicts where the participant felt judged or insulted by the other identity group. What differentiated these three negative outcomes was whether the conflict was resolved or not, and whether there was one isolated conflict or a conflict tied to multiple negative intergroup experiences. The only negative outcome with a resolved conflict was Increased Separation, where enough time had passed that negative feelings dissipated and the person felt reconciled enough to engage with the other identity group again. An example of

Increased Separation came from a woman engineering student in the comparison group, who felt mocked by sexist remarks from men engineering students and professors, so she decided to leave the major and separate herself from the men who belittled her. After some time passed, however, she realized she did like engineering and did not want the treatment of a few men to stop her, so she returned to taking engineering classes.

Increased Resentment results when an unresolved conflict is restricted to an isolated incident. For example, in this study, a White man from a race/ethnicity dialogue reported strong feelings of resentment after being repeatedly stereotyped as someone who had always experienced privilege in life, with everything handed to him on a silver platter. He asked to not be stereotyped in this way, but the group kept dismissing him as someone defined only by privilege. Another student experienced Increased Resentment after feeling forced to "come out" during a sexual orientation dialogue activity. The activity required students to break into two identity groups, one with heterosexuals and one with lesbian, gay, and bisexual students. When the participant tried to tell the facilitators he felt uncomfortable coming out this way, the facilitators showed insensitivity by treating the issue as "no big deal" and instructing him to go to whichever group felt right that day. In both examples, the conflict was never resolved.

Increased Disconnection results when an unresolved intergroup conflict connects to several other negative experiences with the other identity group. For example, an African American man in a race/ethnicity dialogue reported Increased Disconnection from White students. He had felt judged and disrespected by White students before the dialogue, especially from overhearing comments that African American students were not smart enough to be admitted to the university without affirmative action. He had heard this so many times and felt so invalidated on campus that when a White student commented that too many unqualified students were being admitted through affirmative action, he got very angry and developed an animosity toward White students in general. When this participant was interviewed six months after his dialogue, his anger toward White students was still very strong—he expressed both a belief that White students would never understand their privilege, and a desire to get through college with as little interaction with White students as possible.

Summary of Positive and Negative Change Factors

The results of this study reveal that *depth of personal sharing* and the *processing of conflicts* play key roles in shaping dialogue outcomes. Because negative outcomes happened when hurtful intergroup experiences were not addressed, having a *safe dialogue space* and *attending to the signs of negative processes* are two additional factors that shape dialogue outcomes. A fifth factor related to outcome differences was the *identity of the participants as targets*[2] *or agents*,[3] as more agent group members had positive outcomes than target group members (i.e., five out of six Positive Change cases and one out of two Mixed Change cases). Although this study found more positive outcomes for dominant than subordinate group members, my experience teaching dialogue courses for the past 14 years has shown me that a majority of dialogue participants, from both identity groups, experience positive dialogue outcomes. In this study, the differences may have been due to the fact that agents enter the dialogue with more to learn, while targets have more past experiences with oppression that may be retriggered by offensive comments made in the dialogue.

To achieve strong positive outcomes for all dialogue participants, facilitators need to be trained in the skills that promote positive outcomes. Five of these facilitation skills (corresponding to the five factors that shape dialogue outcomes) are described in the section below on implications for facilitator training.

Implications for Facilitator Training

Based on the five factors that shaped dialogue outcomes in this study, there are five facilitation skills that are essential to promoting positive outcomes: (1) creating a safe space, (2) recognizing signs of negative processes, (3) encouraging and supporting depth of personal sharing, (4) engaging conflicts as teachable moments, and (5) attending to identity differences in awareness and experience. These five facilitation skills should be thoroughly addressed in facilitation training, as described in the following sections.

Creating a Safe Space

Dialogue participants can share their honest thoughts and feelings and divulge their personal experiences to their peers *only* if the dialogue is a safe space for sharing. To create a safe space, facilitators need to understand what safety means to their group of participants. They must know how to effectively lead the group in the creation of ground rules in order to make the dialogue a safe, supportive, and respectful space for participants. Facilitators will also need to understand how communication styles, responses to conflict, and signs of respect can vary across cultures or identities. For example, direct eye contact may signify respect in some cultures but feel confrontational in others. For y means having complete honesty (even if the truth hurts), and knowing that everything is out in the open. For others, safety means not having anger or conflict in the dialogue, and keeping the discourse "nice" and polite.

While it is important for the facilitators to understand how the concepts of safety and respect may have different meanings for different participants, it is also important for them to explain that "safety does not mean they will never feel challenged or uncomfortable" (Griffin & Ouellett, 2007, p. 96) and that part of the learning process in dialogue is to step outside of our comfort zones in order to be open to different perspectives, reexamine our assumptions, and use conflict as a learning tool.

Facilitators will also need to understand the safety issues that are unique to a specific dialogue topic. For example, a sexual orientation dialogue will have safety issues around the subject of "coming out" when students are asked to share about their identities. Participants need to be given the full freedom and decision power in whether they "come out" to the group or not, so they never feel forced to reveal their sexual identity or have their sense of safety compromised. Trainers should therefore guide facilitators on how to modify activities so that participants can still share their different perspectives and experiences without having to reveal their sexual orientation. Safety issues also exist for gender dialogue participants who do not identify with the gender binary (e.g., transgender, genderqueer), and for survivors of sexual assault or gender-based violence, because these topics are often discussed in gender dialogues. When survivors do share their stories in the dialogue, it is often very emotional for them, so it is also important for facilitators to know how to access the counseling and support services on campus.

Finally, facilitators need to be able to detect when the dialogue has become "unsafe" by being transformed into a debate. When this happens, it usually means that the ground rules are not being followed. Facilitators will need to know how to revisit the ground rules and inquire if anything needs to be added to restore safety to the group.

Recognizing Signs of Negative Processes

Facilitators need to know when differential outcomes are happening in the dialogue in order to know when they need to intervene in the dialogue process. There are several signs that negative change processes may be unfolding for one or more participants that facilitators should attend to, including the following:

- Hearing complaints or frustrations voiced in the dialogue (e.g., complaints that some participants appear to be holding back)

- Hearing a tone of anger or frustration in a participant's question or response
- Observing body language that indicates a lack of engagement or disrespect of others (e.g., rolling eyes or averting eye contact, turning body away from the group, making facial expressions of displeasure, messaging, or doodling during dialogue)
- Reading comments in journal assignments that express unhappiness or disappointment with the dialogue process (e.g., one participant writes that they feel disrespected and do not want to share anymore, or multiple participants write he or she feels triggered by the same comment)
- Having students drop out or expressing that they are thinking of dropping out of the dialogue

In order to prepare facilitators to intervene appropriately when these signs appear, facilitation training needs to cover how to attend to body language, respond to complaints and give feedback on journals in encouraging and supportive ways, talk one-on-one with participants who are struggling, and process group dynamics issues with the group.

Encouraging and Modeling a Depth of Personal Sharing

As the research findings imply, positive dialogue outcomes are more likely when participants have deeper levels of personal sharing. To achieve this, facilitators must provide a model of deep personal sharing themselves. The facilitator training course should therefore provide as many opportunities for the facilitators to self-reflect and share personal experiences with each other as possible.

Facilitators can guide their participants to deeper forms of personal sharing if they know how to ask "probing" questions—questions that strive to get at the underlying motivations, feelings, and values that have shaped someone's beliefs or perspectives (see chapter 1). Probing questions allow participants to gain a deeper understanding of why someone feels the way he or she does about an issue, even if they disagree with her or him.

Facilitators also need to recognize when personal sharing has been hindered in their dialogue and know what they can do to promote a greater depth of personal sharing. For example, if strong emotions are expressed in the journals but not in the dialogue, the facilitators need to know how to comment on journals so that participants feel encouraged to bring their feelings up to the group. If personal sharing stays at the surface level, the facilitators will need to know how to bring up these concerns and provide the group with direct feedback on how a willingness to take risks and share at a deeper level is a must for getting the most out of their dialogue experience.

Facilitators need to be aware that personal sharing involves different types of risks and emotions for the different identities. For example, target group members' sharing includes experiences with prejudice and discrimination, like being put down or invalidated by privileged group members, or not being allowed access to an activity or a group because of their subordinate identity. Sharing these experiences may feel like airing dirty laundry in front of the agent group and could stir up the target group's emotions of anger and sadness all over again. While the dominant group members also take risks when they admit to stereotypes or reflect on how they have experienced privilege, their sharing usually does not make them as emotional or vulnerable as oppressed group members' personal sharing can.

Engaging Conflicts as Teachable Moments

How intergroup conflicts are treated plays a key role in whether positive or negative outcomes will emerge from an intergroup dialogue. To be able to use conflicts as teachable moments, the facilitators must first be able to detect the signs that a conflict is brewing or needing to surface. This requires developing an awareness of nonverbal cues from the participants, recognizing that looking away, shifting in a chair, or remaining silent may be signs that someone is having a negative reaction to something that was shared in the group. I also encourage facilitators to be aware of their own internal reactions to offensive statements as cues that some of the participants may be experiencing similar tensions and needing to voice their feelings.

A large part of conflict skills training for facilitators focuses on helping facilitators to become more comfortable with conflict themselves. If facilitators can undergo a conflict during their training process, they will know from experience that conflict can be constructive and valuable to the dialogue learning process. With the ground rules and the training leaders as supports, facilitators can also gain an understanding of what their participants will need to feel supported through a conflict.

One of the findings from this research study was that unresolved conflicts produced negative outcomes. This indicates that facilitators need to fully unpack the conflicts that come up in their dialogue, even if it means using another session to revisit what happened. Sometimes facilitators think it is more important to follow the dialogue syllabus or their session plan than to address issues that come up unexpectedly or that require more discussion time than was originally planned for. Therefore, facilitation training should cover the importance of being able to adjust the dialogue agenda according to the pace and needs of the group, and that conflicts, in particular, need to be fully discussed before the group moves on to a new topic.

The facilitators do not need to get everyone in agreement after a conflict. Rather, facilitators will need to provide enough time for everyone to share his or her views and reactions, ask each other questions, and hear the reasons behind different beliefs. If facilitators take the time to fully process everyone's feelings after a conflict, participants will feel heard and better understood, recognize where others' perspectives came from, gain insight into what caused the conflict, and achieve better intergroup understanding.

Facilitators can turn conflicts into powerful teachable moments if they can make connections between the conflict dynamics taking place in the dialogue (e.g., assumptions made, reactions and treatment given to each other, and emotions experienced) and the larger conflicts that take place between their two identity groups within society. If facilitators can show how the dialogue conflict(s) resemble societal-level battles over issues or policies, the participants can see how their intergroup struggles go beyond the individuals in the dialogue group, and how their own interactions have been shaped by deeply ingrained beliefs, feelings, and reactions that have been passed down to them through the cycle of socialization (Harro, 2000).

Attending to Identity Differences in Awareness and Experience

The fifth facilitation skill involves paying close attention to how the identity groups may be experiencing the dialogue differently (e.g., how an activity on sexism may be experienced differently by women compared to men). Facilitators must be able to detect when identity differences begin to replicate oppression dynamics (e.g., men speaking over women), to know when to intervene and regain a balance in the group dynamics between the two identity groups.

First, facilitators need to understand how the two groups often differ in their awareness of oppression when they enter the dialogue group. For example, subordinate group members are often perceived as "experts" on oppression by the dominant group because they are believed to be knowledgeable through personal experience about the impacts of oppression and how it operates through social and political structures (e.g., media portrayals, racial profiling). Dominant group members, in contrast, often enter the dialogue feeling oblivious about privilege, oppression, and what their agent identity means to them. It is helpful if facilitators are trained to challenge these assumptions about awareness and expertise at the beginning of the dialogue because, in fact, everyone has the opportunity to learn from the dialogue, and everyone has personal experiences to contribute to others' learning.

To help facilitators learn how to challenge assumptions about which group should be the "educator" or "expert" in the dialogue, the training instructors can help facilitators look back and recognize how their own assumptions about different levels of awareness changed during their training process. The fact is that every facilitator, regardless of their dominant or subordinate identity status, begins his or her training experience with a lack of understanding on many issues and then has tremendous growth in awareness by the end of the training experience. Facilitators can use this realization to challenge their participants' assumptions and to interrupt the dialogue group process if they see that the target group members are being asked too many questions by the agent group.

Second, facilitators need to be aware of identity differences in experiences with oppression, particularly when conflicts emerge. Biased statements, stereotypes, and offensive comments made in the dialogue are likely to hit the oppressed group members particularly hard, because they can revive painful feelings from past experiences. Facilitation training should therefore cover methods of providing support to oppressed group members, such as affording enough time to process feelings after a conflict and interrupting the educator dynamic when it happens. Methods of providing support to dominant group members will also need to be covered, such as helping them to move beyond feelings of guilt, to see themselves more as allies than oppressors, to acknowledge how they have experienced privilege, and to understand why certain statements can sometimes be offensive or hurtful to target group members.

Facilitators who can distinguish the different support needs of target and agent group members will also be better prepared to consider the role of identity when they are applying the other four facilitation skills. For example, a facilitator who is knowledgeable of target and agent group differences in awareness and experience in a dialogue will be better able to detect how the two identity groups differ in their needs for creating a "safe space," whether personal sharing entails disproportionate levels of risk taking or discomfort, whether one group is showing more signs of negative processes than the other, and whether each identity group responds differently to conflicts.

Although I conducted this study over a decade ago, the same types of positive and negative change processes continue to manifest in the various classroom and community dialogues I have facilitated or supervised since the study. The five facilitation skills that emerged from understanding these processes have also been pivotal for highly successful dialogue experiences every time.

There are similar and distinct aspects to classroom and community dialogues that impact how the five facilitation skills can be applied across different settings. For example, one important factor is whether the dialogue meets over a sustained period, like classroom dialogues, or whether it meets for only one or two days, like many of the community dialogues I have facilitated. The time interval impacts how conflicts can be addressed, because facilitators cannot revisit a conflict in a later session if the dialogue is constrained to one day. Even for community dialogues with more time available, the surfacing of conflicts is still sometimes hindered by participants' relationships with one another if they come from an intact group (e.g., teachers of a school, members of an organization, or employees of a company). Some participants may fear future repercussions for comments they make in front of others who are in a higher position than themselves (e.g., an employer, an administrator, a supervisor, or a police officer).

By considering the shared and unique aspects of dialogues that occur in different settings, facilitators can apply their skills in a more context-specific way, to maximize positive learning outcomes for the participants. The next two sections in the book will showcase facilitation training models in classroom, campus, and community settings. The authors articulate their rationale and approach to training facilitators in these settings, illustrating the differences among as well as within the broader classroom, campus, and community settings.

Notes

1. The term *dialogue* is used interchangeably with *intergroup dialogue* in this chapter. Although the two terms can have different meanings, I use the term *dialogue* frequently as shorthand for intergroup dialogue. Thus, the dialogues mentioned here refer only to intergroup dialogues and, specifically, to intergroup dialogues among college students that are co-facilitated by two trained peers.

2. *Target*, sometimes used to refer to subordinate or oppressed identity groups, refers to social identities that are "disenfranchised, exploited, and victimized by prejudice, discrimination, and other structural obstacles" (Harro, 2000, p. 17). In this study, target identities included women, people of color, lesbians/gay men/bisexuals, and Jews.

3. *Agent*, sometimes used to refer to dominant or privileged identity groups, refers to social identities that have relatively more power and privilege in systems of oppression. In this study, agent identities included men, White people, heterosexuals, and Christians.

References

Alimo, C., Kelly, R., & Clark, C. (2002). Diversity initiatives in higher education: Intergroup dialogue program student outcomes and implications for campus radical climate: A case study. *Multicultural Education, 10*(1), 49–53.

Allport, G. W. (1954/1979). *The nature of prejudice*. Cambridge, MA: Addison-Wesley Publishing Company.

Cook, S. W. (1978). Interpersonal and attitudinal outcomes in cooperating interracial groups. *Journal of Research & Development in Education, 12*(1), 97–113.

Glaser, B., & Strauss, A. (1967). *The discovery of grounded theory: Strategies for qualitative research*. Chicago: Aldine Publishing Company.

Griffin, P., & Ouellett, M. L. (2007). Facilitating social justice education courses. In M. Adams, L. A. Bell, & P. Griffin (Eds.), *Teaching for diversity and social justice* (2nd ed. pp. 89–113). New York: Routledge.

Gurin, P., Dey, E. L., Hurtado, S., & Gurin, G. (2002). Diversity and higher education: Theory and impact on educational outcomes. *Harvard Educational Review, 72*(3), 330–366.

Gurin, P., Nagda, B. A., & Lopez, G. (2004). The benefits of diversity in education for democratic citizenship. *Journal of Social Issues, 60*(1), 17–34.

Harro, B. (2000). Cycle of socialization. In M. Adams, W. J. Blumenfeld, R. Castaneda, H. W. Hackman, M. L. Peters, & X. Zuñiga (Eds.), *Readings for diversity and social justice: An anthology on racism, antisemitism, sexism, heterosexism, ableism, and classism* (pp. 15–21). New York: Routledge.

Hurtado, S. (2003). *Preparing college students for a diverse democracy: Final report to the U.S. Department of Education, OERI, Field Initiated Studies Program.*. Ann Arbor, MI: Center for the Study of Higher and Postsecondary Education.

Nagda, B. A., Kim, C. W., & Truelove, Y. (2004). Learning about difference, learning with others, learning to transgress. *Journal of Social Issues, 60*(1), 195–214.

Pettigrew, T. F. (1998). Intergroup contact theory. *Annual Review of Psychology, 49*, 65–85.

Pettigrew, T. F., & Tropp, L. R. (2006). A meta-analytic test of intergroup contact theory. *Journal of Personality and Social Psychology, 90*, 751–783.

Sherif, M., Harvey, O., White, B., Hood, W., & Sherif, C. (1961). *Intergroup cooperation and competition: The Robbers Cave experiment*. Norman, OK: University Book Exchange.

Yeakley, A. (1998). *The nature of prejudice change: Positive and negative change processes arising from intergroup contact experiences*. Unpublished doctoral dissertation, University of Michigan, Ann Arbor.

SECTION ONE

INTERGROUP DIALOGUE FACILITATION TRAINING FOR CLASSROOM-BASED EXPERIENCES

The chapters in this section help us move from the theoretical considerations and implications for facilitation training outlined in the first two chapters to specific approaches to training facilitators for classroom-based learning experiences. As a whole, the chapters in this section examine the breadth and depth of training facilitators for classroom-based intergroup dialogues. In almost all cases, these intergroup dialogues bring together two different social identity groups (people of color and White people; women and men; lesbian, gay, and bisexual people and heterosexual people; and others) for a sustained period of time (5–15 weeks) in a co-facilitated encounter using a four-stage curriculum (see Zúñiga, Nagda, Chesler, & Cytron-Walker, 2007).

Each chapter emphasizes facilitation training by faculty and practitioners who have trained hundreds of undergraduates, graduate students, and faculty members. The chapters in this section identify a number of critical topics central to the training process of the classroom-based intergroup dialogues and how they each, uniquely, address these issues:

- Structure in training facilitators
- Continued learning about social identities, inequalities, and personal and social change

- Participatory learning and training processes that involve content-based and process-based learning
- Supports for addressing risk taking, from sharing personal stories to working through conflicts

Chapters also address the specific institutional and constituent focus for facilitation training, provide a description of their training components grounded in theory and practice, and offer an illustration of select exercises or practice elements that highlight their training process. Across the chapters, the authors develop a unique picture of the similarities and differences in training undergraduates, graduate students, and faculty or staff.

In Chapter 3, Maxwell, Fisher, Thompson, and Behling introduce the training and support model of the Program on Intergroup Relations (IGR) at the University of Michigan. The longest-running intergroup dialogue program in higher education, IGR utilizes undergraduate peers as facilitators of intergroup dialogues. The chapter describes the foundations of their training model, discusses the importance of both cognitive and affective learning in their two-course sequence, and provides specific examples of ways to engage students in this integrative learning approach.

Chapter 4 continues the subject of working with undergraduate peers but in a distinctive higher education context. Rodríguez, Rodríguez-Scheel, Lindsey, and Kirkland describe the goals and outcomes of a newly established Intergroup Dialogue Program at Occidental College with a focus on facilitator training. The program weaves together dimensions of the intergroup dialogue model with attention to the unique needs and characteristics of facilitators at a small, private, residential, liberal arts college whose institutional mission is diverse democracy.

Zúñiga, Kachwaha, DeJong, and Pacheco shift the focus to a reflective practice training model in chapter 5. Working with graduate students in the School of Education at the University of Massachusetts Amherst, this program relies on the reflective practice tradition in teacher education, which asserts that learning is dependent upon the integration of experience with reflection and of theory with practice. The authors describe a specific case between two co-facilitators and their instructors that illustrates the reflective practice model. They provide a unique opportunity to learn about this process by examining the fears, challenges, and insights gained from a critical examination of a particular facilitation experience.

Chapter 6 examines professionals as facilitators. Because they are de-greed professionals and faculty with significant life experience and institutional power, Wong(Lau), Landrum-Brown, and Walker describe their unique challenges to intergroup dialogue facilitation. This chapter focuses on the tacit theoretical and practical knowledge that faculty and practitioners in social justice–related work and disciplines bring to intergroup dialogue work, as well as the distinctive challenges these same professionals have when facilitating classroom-based intergroup dialogues. Instead of participating in a traditional training program, the authors share how their professional development, practice, and reflection have given them the tools to successfully facilitate intergroup dialogues.

Reference

Zúñiga, X., Nagda, B. A., Chesler, M., & Cytron-Walker, A. (2007). Intergroup dialogues in higher education: Meaningful learning about social justice. *ASHE Higher Education Report Series*, *32*(4). San Francisco: Jossey-Bass.

3

TRAINING PEER FACILITATORS AS SOCIAL JUSTICE EDUCATORS

Integrating Cognitive and Affective Learning

Kelly E. Maxwell, Roger B. Fisher, Monita C. Thompson, and Charles Behling

Intergroup dialogue demonstrably benefits participants cognitively, affectively, and behaviorally. Participants show increased interest in political issues and awareness of institutional and structural causes of group differences as a result of participation in intergroup dialogue. They deepen their understanding of the perspectives of others and appreciate more the commonalities and differences between and within groups. They also increase their participation in college and community activities. Overall, participation in dialogues fosters active thinking and preparation for citizenship in a diverse democracy (Dessel & Rogge, 2008; Gurin, Nagda, & Lopez, 2004; Nagda, Gurin, Sorensen, & Zúñiga, 2009).

As positive as these effects are for participants, an even stronger and more long-lasting impact of dialogue is found with the *facilitators themselves*. One recent facilitator at the University of Michigan notes:

> As a facilitator, I took a journey with my participants through our social identities and their impact on our lives as well as the lives around us. . . . I have developed a newfound respect for oppressed groups, individuals, and even myself. Surely, my experience with intergroup relations will not end at the closing of this semester. I hope to continue to explore different areas of awareness, and I am committed to a lifelong pursuit of combating social injustice. (White woman facilitator)

Facilitators experience learning that is deeper and more intense than simply participating in intergroup dialogues; they are empowered by their experiences to act in their post-college communities (Vasques-Scalera, 1999; also see chapter 13 for more detail on this experience).

The preparatory training and facilitating of intergroup dialogues leaves a deep impact as expressed by another facilitator:

> I am very thankful for the lessons learned and the degree to which I understand important concepts regarding isms, target/agent identities, privilege/power, and dominant narratives. . . . Overall it's been an amazing semester, with a lot of learning. . . . I do feel that I have learned a ton as a facilitator, and I want to continue improving. [Being a facilitator] was a great choice, and my learning does not end here. (Arab American woman facilitator)

In this chapter, we focus on a peer facilitation model of intergroup dialogue. Peer facilitation, skilled undergraduates working with other undergraduates, is an important educational experience for both sets of students—facilitators and participants. Micari, Streitwieser, and Light (2006) assert that undergraduates who lead their peers make gains in cognitive, personal, and professional development areas. For facilitators, training in itself coupled with applied practice of new skills and insights is a critical opportunity to deepen their learning about social justice. Furthermore, intergroup dialogue by design is a democratic space for mutual learning of all participants. Peers as facilitators actualize this democratic, multicultural arena. Undergraduate facilitators' leadership in dialogue minimizes hierarchy and seeks to provide more egalitarian ownership in the dialogue. There is a shared identification between participants and facilitators that leads to an ease of interaction and greater commitment from participants (Chesler, Kellman-Fritz, & Knife-Gould, 2003). We describe in more detail the facilitator training and support necessary to create a positive intergroup dialogue environment.

A Model of Social Justice Education

The Program on Intergroup Relations (IGR) at the University of Michigan is supported and staffed as a collaboration of the Division of Student Affairs and the College of Literature, Science, and the Arts. As a result, IGR's curriculum and programming are influenced by multidisciplinary theoretical perspectives including theories of student development, social identity, social and clinical psychology, conflict studies, and sociology (e.g., Baxter Magolda &

King, 2004; Chickering & Reisser, 1993; Dovidio & Gaertner, 2004; Evans, Forney, & Guido-Dibrito, 1998; Harro, 2000; Keagan, 1994; Torres, Howard-Hamilton, & Cooper, 2003; Wijeyesinghe & Jackson, 2001).

The undergraduates who act as peer facilitators of IGR dialogues typically participate in at least three of the courses in IGR's curriculum: a dialogue course, a training course, and a practicum course. These courses offer options designed to "meet students where they are," building upon a variety of approaches to social justice (Potapchuk, 2002) and student development (Chickering & Reisser, 1993), permitting students to locate their own developmentally appropriate level of study. In the following sections we will examine the six spheres of development (individual, interpersonal, intergroup, institutional, structural, and cultural) and the cognitive and affective learning promoted during facilitator training.

Spheres of Development

IGR conceptualizes social justice education as occurring along a continuum of six overlapping domains: individual, interpersonal, intergroup, institutional, structural, and cultural spheres. (This framework was conceptualized in IGR using Potapchuk, 2002, as an initial reference point.) Depending on their prior experiences and awareness, students typically begin their studies by focusing on individual and interpersonal issues, then progress to intergroup and institutional issues, and finally structural and cultural issues. Breadth and depth are added as students progress through the course sequence and ultimately become facilitators. Students are encouraged first to develop an understanding of self and their social identities within the individual sphere. They learn interpersonal skills and how to communicate with members of other social identities. They then begin to understand the broader implications of social identity for their own groups and others in the intergroup sphere and move toward an understanding of power and society at large in the institutional sphere. Structural and cultural spheres focus on a web of institutions and structures, the unquestioned norms and assumptions that underlie those structures, and the ways the structures socialize our judgments of what is "good," "right," and "valued" in our society. The IGR facilitation training sequence focuses primarily on the first four spheres (intrapersonal, interpersonal, intergroup, and institutional). Many undergraduates enter their studies of diversity and justice at these levels, so exploration of these spheres seems essential. Each domain builds upon the processes associated with the previous ones as students move developmentally through the sequence. For example, individual learning and action persist through the interpersonal sphere, which continues through the intergroup sphere and builds in each subsequent sphere. Of course, a student's learning is rarely linear, and there are rich and complex interactions occurring as the courses progress across spheres. Although structural and cultural spheres are less emphasized in the courses, they become part of these interactions between domains: individual, interpersonal, intergroup, and institutional domains exist within structural and cultural contexts.

Affective and Cognitive Learning

Two learning frameworks inform our training approach. First, we draw upon Jackson's framework of multicultural competencies comprising Passion, Awareness, Skills, and Knowledge, or "PASK" for short (Beale, Thompson, & Chesler, 2001; Jackson, n.d.). PASK serves as a foundation for the competencies needed in facilitation. Second, Keagan (1994) suggests that there are three dimensions of learning: cognitive, intrapersonal, and interpersonal. This framework stresses the convergence of the three dimensions to provide optimal learning. We integrate the two frameworks. It is not enough for students to experience cognitive learning exclusively (knowledge, skills, and factual awareness). They must also experience the affect or emotion tied to these issues (passion and personal awareness). Integrating cognitive knowledge with personal passion and empathy (the intrapersonal and interpersonal) therefore becomes a central learning goal of the IGR training process.

Dovidio and Gaertner (2004) provide an empirical basis for understanding the importance of affective experience in diversity and justice education. They hypothesize that there is widespread acceptance of principles of equality and justice in contemporary society, which makes it easy to believe that one is not complicit in continued social injustice. However, one is also influenced by negative factors, for example, knowledge of stereotypes of social groups, anxiety and fears regarding some groups, enjoyment of privilege, ingroup-outgroup processes, and other factors that contribute to prejudice and discrimination. Since these processes violate one's conceptions of justice, they often operate at an unconscious level. In short, "modern discriminators" may engage in discrimination even when they believe that they are advocates for justice (Gaertner et al., 1997; Stephan & Stephan, 2000).

In social justice education, therefore, cognitive instruction is important but not enough. Cognitive instruction lays the foundation for social justice learning. "Content" aspects of training include information about the history and contemporary state of relations among the groups of interest; facts about privilege and stigmatization of the groups; and the dynamics of interpersonal, institutional, and cultural discrimination. In addition, content includes detailed instruction in technical skills of facilitation, group processes, and dialogue methodology. Such instruction, as important as it is, confronts and enriches students mostly on a conscious level of awareness. However, the real problem of prejudice and discrimination may often be on a deeper, less conscious level. One way to surface unconscious prejudice is by personal exploration, including emotional processes such as building empathy between groups. Stephan and Finlay (1999) discuss the role of empathy in intergroup relations and suggest that there must be explicit opportunities for groups to identify with members of the other group. Much of this is done by providing emotionally challenging experiences—involving doing and feeling, not merely thinking—to confront this unconscious level. It is in this space of self-exploration that one finds, first, one's own complicity in injustice, and then, the power to create better communities. As such, IGR's model for social justice education challenges students on both affective and cognitive levels.

A Sim(ulation) City Exercise

One exercise that bridges the cognitive and affective processes in the training course is called "Sim City." Short for "simulation," this exercise places students in a mock situation with an unequal distribution of "land" and "resources" to create their city. Paper, index cards, tape, cups, and other materials make up the resources to build their city. A city director gives permits for buildings. Students have to create towns with less land, fewer resources, less time, and more constraints, respectively. The students are subdivided into four groups (Vanilla, Strawberry, Banana, and Chocolate) and instructed to build cities on adjoining "land." The total space is divided into separate "parcels" with differences in land mass (Vanilla having the majority of land space, about half, with Strawberry having one-third of the remaining land, and Banana and Chocolate dividing the other parcels 60/40, respectively). Groups are brought into the room at intervals, Vanilla first, having the most time to create its "city" and community, then Strawberry, Banana, and last, Chocolate. The city director has discretion and power over what can be constructed in the various cities. The director's decisions are reinforced by simulated police officers. Both the city director and the police officers give preferential treatment to the Vanilla group. Participants may or may not recognize what is going on based on their relative privilege and, therefore, differential treatment occurs in the exercise (Pittman, 2002).

Students come to the simulation having read and discussed a number of articles about privilege, institutional discrimination, power, classism, and racism. While vivid classroom discussions often occur before the simulation, it is the actual experience of the simulation that codifies the students' learning about injustice. Students who have come from privileged backgrounds often begin to understand the frustration, anger, or helplessness of living in an inequitable system. Prior to the simulation, participants who have salient targeted identities often wonder how privileged people can "not know" what is going on. Experiencing the Vanilla or Strawberry groups, who have relative privilege, allows them to begin to understand how institutions are built to disguise injustice and separate people.

While the simulation itself is a provocative experience, it is the debriefing (often lasting as long as or longer than the simulation itself) in which trainees begin to make connections between the exercise, their life experiences, the course readings, and what others have shared about their lives. The debriefing also serves to elucidate participant emotional feelings about the exercise as it relates to real-life experience. We typically begin with questions about how participants feel and then move to questions about what happened in the exercise itself such as:

- What did you and others do in the simulation?
- What did you observe happening around you?
- What were the consequences of unequal treatment experienced by each group?

We then move to relating this exercise to real-life experiences and how new insights can be applied to spheres of influence in their own lives.

- How does this exercise relate to real-life experiences?
- What did you learn that you can use in your sphere of influence?

Finally, because students are training to become facilitators, we process the facilitator roles:

- What impact, if any, did the social identities of the exercise facilitators have on their roles in the simulation?
- What facilitation techniques did you notice in the debriefing?
- What other questions would you have asked or explored?
- How would you have handled debriefing?

The full debriefing is an integration of cognitive, analytical, and emotional learning.

In short, the pedagogy of IGR assumes that the learning of content information is most effective when it takes place in the context of carefully facilitated experiential exercises requiring trainees to examine their own attitudes, emotions, behaviors, perceptions, and life stories. When time constraints require that some aspects of training be compromised, IGR typically chooses not to compromise affective components. The experiential and affective learning of trainees continues after the training class and is reinforced during their leadership of the dialogues themselves.

The IGR Training Sequence

Facilitation training and support are conducted through a two-course sequence. Students apply for an initial three-credit, letter-graded course called "Training Processes for Intergroup Dialogue Facilitation." During a subsequent semester, most trainees apply for a facilitation position and, if accepted, enroll in a three-credit "Practicum in Intergroup Dialogue Facilitation." Referred to as "training" and "practicum," respectively, these courses are the mechanisms for training and supervising undergraduate peer facilitators in intergroup dialogue.

Students who apply for the training course participate in a group interview process. Once students are admitted, the program commits to enrolling students for at least two semesters (training and practicum) and requests the same two-semester commitment from them. Should a student not be prepared or eligible to facilitate in a future term, IGR faculty and staff will work with the student through independent studies or other continued course or practice work.

We now turn to a discussion of four primary learning/teaching goals for the IGR training/practicum courses and the IGR pedagogy concerning them: understanding social identity; learning about social justice, privilege, and discrimination; developing facilitation skills; and increasing the ability to analyze and understand interpersonal and intergroup relationships. Each goal integrates the cognitive and affective learning components previously described.

Understanding Social Identity

The training course includes opportunities to engage in personal work to discover the multiplicity of one's social identities, including the fluidity and intersectional natures of identities, and their relationships to inequalities. Students often enter the training course focused on one or a few identities, such as race or gender. They are helped in the course to see a broad spectrum of identities and to expand their understanding of the impact of their own and others' multiple social identities.

It is important that facilitators recognize their own developmental paths regarding their social identities (Tatum, 2003). Trainees are challenged to reconsider the socialization they have received as members of certain identity groups in society and are encouraged to engage in critical reflection about both positive and negative aspects of that socialization process (Harro, 2000). This exploration of identity begins at an overnight retreat early in the training course. Both trainees and instructors attend this retreat at a comfortable, off-campus lodge. The retreat agenda includes numerous structured activities about identity and other issues and emphasizes extensive debriefing following the activities. There is a balance among deepening knowledge about intergroup dialogue, individual identity examination, and introduction to the major social justice concepts of the course. One example of further identity examination linked to concepts is the Four Corners exercise (Kardia & Sevig, 2001), where small groups physically move to each corner of the room and share personal stories of a time when they were a target of oppression or discrimination, a perpetrator of oppression or discrimination, a witness to oppression or discrimination, and an intervener in oppression or discrimination. This helps students consider themselves within a multiple identity framework and helps them concretely link systems of oppression to real-life issues that we have all experienced. The multiple, interconnected experience of identities in the context of systems of inequality is more advanced than the single-identity focus of intergroup dialogues. Debriefing this exercise focuses on how facilitators will need to understand this complexity as they help students navigate in-depth single-identity learning in the context of multiple identities within their dialogues.

Additional nonstructured time allows for group formation to occur and for issues of trust to emerge and be explored. Subsequent activities, debriefing, and exploration of identity issues continue throughout the training course. In addition to weekly classes following the overnight retreat, there is a second one-day, on-campus, midsemester retreat that permits intensive learning about identity and facilitation issues.

Later during the practicum course, student facilitators continue their development by considering the impact of their identities on their own leadership roles and styles. They also observe identity development processes in their participants and thereby gain a different perspective on identity issues from the vantage point of their roles as facilitators. (See chapter 11 for more on social identities and the facilitation role.) Facilitators are trained to recognize and respond to the developmental stages that may be influencing their dialogue participants. For example, resistance from dominant group members and collusion from subordinate members may be especially pronounced in early stages of identity development. The weekly practicum sessions also help students explore the identity issues that arise within their dialogue groups.

Learning About Social Justice, Privilege, and Discrimination

The second goal of the training and practicum sequence is to learn more about issues of social justice within the larger society. This includes explorations of concepts regarding social power, inequality, privilege, and oppression, and how these factors may connect to various social identity memberships. There is a heavy content focus in the training course on these issues, beginning at the two-day retreat mentioned earlier. The initial work in these areas is focused on awareness and knowledge building. Trainees must become aware of their conscious and unconscious perceptions and stereotypes about participants and of participants' perceptions and stereotypes about the facilitators. This is sometimes addressed as overt bias, but it more often occurs as subtle behaviors that emerge in dialogue (Dovidio & Gaertner, 2004). For example, some participants may largely ignore a female facilitator's instructions but respond immediately to a male facilitator's. Discussion and analyses of such behaviors when conducted in a safe, nonjudgmental atmosphere can provide important learning opportunities about implicit stereotyping and may help both facilitators and participants deepen their own learning about these topics. .

Through such analyses and discussions, trainees develop both cognitive and emotional understandings of the power, privilege, and stigmatization embedded in different aspects of their social identities (Johnson, 2006). Exercises like "Sim City" (described earlier) or StarPower by R. Garry Shirts (1969) (another simulation exercise emphasizing inequalities) help students codify their learning of social justice concepts by experiencing the feelings associated with privilege and oppression. In-depth debriefing helps students make connections between the feelings they experience and the concepts important for their learning. Trainees also explore the impact of their identity status in making decisions about social action. For example, both cognitive and affective experiences can be triggered when trainees are faced with deciding whether to use their privileged identity(ies) actively or passively as an ally (or allies) or their target identity(ies) to resist negative categorization. These decisions involve a nuanced understanding of one's own identities and awareness, if not empathy, for both target and agent groups and the role that each plays in systems of both oppression and justice.

Crucially, students practice analyzing and discussing the social power and hegemony that occur between groups engaged in intergroup dialogue. Trainees learn to look for systemic power asymmetry expressed in "airtime," decision making, verbal acuity, English proficiency, and other factors. While students often gain a conceptual understanding of these factors during the training course, their understanding is enhanced during practicum when they have a more intensive experience of facilitating other students in dialogue. Practicum serves to reinforce earlier learning, clarify questions, and push facilitators to grapple with these issues on a metalevel outside their dialogue facilitation.

Developing Facilitation Skills

A third goal relates to the development of specific facilitation skills in trainees and connects significantly to power and privilege issues addressed above. While skill building involves learning how to manage and lead group processes in general, it also involves learning how to facilitate groups with content specifically about social inequality. Social power among both participants and co-facilitators is analyzed.

An important way for trainees to learn to manage the influence of social-ization and oppression is by making conscious decisions about their facilitator style. In considering differing power among participants, Wing and Rifkin (2001) suggest a mediator/facilitator technique they term "multipartiality." They hypothesize the presence of a "master narrative" in every setting. The master narrative is a form of hegemony that enters the dialogue by providing immediate legitimacy for a dominant social position. Thus, it creates "co-herence" for the agent group and "incoherence" for the target group(s). This "coherence" is the degree to which the participants' experiences or perspec-tives seem consistent with the socially accepted view of an issue or a situation. Often, this is expressed by privileged groups referring to the experiences of targeted groups as "unusual," "isolated incidents," and even "unbelievable or delusional."

A traditional "neutral" facilitation style not only does not counter the influence of the master narrative but also actually serves to advantage the agent perspective by allowing this narrative to remain central in the dialogue. "Multipartial" facilitation (Wing & Rifkin, 2001), on the other hand, simul-taneously challenges the master narrative, supports the target narrative, and invites the agent group's experiences to be a participatory element, which creates a more productive and healthy environment for dialogue.

Conceptually, trainees understand multipartiality easily. However, facili-tating in a multipartial way takes skill and nuance. The concept is introduced very early in the semester. During this initial presentation, trainees brain-storm examples of dominant narratives and discuss ways that they manifest in dialogues. Facilitators are given scenarios that indicate the presence of dominant narratives in the dialogue. For example, one scenario is that the group with privilege is driving the dialogue to learn from and about the subordinate group. Trainees brainstorm facilitation responses to recenter the dialogue on both groups learning from one another. Later in the term, they role-play scenarios to practice multipartiality. Follow-up peer and instructor-led feedback helps trainees refine their multipartial facilitation skills. This continues in the practicum course when real scenarios challenge facilitators in their dialogues. Coaching groups help facilitators to replay portions of their dialogue to improve skills further.

In the training course, students have several major opportunities to practice facilitation. The midsemester retreat emphasizes specific facilitation skills. Trainees also facilitate an in-class session in which their peers serve as "participants" during exercises and discussion. Along with the instructors, peers give feedback to one another about their facilitation. A third major assignment is an out-of-class intergroup co-facilitation project. In pairs, students invite six to eight people for a one-hour audiotaped discussion about a social identity topic. Co-facilitators plan, prepare, and implement the dialogic conversation. They transcribe their discussion and comment about process issues (where facilitation was particularly strong, where participants were off topic, where power was enacted in the setting, etc.) and content issues (how the topic was covered in the discussion).

In the practicum course, concrete skills take on a special urgency for the facilitators and learning is accelerated. Facilitators meet weekly with their practicum coaching group (other facilitators and an instructor) to debrief their dialogues, strategize for improvement, continue to develop their skills, and learn how to adjust their facilitation to the needs of participants.

Increasing the Ability to Analyze and Understand
Interpersonal and Intergroup Relationships

Finally, interpersonal and intergroup relationship issues are examined in both the training and practicum courses. Students spend time building and discussing relationships in both intragroup and intergroup identity settings. Several training strategies attempt to deepen the empathy, perspective taking, and emotional learning of facilitators. Trainees are invited to use first-person narratives as a method of creating dialogue. The emphasis here is on helping students see themselves as subjects (not objects) of a coherent autobiographical story. They are encouraged to speak in somewhat vulnerable terms of self-disclosure. We begin this emphasis at the initial training retreat. At the beginning we do an icebreaker called, "If you knew me, you would know that . . ." Students fill in the blank with personal information like the type of music they like, their hobbies, a significant event in their lives, and so forth. At the end of the retreat we do a similar exercise, "If you *really* knew me, you would know that . . ." This time students often share deeper, more personal stories of facing discrimination, overcoming challenges, and other struggles they endure. The instructors model appropriate levels of sharing, and the students often feel that this is the most significant and intimate sharing of the retreat. It is built on two days of increasingly rich conversations and sets the groundwork for personal sharing throughout the rest of the semester.

In the practicum course, students learn about working with a co-facilitator and how their identities and personalities impact the co-facilitation and facilitator-participant relationships. During a 1-day retreat at the beginning of practicum, co-facilitators discuss their facilitation styles and engage in relationship-building exercises. For example, they explore how they might best support one another, what their points of tension and disagreement might be, and how their comfort levels with conflict might impact both dialogue and co-facilitation.

Students are trained to utilize conflict as an educational tool, and they practice responding to conflict in ways that are both honest and productive. Since dialogues about social power, privilege, and oppression often generate conflict (Zúñiga, Nagda, Chesler, & Cytron-Walker, 2007), facilitators are encouraged to see conflict as an opportunity, not something to be avoided or repressed. Both interpersonal and intrapersonal (e.g., dissonance) conflict helps to challenge the assumptions, biases, and socialization/hegemony of participants. Through role plays, ongoing feedback from peer facilitators, and coaching support from their instructors, facilitators explore how to use conflict in their dialogue to build constructive relationships and deepen the dialogue experience for their participants.

Each goal highlights a specific and important aspect of the training sequence. Yet, all four goals work together to create an integrated experience for students. For example, when practicing facilitation skills (goal 3), we ask trainees about how their social identities and social power positions (goals 1 and 2) interact to enhance or detract from the relationships in the dialogue (goal 4). This process highlights the complexity of both the facilitation experience and the social justice education more broadly. These goals provide the foundation for peer facilitators' continued learning. Furthermore, the integration of cognitive and affective learning approaches throughout the course helps students discover unconscious prejudice and advance their skills to work in an increasingly diverse society. By learning about social identity and social justice concepts, developing facilitation skills, and increasing the ability to analyze and understand interpersonal and intergroup relationships, undergraduates gain the skills to work in an increasingly diverse society. Peer facilitators not only guide others in an important change process, but they, too, are companions on a journey of social justice learning through their own training and support. While practicing these skills as facilitators, they are developing the leadership needed for decades to come.

References

Baxter Magolda, M. B., & King, P. M. (Eds.). (2004). *Learning partnerships: Theory and models of practice to educate for self-authorship*. Sterling, VA: Stylus.

Beale, R. L., Thompson, M. C., & Chesler, M. (2001). Training peer facilitators for intergroup dialogue leadership. In D. Schoem & S. Hurtado (Eds.), *Intergroup Dialogue: Deliberative democracy in school, college, community, and workplace* (pp. 227–246). Ann Arbor: University of Michigan Press.

Chesler, M. A., Kellman-Fritz, J., & Knife-Gould, A. (2003). Training peer facilitators for community service learning leadership. *Michigan Journal of Community Service Learning, 9*(2), 59–76.

Chickering, A. W., & Reisser, L. (1993). *Education and identity* (2nd ed.). San Francisco: Jossey-Bass.

Dessel, A., & Rogge, M. (2008). Evaluation of intergroup dialogue: A review of the empirical literature. *Conflict Resolution Quarterly, 26*(2), 199–238.

Dovidio, J. F., & Gaertner, S. L. (2004). Aversive racism. *Advances in Experimental Social Psychology, 36*, 1–52.

Evans, N. J., Forney, D. S., & Guido-Dibrito, F. (1998). *Student development in college: Theory, research, and practice* (Jossey Bass Higher and Adult Education Series). San Francisco, CA: Jossey-Bass.

Gaertner, S. L., Dovidio, J. F., Banker, B. S., Rust, M. C., Nier, J. A., Mottola, G. R., et al. (1997). Does white racism necessarily mean antiblackness? Aversive racism and prowhiteness. In M. Fein, L. Weis, L. C. Powell, & L. M. Wong (Eds.), *Off White: Readings on race, power, and society* (pp. 167–178). New York: Routledge.

Gurin, P., Nagda, B. A., & Lopez, G. (2004). The benefits of diversity in education for democratic citizenship. *Journal of Social Issues, 60*(1), 17–34.

Harro, B. (2000). Cycle of socialization. In M. Adams, W. J. Blumenfeld, R. Castañeda, H. W. Hackman, M. L. Peters, & X. Zúñiga (Eds.), *Readings for diversity and social justice* (pp. 15–20). New York: Routledge.

Jackson, B. W. (n.d.). *PASK: Framework for multicultural competency*. Amherst, MA: New Perspectives. Mimeograph.

Johnson, A. (2006). *Privilege, power, and difference* (2nd ed.). Boston: McGraw-Hill.

Kardia, D. & Sevig, T. (2001). Embracing the paradox: Dialogue that incorporates both individual and group identities. In D. Schoem & S. Hurtado (Eds.), *Intergroup Dialogue:*

Deliberative democracy in school, college, community, and workplace (pp. 247–265). Ann Arbor: University of Michigan Press.

Keagan, R. (1994). *In over our heads: The mental demands of modern life.* Cambridge, MA: Harvard University Press.

Micari, M., Streitwieser, B., & Light, G. (2006). Undergraduates leading undergraduates: Peer facilitation in a science workshop program. *Innovative Higher Education, 30*(4), 269–288.

Nagda, B. A., Gurin, P., Sorensen, N., & Zúñiga, X. (2009). Evaluating Intergroup Dialogue: Engaging diversity for personal and social responsibility. *Diversity & Democracy, 12*(1), 4–6.

Pittman, C. (2002). Sim(ulation) City Instructions. The Program on Intergroup Relations, Ann Arbor: University of Michigan. Unpublished PDF.

Potapchuk, M. (2002). *Holding up the mirror: Working interdependently for just and inclusive communities.* Washington, DC: NABRE/Joint Center for Political and Economic Studies.

Shirts, R. G. (1969). *Star power simulation game.* Retrieved from http://www.stsintl.com/schools-charities/star_power.html.

Stephan, W. G., & Finlay, K. (1999). The role of empathy in improving intergroup relations. *Journal of Social Issues, 55*(4), 729–743.

Stephan, W. G., & Stephan, C. W. (2000). An integrated threat theory of prejudice. In S. Oskamp (Ed.), *Reducing prejudice and discrimination* (pp. 3–45). Mahwah, NJ: Erlbaum.

Tatum, B. D. (2003). *"Why are all the Black kids sitting together in the cafeteria?" And other conversations about race* (Rev. ed.). New York: Basic Books.

Torres, V., Howard-Hamilton, M. F., & Cooper, D. L. (2003). *Identity development of diverse populations: Implications for teaching and administration in higher education.* ASHE-ERIC Higher Education Report (A. J. Kezar, Series Ed.). Hoboken, NJ: Wiley Periodicals.

Vasques-Scalera, C. (1999). *Democracy, diversity and dialogue: Education for critical multicultural citizenship.* Unpublished doctoral dissertation, University of Michigan. Ann Arbor.

Wijeyesinghe, C. L., & Jackson, B. W., III (Eds.). (2001). *New perspectives on racial identity development: A theoretical and practical anthology.* New York: New York University Press.

Wing, L., & Rifkin, J. (2001). Racial identity development and the mediation of conflicts. In C. L. Wijeyesinghe & B. W. Jackson, III (Eds.), *New perspectives on racial identity development: A theoretical and practical anthology* (pp. 182–208). New York: New York University Press.

Zúñiga, X., Nagda, B. A., Chesler, M., & Cytron-Walker, A. (2007). *Intergroup dialogues in higher education: Meaningful learning about social justice.* ASHE Higher Education Report Series, *32*(4). San Francisco: Jossey-Bass.

4

FACILITATOR TRAINING IN DIVERSE, PROGRESSIVE RESIDENTIAL COMMUNITIES

Occidental College as a Case Study

Jaclyn Rodríguez, Andréa C. Rodríguez-Scheel,
Shaquanda Lindsey, and Ariel Kirkland

O ccidental College is a diverse, residential institution located in Los
Angeles. Its institutional mission links intellectual goals with democratic ideals and consequently attracts students who are interested
in diversity. This reputation, together with Occidental's structural and curricular diversity, simultaneously supports and challenges intergroup relations on
campus. For example, in a recent National Survey of Student Engagement of
graduating seniors, nearly all students agreed that Occidental's emphasis on
multiculturalism had contributed significantly to their knowledge and personal development concerning diversity. However, significantly fewer students
reported having serious conversations with others whose beliefs differed from
their own (*National Survey of Student Engagement*, 2000). This pattern—
an intellectual interest in diversity that might be theoretically or passively
consumed rather than authentically practiced as part of the educational process—is not unique to Occidental. What is distinctive at Occidental is the
coalescence of an institutional ethos, creative pedagogies, and a handful of
exceptional students prepared to engage in interpersonal risk to transform
intergroup relationships on campus.

This chapter examines the strategies used to train these students. We contextualize our approach with a brief description of Occidental's Intergroup

Dialogue Program (IDP), then discuss how three classic dialogue themes are uniquely addressed at Occidental: setting the context for training; guiding inclusive, reflective practice; and nurturing constructive co-facilitation relationships. Where helpful, quotations from students' reflection papers are shared.

Components of Occidental's Intergroup Dialogue Program

At Occidental, IDP consists of three credit-bearing courses, two of which are devoted to facilitator training. *The Social Psychology of Intergroup Relations and Dialogue* (Psychology 223) serves as the program's facilitator "training" course and earns students full course credit. *Practicum in Intergroup Dialogue Facilitation* (Psychology 325) provides additional instruction in content and skills as well as support for facilitators during the facilitation semester. Students in this course earn partial course credit, and co-facilitators earn a small stipend.

This incentive structure is appropriate for the workload but unusual for an academic institution. Whereas many institutions offer full course credit for training and peer-led dialogue courses, few augment training with stipends for actual facilitation work. These incentives help to bridge the conceptual and applied dimensions of diversity education at Occidental by institutionalizing a distinctive, experiential course structure; attracting diverse facilitators with work study responsibilities; and formally recognizing the importance of knowledge and skill development in diversity instruction.

Training Course Content, Composition, and Structure

The following sections detail distinguishing features of Occidental's IDP facilitator training course content, student composition, and overall structure.

Content

Psychology 223 is designed to provide background in intergroup relations theory and experience in meaningful dialogue about difficult issues. The course was developed in consultation with national experts in the field of intergroup dialogue (Schoem, Hurtado, Sevig, Chesler, & Sumida, 2001; Yeakley, 1998; Zúñiga & Nagda, 2001; Zúñiga, Nagda, Chesler, & Cytron-Walker, 2007).

At Occidental, examination of multiple identities is an essential feature of our training. The course addresses sexism, classism, heterosexism, ableism, racism, and anti-Semitism. Inclusion of multiple identities and their intersections enriches and complicates the curriculum as students find themselves moving between positions of relative power and privilege while they critically examine their assumptions, knowledge, and experiences. Most students enter the course with limited knowledge about a "lower-status" identity. Few have explored "higher-status" identities in depth, fewer have examined the implications of multiplicity in a structured society, and fewer still have considered the processes and dynamics involved in forming intergroup alliances across differently configured identities.

> As a racial minority conscious of the existence of racism and oppression . . . I spent a lot of time trying to learn about my racial identity and its history. . . . It seemed too time consuming to learn about other groups. . . . (Black man)

> I . . . realize that I kept myself at least somewhat comfortable with my identity by taking a dialogue where I would be considered in the "minority" group. (White woman)

> I consciously avoided my agent identities because I did not want the responsibilities associated with power and privilege. (Asian American woman)

Because students' learning about multiple identities invariably involves spiraling within and between intrapersonal, interpersonal, and intergroup processes, we offer frameworks that help them work through these shifting and challenging ideas, feelings, and group dynamics. Particular attention is devoted to the intrapersonal and interpersonal processes delineated in identity development models (Cross, Parham, & Helms, 1991; Helms, 1990); increased familiarity with intergroup relations paradigms (Brewer & Miller, 1984; Gaertner & Dovidio, 2000; Tajfel & Turner, 1986); and awareness of antioppression literature that bridges personal experience, social structure, and resistance (Adams et al., 2000). Because our course satisfies a departmental requirement, special efforts are made to link course themes to psychological research (Aries, 2008; Dovidio, Glick, & Rudman, 2005).

Composition

Enrollment in the training course is open to 16 students who have completed an introductory-level psychology course and a short online placement form. The form surveys social identity demographics and asks students to state the importance of several goals: developing of knowledge and awareness in the area of intergroup relations, working to form social justice alliances, honing communication and inquiry skills, preparing to peer facilitate, and satisfying a departmental requirement.

The survey assessment serves three key purposes. First, demographic data help to assemble a class inclusive of Occidental's gender and racial diversity and to provide multiple perspectives. Second, asking students to consider their educational goals introduces the practice of self-reflection. Third, sharing students' reported goals in aggregate form nurtures a culture of openness, hope, and commitment to social justice among diverse participants. Our approach yields and highlights a class that is diverse and similar, comprising unique individuals with a shared desire to bridge theoretical support for diversity with informed, personal practice.

Structure

An unusual feature of Occidental's training course is a weekly, three-hour, experiential laboratory. The laboratory emerged out of repeated student requests to create additional opportunities for semistructured dialogue involving the entire class. While additional time is often useful in working with the natural resistance that students experience during discussions of difference, power, and identity, we believe that it may be essential on small campuses. In such communities, identities and group boundaries are often publicly presumed by oneself and imposed by others. Students need dedicated time and space to shift from the comfortable role-playing that often characterizes diversity education into deeper, more personal learning modes. The quotations below reveal some of the tensions students experience as they reflect on the relationship between dialogue and their identities in a small, relatively enclosed community.

> I had engaged in dialogues . . . and felt quite comfortable in that place. . . . This is the case that I often presented to the public, yet . . . (Latino man)

> I found myself in a comfort zone as my experience served as the main educational tool, albeit in a somewhat voyeuristic manner. (Black man)

> During a reflection activity in which we were challenged to be "real," I was triggered by my inauthenticity, by the inconsistency between my so-called social justice beliefs and my friends and actions outside of dialogue class. (White woman)

Our structure enhances the potency of the course by allocating shared time and space to readings, experiential activities, reflection, and dialogue. It offers an unusual educational prototype—an uninterrupted flow within and among theory, narrative, research, and experiential learning. Within this framework, even a simple "check-in" at the end of a laboratory session presents an important learning opportunity as students are encouraged to take time to synthesize and voice their thoughts and feelings in the moment.

Within this course configuration, students are more introspective and open to risky conversations than in previous nonlaboratory iterations. Early sessions may appear more frustrating than productive as students learn about and work through resistance and communication challenges. However, returning time and again to the same communal space conveys dedication to the process, respect for the material, and respect for one's peers. In total, the training class meets three days per week for approximately six hours. Predictably, the content, composition, and structure of the course establish a compelling context for facilitator training.

Guiding Inclusive, Reflective Practice

At Occidental, we face the challenge of facilitating progress from various points of entry—perhaps more points of entry than are characteristic of institutions with lesser structural and curricular diversity and a different institutional mission. Vastly discrepant starting points within the same classroom can trigger behavioral and emotional resistance including boredom, withdrawal, anger, and guilt (Tatum, 1992). Students tend to be impatient, particularly when they believe that what they are learning is ineffective, insufficient, or at the expense of specific identity groups. The following quotations illustrate some of these entry-level dynamics and sentiments:

> I always knew there was a lot of difference in the world. My school emphasized this with deafening intensity. . . . I had a pretty good theoretical foundation, but . . . as I left the room so did the lessons. . . . (White man)

> As a Black, queer woman I have developed an acute awareness of the ways that oppression affects my life. . . . While I was extremely passionate about social justice . . . I was skeptical as to whether dialogue was going to be a strong enough catalyst for self-reflection. . . . (Black woman)

> Throughout the race dialogue . . . I remember thinking to myself, I have been here before. . . . I saw the eyes of other students of color. . . . Here we go again . . . another learning activity at our expense. . . . (Multiracial man)

How do we structure learning in a manner that engages and respects differences *and* deepens reflection regardless of one's starting point? Initially, our lessons were carefully sequenced from lesser to increased risk. More recently, a deep sense of responsibility to students who enter training with enhanced knowledge, as well as an appreciation for Occidental's curricular success in preparing students for more complex diversity education, has compelled us to rethink this strategy. We now intersperse lower-risk activities with higher-risk activities throughout the semester. This combination is illustrated in two assignments scheduled early in the semester—a low-risk self-assessment inventory and a high-risk multiple identity laboratory activity—described in the following sections.

Low Risk: Self-Assessment Inventory

We have found it helpful to students' learning if they begin the course by reflecting concretely on what they know and feel about various social justice issues as well as why. To accomplish this we adapted a self-assessment inventory from the University of Michigan (Beale, Thompson, & Chesler, 2001). This instrument guides, refines, and synthesizes students' thinking about intergroup relations and social justice by asking them to assess specific knowledge held about their own and other groups' histories, social justice terminology and paradigms, and group processes. This entry-level exercise invites students to consider their assumptions and values, to embrace inquiry, and to practice precision as they produce contemporary judgments about past experience. The assessment provides a record of students' thoughts and feelings at a particular point in time and prepares them to view their own learning as a dynamic and continuous process.

Until recently, we reserved self-assessments for the "end-of-semester" reflection papers. However, in line with our decision to promote early, broader engagement among students and make our learning goals explicit, we "revisit" self-assessments throughout the semester. In addition to providing an informative instructional portrait of students' initial attitudes, skills, and course expectations, deliberate reexamination of entry-level assessments models the value of reflecting backward and forward to gain new insights about challenging content. Self-assessments are now completed online, where they can be easily stored disaggregated by identity groups and recalled as needed during the semester.

High Risk: The Identity Shield

Two laboratory sessions are dedicated to an identity exercise. The first session focuses on introducing and modeling the activity, the second on sharing and debriefing. Our exercise is based on the "Coat of Arms—Shield Activity," a popular icebreaker. The activity is named after the template used to structure the assignment, a four-quadrant image that resembles a coat of arms shield. Shield activities allow students to examine and share parts of the self through drawing and speaking. Our version asks students to represent and share three important aspects of their lives in the first three quadrants: where they grew up, with whom they lived, and an early memory in which two social identities figure prominently. The fourth quadrant is reserved for text; students are asked to identify three conceptual connections between their representations and course readings.

The exercise develops students' awareness about the relationships between identity and group membership. Students become increasingly knowledgeable about the distinction between personal and social identity, broaden the types of social identities deemed significant, recognize developmental influences on identity, and consider how identification with a social category emerges in a structured society.

The multidimensional character of the activity invites thoughtful reflection among all students, even among those with a history of diversity work. It facilitates viewing the self as an object over time and searching for evidence of patterns in one's life. Asking students to consider the significance of two social identities encourages them to construct fuller, more dimensional portraits of the self. Embedding this reflection in a series of social systems (cities, communities, and families) allows students to become more mindful of developmental and structural forces that socialize the self. The opportunity to reflect back on key moments in one's life allows students to weave together a coherent narrative whose roots extend farther back in time than they might initially realize. Some students come to understand their own and others' passion (or apathy) toward certain forms of oppression. Some offer vivid examples of heterosexism or sexism in their homes and segue into internalized oppression and dominance. Others reflect on communities of hope and justice. Often, this activity helps students understand the origins of their presence in this dialogue course.

Inevitably the exercise generates emotion and provides a mechanism for examining affect in students' lives. Some students become highly emotional as they revisit and share their pasts, whereas others appear unmoved by the activity. These differences affect group dynamics in important and predictable ways and provide important topics for dialogue. Should emotions be shared or managed? What are the costs of emotional vulnerability in this class with these people at this time? How does emotion impact students' ability to "hear" others' stories?

This exercise impacts students at all entry levels. Most find it challenging. Some find it risky. Challenges include discomfort with a less traditional form of expression and an inability to think about the self in group terms. Risks include revisiting and sharing painful secrets, emotional vulnerability, and ability to empathize. Confronting and working through these challenges can generate awareness about diversity within previously aggregated social groups and increase students' understanding of the lived implications of group membership, highlight commonalities across groups, and enlighten us about emotional triggers and perspective-taking skills. Ultimately, the shared risks associated with this identity exercise strengthen students' connections to one another as social justice advocates and cultivate key competencies in future facilitators.

Guiding Inclusive Reflection: Linking Low- and High-Risk Activities

How do we deepen students' understanding of the *Identity Shield* exercise by drawing on an earlier low-risk assessment? We begin by allowing students to share their work as we listen for emerging patterns. Most students complete the first two quadrants of the shield—depicting their home and family environments—quickly and easily, in fact, rather mechanically. Some, however, highlight the role of social structure in early childhood by drawing attention to the lack or relocation of homes as a consequence of social class, impinging highways, the presence or absence of yards, and various family configurations. While listening to other members of the group, students become acutely aware that what is imperceptible to some is painfully obvious to others.

The third quadrant disrupts most students' complacency. On the surface, representing an early memory in which two social identities figure prominently appears "easier" for some students to generate than it does for others. Predictably, these tend to be students with extensive diversity knowledge. Indeed, women of color who have both intellectual and personal experience with race and gender have generated some of the richest and most eloquent representations of the *Identity Shield*. Unsurprisingly, students with less diversity experience struggle with this assignment, noting that significant identity-related memories are rare. The poignant experience of individuality for some, but "group-ness" for others, emerges in this session. Reflecting on these distinct patterns as a class generates new insights among most students. In response to the debriefing question, "What did you notice about this activity?" people generally report that

- students of color volunteer to share earlier in the session and divulge riskier memories than do White students;
- this is particularly true among women of color;
- race and gender identities are represented in people's memories more often than other social identities;
- shared recollections generally emphasize lower rather than higher social status group memberships; and
- emotional expression produces discomfort.

In some ways these perceptions confirm experienced students' initial concerns about facilitator training—that it will be familiar and occur at their expense. In other ways they disrupt expectations by highlighting the pervasive invisibility of privileged identities such as social class, ability, and sexual orientation in most students' lives.

The vivid and dislocating immediacy of the *Identity Shield* testimonials can compel students to reconsider their presumed knowledge, receptiveness to diversity education, and motives for enrolling in the course. Revisiting the *Self-Assessment Inventory* after such a challenging, emotional activity provides perspective and opportunities for guided introspection. We facilitate introspection by connecting students' responses to the *Identity Shield* with early semester self-assessment data. This focus encourages students to reflect back on their commitment to personal and social change, develop intergroup friendships, and work across difference to form alliances. Data usually reveal that most enrolled students believe they have much to learn about the depths of their stereotypes, their role in perpetuating oppression, their knowledge about other groups' histories and cultures, and their familiarity with systemic bases of oppression. Overall, the portrait that emerges from students' self-assessments is one of humility, openness, and a commitment to learn within the group. This portrait offers a humane, student-generated framework from which to reexamine students' shields.

Because journals offer a space to process honest self-reflections, we close our laboratory by inviting students to journal about their activity-related thoughts, feelings, and questions. These privately generated thoughts often surface in later dialogues and reflection papers. A woman of color who had shared a vivid memory of racism in her *Identity Shield* later noted that "while painful in lots of ways, at another level the task was easy" because it is "the part of my story that I share at Oxy." A White student wondered whether her discomfort with emotion reflected a deep-seated unwillingness to work across difference. Another White student reported that the initial anger he felt because the assignment was so "hard for me and so easy for the minority students" made him realize this was a "first for me." Another student inquired, "Are we trying to become allies too quickly?"

Our linked assignments—*Self-Assessment Inventory, Identity Shield,* and *Reflective Journal Prompts*—guide future facilitators through the process of self-reflection. By making their assumptions the object of inquiry, students enhance active listening, inquiry, and perspective-taking skills. We close this section by sharing excerpts from the final reflection papers of the students. Their concerns about Psychology 223's capacity to engage and deepen their understanding of intergroup relations appear somewhat alleviated.

Before . . . I was aware of my privilege to a very shallow degree. . . . I was aware of stereotypes in the world, but not so much those that I held. . . . (White man)

My experience this semester . . . has challenged me to think about myself in a much more complex and complete way . . . encouraged me to develop awareness of my many identities—not just race. (Black woman)

I was on my way to becoming an expert in comprehending the systems of power from a theoretical level. . . . What was lacking was my understanding of my own complicit relationship to the very oppression I was so eager to combat. (Multiracial man)

Nurturing Constructive Co-facilitation Relationships

Students who successfully complete Psychology 223 may apply for a peer-facilitator position. Because we work with undergraduate students, deliberate attention is paid to the co-facilitation relationship. In this section we offer strategies developed to inform and strengthen co-facilitation across three different training phases: Psychology 223, Psychology 325, and the retreat that connects them.

Phase One: Psychology 223

Practice in co-facilitation begins with a required exercise in Psychology 223. The goals of the exercise are to plan, co-facilitate, and assess a meaningful social identity dialogue with peers. The co-facilitation is scheduled during the second half of the semester, after students have acquired an intellectual understanding of identity, privilege, oppression, and resistance; participated in multiple experiential activities (e.g., dyads, gallery walk, caucus groups, fish bowls); and been introduced to key themes in social justice pedagogy.

Successful facilitators attend to group dynamics at the planning, implementation, and assessment stages. We nurture constructive collaboration by requiring submission of a proposed session agenda in advance of the facilitation and at least one minidialogue that explores power and identity, knowledge about the dialogue theme, and dialogue skills and anxieties within the co-facilitation team. This process builds dialogue skills, trust, and openness among co-facilitators and deepens knowledge about the facilitation topic.

While planning and implementation heighten students' awareness of the intricacies of dialogue pedagogy, the self-assessment portion of the assignment encourages facilitators to reexamine dialogue dynamics. One student noted that "the experience of being a facilitator was ... more complex. ... It highlighted a lot of intricacies of dialogue that I had never previously noticed." This individual named the delicate and supportive balance required of co-facilitators who are simultaneously in and on the edge of personally meaningful dialogues: "I found it emotionally difficult to be in the space, especially when talking about my sister." She was appreciative that her co-facilitator "decided to share his experience with learning disabilities" because it "helped balance the sharing that I did ... and ... helped to augment our theme of the multifaceted nature of disabilities and abilities." This exercise generally nurtures and demystifies constructive co-facilitation, promotes collaborative relationships within the class, and generates effective dialogues.

Phase Two: Retreat

The second phase of facilitator training begins with a three-day off-campus retreat just prior to the facilitation semester. While our overarching goal is to come together as a group capable of meaningful support, specific attention is devoted to the facilitation team. One assignment, designed to encourage awareness and perspective taking within co-facilitation teams, involves reflecting on one's own identities from within an identity development model (Cross et al., 1991; Helms, 1990; Tatum, 2003), reflecting on one's co-facilitator's identities, and reflecting on assumptions about how each sees the other. Among the prompts we offer are the following:

- Locate yourself in the model for both Gender and Race/Ethnicity. Briefly explain the reasons for your self-assessment. How do these different identities contribute to your self-image as a social justice advocate? What consistencies and inconsistencies do you notice across identities? How do you feel about this assessment? How might this influence your facilitation of this particular dialogue theme?
- Having worked briefly with your co-facilitator and focusing only on the identity theme of your dialogue (Gender or Race/Ethnicity), try to locate him or her in an identity development model. Share your thinking. How might this knowledge shape your co-facilitation relationship?
- Finally, how do you think you are "seen" by your co-facilitator? How do you anticipate working with this "knowledge"?

This assignment provides a framework that guides students' thinking about the relationships between multiple identities and facilitation. It offers a mechanism for thinking analytically and objectively about the self, challenges students to wrestle with the intersection of race and gender, and addresses the politics of identity on a small campus. The process also helps facilitators practice inquiry, perspective taking, and stereotyping within their working relationship. For example, a White woman who located herself at a more "advanced" stage for racial identity than gender identity noted that while she felt prepared to facilitate a race dialogue, she knew that she could not contribute effectively to a gender dialogue. She also recognized that her internalized sexism inhibited constructive working relationships with women, prompting her to choose men of color as her co-facilitators. This exercise helped her begin to address this dynamic.

Phase Three: Psychology 325

The third phase of facilitator training is rooted in the practicum course and occurs during the semester of peer-dialogue instruction. Weekly training and supervision continue in two forms: a two-hour group meeting with all facilitators and a one-hour meeting with each co-facilitation dyad. A component of practicum includes assessing and discussing ongoing co-facilitator interactions.

Most facilitation teams experience some conflict during the semester. To constructively address team dynamics we developed a *Co-facilitation Inventory* (see Table 4.1).

Five inventory-linked assignments are scattered across the first half of the semester: inventory completion, individual reflective journal, co-facilitation sharing and discussion of completed inventories, reflective journal on co-facilitation strengths and challenges, and co-facilitation affirmations in practicum setting.

This structure normalizes and formalizes assessment across teams, allows potential conflicts to surface constructively, focuses attention on facilitation strengths, and provides affirmation opportunities. The inventory increases facilitators' sensitivity to and awareness of unconscious power dynamics that may shape intergroup interactions in the dialogue. In one team the process proved particularly helpful early on. The more assertive member of the dyad observed her regular enactment of privilege in communication and organization dynamics after completion of her own self-assessment. Recognizing her tendency to interrupt, arrive late for meetings, and make unilateral decisions in class, she said, "I guess I really do work as an individual. I need to watch that." Her co-facilitator appreciated this and acknowledged that she herself had a deferential style that also needed attention. Their working relationship, and their dialogue, improved significantly. This inventory works best with

TABLE 4.1
Co-facilitation inventory

1. Which social identities do you believe are most important to you? Discuss two ways they shape your interactions:
   a. as a facilitator navigating your peer dialogue
   b. as a facilitator relating to your dialogue co-facilitator
2. Which social identities do you tend to minimize or ignore in your interactions? Identify two ways these identities shape your interactions:
   a. as a facilitator navigating your peer dialogue
   b. as a facilitator relating to your dialogue co-facilitator
3. What are some of your "buttons"—soft and hot? Identify a time when these buttons were pushed within any context of the dialogue program.
4. With your dialogue theme in mind, assess your personal knowledge about the following dimensions of intergroup relations. Use a 1–10 scale (10 = perfection) to assign a score to each of the dimensions below. Next identify two with which you would most appreciate assistance/support from your co-facilitator.

Dimension	Score	Co-facilitator Support
• Group Histories		
• Knowledge and Terminology		
• Intergroup Relations Privilege, Oppression		
• Group Communication (Talking Space, Inquiry)		
• Group Formation (Engagement, Marginalization, Cohesion)		
• Group Conflict (Emotion, Invisibility, Empathy)		
• Group Collaboration (Alliances, Bridging Difference, Cohesion)		

5. Reflect on your own "passion" for social justice. How is this passion related to your decision to facilitate? How is it related to the typical way you respond to important issues on campus? In the Dialogue?
6. Grade your "co-facilitation" on each of the following qualities to date (1–10, 10 = perfect):
   • Listening to my co-facilitator
   • Showing my respect for my co-facilitator
   • Being on time for set appointments with my co-facilitator
   • Accommodating my co-facilitator
   • Sharing the work equally with my co-facilitator
   • Serving as an ally to my co-facilitator
   • Completing my assessment of student journals

(*Continued*)

TABLE 4.1
Co-facilitation inventory (*Continued*)

Dimension	Score	Co-facilitator Support
• Designing class activities/questions		
• Confiding in my co-facilitator		
• Preparing for class—handouts, videos, questionnaires, e-mails		
• Holding office hours		
• Effectively adhering to our prepared agenda		
• Effectively sharing space in the Dialogue		
• Understanding the power of my communication style as a member of group(s) _____		
• Communicating openly with my co-facilitator		

7. Reflect on your co-facilitation experience thus far.
   a. Identify one specific constructive behavior you've enacted as a facilitator IN CLASS.
   b. Identify one specific constructive behavior you've enacted as a facilitator OUTSIDE of class.
   c. Identify one specific behavior you enacted as a facilitator that you regret/wish you had executed differently.
   d. Identify and explain two specific qualities you have come to appreciate in your co-facilitator.
8. Reflect on what you have learned from this self-assessment tool as a whole.
   a. Identify two of your strengths. Discuss ways that you can draw on and use your strengths more effectively as a co-facilitator.
   b. Identify two personal challenges or limitations. Discuss how you can work as a team to address these challenges.

well-communicating facilitators. Others who lack insight or have a tendency toward defensiveness are less changed by or invested in this activity. Instructor comments on reflective journals are helpful in generating perspective and honing facilitation skills.

Final Reflections

Occidental is among a handful of small residential colleges that offer peer intergroup dialogue courses. Facilitator training is essential for the success of our program. Our current structure and pedagogy have transformed intergroup relations among participants, who, in turn, have transformed campus culture by designing and implementing impressive programs (Exploring Blackness Week, Exploring Whiteness Week); institutionalizing counterspaces for underrepresented students (Black Men's Group, Science Academic Support); forming bridges between cultural groups; and, of course, facilitating dialogues on race, gender, and sexual orientation.

Our program and pedagogy are neither effortless nor guaranteed. Sustaining the IDP, including facilitator training, is dependent on continued structural diversity, student interest, and institutional support. While some of these dynamics may be an inevitable part of diversity education, we wonder whether they are exacerbated in a small residential setting where anonymity and personal space are rare. Small liberal arts colleges often compete to attract the same small pool of diverse students; a critical mass of diverse students cannot be presumed. Some of our training techniques gain their potency from students with rich and varied diversity experiences, and over the past five years the spectrum of experience among students on campus appears to have narrowed. Still, increasing perceptions of a "postracial society" have impacted interest in engaging diversity. We are hopeful, however, that President Obama's election and his repeated call for dialogue across diverse groups will stimulate increased interest in and commitment to authentic intergroup relations and dialogue. We remain committed to maintaining the IDP as a transformative intellectual space, allowing our pedagogy to evolve, and seeking continued institutional support for this important educational experience.

References

Adams, M., Blumenfeld, R., Castañeda, R., Hackman, H. W., Peters, M. L., & Zúñiga, X. (Eds.). (2000). *Readings for diversity and social justice: An anthology on racism, sexism, anti-Semitism, sexism, heterosexism, ableism, and classism.* New York: Routledge.

Aries, E. (2008). *Race and class matters at an elite college.* Philadelphia: Temple University Press.

Beale, R. L., Thompson, M. C., & Chesler, M. (2001). Training peer facilitators for intergroup dialogue leadership. In D. Schoem & S. Hurtado (Eds.), *Intergroup dialogue: Deliberative democracy in school, college, community, and workplace* (pp. 227–246). Ann Arbor: University of Michigan Press.

Brewer, M. B., & Miller, N. (1984). Beyond the contact hypothesis: Theoretical perspectives on desegregation. In N. Miller & M. Brewer (Eds.), *Groups in contact: The psychology of desegregation.* New York: Academic Press.

Cross, W. E., Jr., Parham, T. A., & Helms, J. E. (1991). The stages of Black identity development: Nigrescence models. In R. Jones (Ed.), *Black psychology.* Oakland, CA: Cobb & Henry.

Dovidio, J. F., Glick, P., & Rudman, L. (2005). *On the nature of prejudice: Fifty years after Allport*. Malden, MA: Wiley-Blackwell.

Gaertner, S. L., & Dovidio, J. F. (2000). *Reducing intergroup bias: The common ingroup identity model*. Philadelphia: Psychology Press.

Helms, J. E. (Ed.). (1990). *Black and white racial identity: Theory, research and practice*. Westport, CT: Greenwood Press.

National Survey of Student Engagement. (2000). Los Angeles: Occidental College.

Schoem, D., Hurtado, S., Sevig, T., Chesler, M., & Sumida, S. H. (2001). Intergroup dialogue: Democracy at work in theory and practice. In D. Schoem & S. Hurtado (Eds.), *Intergroup Dialogue: Deliberative democracy in school, college, community, and workplace*. Ann Arbor: University of Michigan Press.

Tajfel, H., & Turner, J. C. (1986). The social psychology of intergroup behaviour. In S. Worchel & W. G. Austin (Eds.), *Psychology of intergroup relations* (pp. 7–24). Chicago: Nelson-Hall.

Tatum, B. (1992). Talking about race, learning about racism: An application of racial identity development theory in the classroom. *Harvard Educational Review, 62*(1), 1–24.

Tatum, B. (2003). *"Why are all the Black kids sitting together in the cafeteria?" And other conversations about race*. New York: Basic Books.

Yeakley, A. (1998). *The nature of prejudice change: Positive and negative change processes arising from intergroup contact experiences*. Unpublished doctoral dissertation, University of Michigan.

Zúñiga, X., & Nagda, B. A. (2001). Design considerations for intergroup dialogue. In D. Schoem & S. Hurtado (Eds.), *Intergroup Dialogue: Deliberative democracy in school, college, community, and workplace* (pp. 306–327). Ann Arbor: University of Michigan Press.

Zúñiga, X., Nagda, B. A., Chesler, M., & Cytron-Walker, A. (2007). *Intergroup dialogues in higher education: Meaningful learning about social justice*. ASHE Higher Education Report Series, *32*(4). San Francisco: Jossey-Bass.

5

PREPARING CRITICALLY REFLECTIVE INTERGROUP DIALOGUE FACILITATORS

A Pedagogical Model and Illustrative Example

Ximena Zúñiga, Tanya Kachwaha, Keri DeJong,
and Romina Pacheco

S killed and thoughtful facilitation is key to encouraging a dialogical relationship and increasing understanding across social identity groups in intergroup dialogues (IGDs). This task can be both rewarding and daunting, as facilitators must simultaneously guide the process of conversation through reflection and inquiry and explore issues of identity and power in a dialogical manner. Because of the complex and multilayered nature of intergroup dialogue facilitation, IGD programs need to offer facilitators both comprehensive preparation and ongoing support. This chapter describes and discusses a facilitator preparation model that blends dialogic and social justice education pedagogies with critically reflective practices. It is organized into four sections. The first section briefly describes the graduate course sequence used to prepare IGD facilitators. The second section introduces the conceptual frameworks informing a critically reflective practice approach to preparing IGD practitioners. The third section uses a specific critical incident in dialogue facilitation to illustrate how reflective practice methods are used to support and challenge graduate students' growth and development as IGD facilitators. The final section briefly discusses key practice implications.

The Program: Goals and Location

The IGD program described in this chapter is part of the Social Justice Education (SJE) master's program within the Department of Student Development and Pupil Personnel Services, School of Education, University of Massachusetts Amherst. The SJE master's program focuses on preparing reflective practitioners who can demonstrate competency in the knowledge, awareness, and skills needed to plan, implement, and evaluate effective social justice education programs in K–16 settings (for more detailed information, see http://www.umass.edu/sje).

Learning to plan, facilitate, and assess intergroup dialogues is one of two elective practicum sequence options offered in the master's program of study. The intergroup dialogue sequence consists of two graduate courses and an undergraduate course that serves as a practice site for the practicum course. The first course, *Educ 795E, Theory, Practice, and Research on Intergroup Dialogue in Schools, Workplaces and Communities,* provides the historical, theoretical, pedagogical, and empirical foundations for the intergroup dialogue sequence. Graduate students learn and apply conceptual, empirical, and practical knowledge and develop self-awareness and skills through IGD practice sessions, reflective writing, and the completion of a theory-practice-research paper. The following semester, students taking *Educ 692B, Practicum in Intergroup Dialogue Facilitation,* co-lead sections of the undergraduate intergroup dialogue course described in the following section. This course focuses on design and facilitation of an intergroup dialogue curriculum and starts with a four-day retreat that emphasizes principles for developing and sustaining diverse learning communities and engages facilitators in goal setting, team building, and IGD facilitation practice sessions. For the rest of the semester, participants in the practicum meet weekly for three and a half hours. For the first hour, co-facilitation teams meet with a consultant, usually an experienced intergroup dialogue facilitator, who assists with team development, debriefing, planning, and facilitation. Next, with the instructor's guidance, co-facilitators engage in collective reflection, dialogue, and inquiry into practice with their peers and participate in coaching and skill-building sessions. This course expands trainees' awareness, knowledge, and skills in dialogue facilitation, curriculum design, and small-group leadership through team consultation, individual and collective reflection, and discussion of readings. Participants write reflective logs, a three-step reflective practice assignment, and a theory-practice paper. The course is co-taught by one faculty member and a graduate teaching assistant.

Educ 395Z, Exploring Differences and Common Ground, a multisection undergraduate intergroup dialogue course, is offered concurrently with the practicum course. Two graduate students participating in the practicum course co-facilitate each of the sections of the course. Similar to other IGD programs, facilitators lead the sections with the support of a curriculum guide that draws from a "classic" four-stage curricular model of intergroup dialogue: (1) group beginnings, (2) exploring differences and commonalities of experience across and within social identity groups, (3) exploring and discussing controversial issues or "hot topics," and (4) action planning and alliance building for creating change (Zúñiga, Nagda, Chesler, & Cytron-Walker, 2007). Sections meet two and a half hours a week for 10 weeks in addition to a full-day retreat early in the semester. In addition to participating in weekly sessions, participants are expected to complete weekly readings, weekly reflective logs, a collaborative action project, and a final reflection paper. Each section has a specific social identity group focus (e.g., race/ethnicity or gender) and enrolls 14–16 students, ideally with each of the social identity groups participating in the dialogue represented equally (for detailed information about course goals and assignments, see http://courses.umass.edu/educ395z/).

Approach to Facilitator Preparation

Intergroup dialogue facilitation involves "active, responsive guidance, not formal instruction" (Zúñiga et al., 2007, p. 39). It focuses on active engagement—cognitive, affective, and kinesthetic—across multiple learning domains and goals (Bloom, 1956). Learning how to actively guide and support the development of dialogic conversations that invite honest sharing, deep listening, and reflection and inquiry, while also examining issues of identity and power in a small and diverse group setting, inevitably raises questions related to pedagogy—how and why we teach what we teach (Adams & Marchesani, 1992). In addressing these questions, the facilitator preparation program described in this chapter draws conceptual and practice principles from social justice education, prejudice reduction, and dialogue theory and practice, as well as the emerging literature on intergroup dialogue inside and outside the United States. In developing the curriculum of the training sequence, particular attention is paid to content and process goals related to dialogue planning and facilitation from a social justice and experiential learning perspective. Because intergroup dialogue facilitation calls for active and responsive guidance across social identity–based differences, we blend traditional approaches to group work (Ellinor & Girard, 1998; Hunter, Bailey, & Taylor, 1995) with social justice education (Arnold, Burke, James, Martin, & Thomas, 1991; Griffin & Ouellette, 2007; Hooks, 1994) and conflict transformation approaches (Lederach, 1995, 2003).

Two conceptual frameworks guide our dialogue facilitation sequence. The *multicultural competency training model* (Beale, Thompson, & Chesler, 2001; Jackson, n.d.), which draws heavily from social justice education (Adams, Bell, & Griffin, 2007) and human relations training (Cooke, Brazzel, Craig, & Greig, 1999), helps to clarify which content areas and skill sets need to be covered by the two-semester sequence and identifies the competencies needed to prepare intergroup facilitators. It guides the content and process of our sequence in four competency areas—Knowledge, Awareness, Skills, and Passion (Jackson, n.d.) (see chapter 3 for more information about this model). The second framework, *critical reflective practice* (Brookfield, 1995; Ghaye & Ghaye, 1998), is rooted in action learning and critical reflective learning. It demonstrates how we guide and structure the learning process to encourage and support reflective practice. While both frameworks are important, critical reflective practice is the primary focus of this chapter.

Critical reflective practice can be defined as both a *method* and a *process* of action learning. This approach to learning encourages trainees to learn from their experiences facilitating the undergraduate intergroup dialogue sections. It asks trainees to notice and examine their personal motives, reactions, skills, and/or experiences in the moment (reflection-in-action) and after a dialogue session took place (reflection-on-action) (Schon, 1983). As such, critical reflective practice can help foreground questions concerning how facilitators' unexamined assumptions and actions may support or work against personal and professional goals, and how issues of identity and power may impact how they make meaning of educational processes and interactions in democratic and diverse classrooms (Brookfield, 1995). For instance, one of the hardest challenges intergroup dialogue facilitators face is learning to notice, describe, and examine the gaps or tensions that often exist between their intentions in making a facilitation move (or abstaining from making one) and the impact of what actually happens in the "here and now." A critical reflective stance can help practitioners gain insight into self and others' intentions (e.g., assumptions and motivations) during a difficult or confusing moment. It can also help facilitators identify what may have led to "what happened," including the extent to which social identity–based processes may have influenced what happened, and help them explore what they could have done differently and why.

In many ways, critical reflective practice mirrors many of the principles guiding dialogue practice (Ellinor & Girard, 1998) and the development of diverse learning communities (Wasserman & Doran, 1999), including the need to create a safe and caring environment that encourages and supports listening deeply, identifying and checking assumptions, asking questions, sharing observations and perceptions, taking risks, and giving and receiving feedback. To frame assignments and guide critical reflective learning, we draw from Brookfield's (1995) four lenses of critical reflective practice: (1) one's autobiography, (2) one's students' eyes, (3) one's colleagues' and peers' eyes, and (4) relevant literature. For instance, facilitators engage in self-study to develop insight into sociocultural and family influences shaping their own perspectives and experiences related to identity, power, and privilege as well as communication, conflict, and leadership styles in groups. In the practicum, facilitators share and explore with peers their thoughts, feelings, dilemmas, and insights and use relevant literature to help contextualize or explain specific moments in the dialogue. In sum, a critical reflective practice approach invites dialogue group facilitators to use multiple lenses to inquire and reflect upon the interactions and processes in the dialogue.

Learning From Action: Using Reflective Practice to Examine Co-facilitation Roles in Dialogue Facilitation

In this section, we illustrate how critical reflective practice is used in the IGD facilitation practicum course to help facilitators make meaning of significant events while co-facilitating the undergraduate intergroup dialogue course. We chose to describe a co-facilitation event experienced by two of the authors of this chapter while trying to *negotiate co-facilitation roles in the dialogue group*. We selected this example because we recognize that IGD facilitation requires the ability to enact and share facilitation roles in the moment in order to provide support and guidance. As we prepared to write this chapter, we all knew that the challenges presented by this episode were not unique. In IGD, co-facilitation teams are often challenged by questions related to equalizing their participation and influence in the dialogue, particularly during stage three, "Exploring and discussing 'hot topics.'" In this stage, the role of facilitator shifts from facilitating fairly structured activities to guiding open conversations about controversial topics. This shift challenges facilitators to communicate with each other clearly and authentically across lines of difference in the moment, as well as before and after the session. It challenges consultants and instructors to also communicate authentically and clearly across lines of difference and provide caring, balanced, and timely guidance and feedback during weekly consultation and practicum sessions.

As we describe this episode, we demonstrate how one co-facilitation team engaged in an in-depth critical reflective practice process of self-study and critical analysis involving the following five methods: (1) microteaching, (2) peer debriefing, (3) reflective writing, (4) weekly consultation sessions, and (5) using inspiring and thought-provoking literature for guidance and further reflection. Although we describe and illustrate the methods we use to support dialogue and critical reflections separately, they are often used together.

Critical reflective practice is not a linear process but an iterative process that requires the use of multiple lenses and methods to inquire into practice (Brookfield, 1995).

Description of the Episode and Methods Used to Support Dialogue and Critical Reflection

Keri, a White woman born in the United States, and Romina, an Afro-Latina immigrant woman born in Venezuela, co-facilitated a 10-week race/ethnicity intergroup dialogue together. During stages one and two of their dialogue, Keri and Romina guided participants through group building and intergroup awareness activities, facilitated group processes, encouraged participant involvement, and helped identify and debrief new learning. In these stages, Romina and Keri developed a pattern of taking turns in leading activities, which helped them to take up equal space and time in each dialogue session. During the third stage, where relevant controversial topics are explored, the design called for a more open, fluid, emergent facilitation style that is less directive and structured and harder to delineate. The first controversial topic session that semester focused on interracial/interethnic relationships. The practice of *microteaching* allowed Keri and Romina to use this session as an opportunity for reflection that began to prepare them for the challenge of facilitating the second controversial topic session.

Microteaching provides an opportunity for facilitator teams to choose and present a snapshot of their facilitation in a videotaped practice or dialogue session, with the purpose of critically reviewing it with the co-facilitation partner and a consultant or course instructor (Allen & Ryan, 1969). By putting the facilitation of a session "under the microscope," facilitators can identify and examine what aspects of their facilitation seem to be working well and why; what is not working, or perhaps missing, and why; and what could be done differently. They can also examine what else may be influencing their facilitation in the moment (e.g., assumptions, perceptions, and reactions) and incorporate input from other lenses (e.g., co-facilitator feedback, participant feedback, consultant, literature). As Brookfield (1995) put it, the integration of multiple lenses can strengthen practitioners' ability to inquire into practice after the experience happened.

In reviewing the material generated by the "microteaching" assignment, Keri and Romina were able to examine and reflect upon their co-facilitation roles and relationship during the "interracial/ethnic relationship" dialogue session. They realized, after reviewing videotaped material from the session, that the conversation had been stilted and disconnected. In discussing why this might have happened, they realized that their "turn-taking" pattern for sharing co-facilitation roles in the dialogue was not well suited for facilitating open dialogic structures and discovered that neither of them had been sure how or when to enter as facilitators in a different way. As a result, they decided to work toward using a more active and organic co-facilitation style during the upcoming dialogue session.

The second open session focused on the controversial topic of immigration. To help start the conversation, the session began with a gallery walk (see Goodman & Shapiro, 1997) facilitated by Romina. As planned, Keri took the lead facilitating the first part of the open dialogue. After facilitating the open conversation for some time, Keri noticed that Romina had not said anything. She asked Romina if she would like to add to the conversation, but Romina just shared some of the information she had been gathering on immigration policy and then remained unusually quiet for most of the session. Keri and Romina both left the immigration session feeling unsettled and uncomfortable. In their *peer debriefing* session, both tried to be open and honest about how they experienced the episode, how their perceptions and feelings affected their behavior in the moment, and how their participants had been impacted. Peer debriefing provides an opportunity to see the experience from the perspective of one's colleague (Brookfield, 1995). It encourages dialogue and feedback about what the experience means and some of the challenges involved.

Keri expressed how she felt very uneasy about being more "out in front" as the U.S.-born White co-facilitator in an open dialogue on immigration. She also felt worried about what led Romina to step back during that session. Up to this point, Keri's perception of herself as a "good" co-facilitator (one who shares space fairly) and a "good" White ally (one who does not take up too much space) in the dialogue and in the co-facilitator relationship came into conflict during this incident. She had been able to share space with her co-facilitator and was trying hard to practice active dialogue co-facilitation in the open dialogue but struggled with how to negotiate roles and power in the moment.

> I found myself in a bind. I was worried about what had caused Romina's silence and her reactions to the content of the conversation but felt unsure about how to support her, or how to make space so that we could check in with each other. I feared that our inability to negotiate roles in the moment would get in the way of our goals of building participants' dialogue skills. However, I tried to make the best out of the situation by staying focused on asking questions and guiding the conversation. (Keri, postdialogue reflection)

Keri worried that what she had perceived as taking a more prominent role during such a difficult and emotionally loaded topic may convey the wrong message to both White students and students of color. By taking such a role, she worried that she was not co-facilitating well. Nonetheless, the participants all seemed very engaged and active during the open dialogue, partly due to Keri's active and responsive guidance in asking clarifying questions, noting and naming patterns in the group, and moving the conversation. On the other hand, Romina was taken aback at hearing Keri's feedback because Romina thought participants were very engaged, despite the fact that she had remained quiet. Romina had been acting on the belief that a "good" facilitator creates space for all students to freely participate without feeling the pressure to self-censor because their views or experiences may be very different from those of the facilitator:

> For me, it was important to not let my emotions, thoughts, and experiences with immigration "take over" when facilitating a dialogue on this controversial topic. I was concerned about communicating in a manner that would not be perceived as biased or "lashing out." Furthermore, I wanted to convey accurate information that would demystify some of the myths about immigration circulating in the media at the time. Not being sure about how to clearly articulate my thoughts, questions, and emotions led me to step back and remain quiet because I wasn't sure how to enter the conversation or what to say. (Romina, postdialogue reflection)

Therefore, in the midst of the moment, Romina did not consider how stepping back was impacting participants' learning and her co-facilitator's role in the dialogue. Hence, the practice of peer debriefing allowed them to share and expose their experiences and emotional reactions to the episode. As they shared their perceptions and experiences, they were able to also begin to acknowledge and validate each other's feelings and experience and develop an increased shared understanding about what happened, thus strengthening their ability to negotiate and share facilitation roles more effectively in the future.

In preparation for the next consultation and practicum session, Romina and Keri used the opportunity provided by bimonthly reflective log assignments to continue to make meaning and reflect on their co-facilitation of the immigration episode. In her log, Keri shared the following thoughts:

> I felt like she [Romina] might have been shutting down a little bit. She was pretty quiet, so I started asking more [probing] questions [to the group]. . . . I started to worry about her. . . . I did not feel like I was able to support her and was feeling like I over-facilitated. I think one of my biggest fears is letting her down in the dialogue.

In her own log, Romina also expressed uncertainties:

> Since I had so much at stake [being an immigrant myself] during that session, I did not feel I could express myself without making some of our students feel as if I were attacking them. Looking back, I realize that I should have better communicated my thoughts around this to Keri before our dialogue. But how to do so when I was not as aware of them then?

Their written reflections in the logs suggest that they shared the common goal of effective facilitation but had different perceptions and concerns about what happened in the dialogue during the immigration session. Log writing provided a structure and a space for Keri and Romina to engage in deeper analysis of what they had each experienced and to explore what they wanted to keep or change about their facilitation. This kind of *reflective writing* helps facilitators take stock, describe, analyze, and reflect on the experience using multiple lenses or standpoints. In this kind of writing, learning to describe and dissect moments in the experience (e.g., What happened and what events may have led to it? How do specific readings or other sources help you interpret what happened?) is as important as learning to "think about the experience, what the experience means, how it felt, where it might lead, and what to do about it" (Posner, 2005, p. 21). Specific prompts are used to guide facilitators in providing detailed descriptions and analysis of a moment in the dialogue, a particular group dynamic, or a certain facilitation behavior or skill, and to extend the analysis building on specific readings. In this way, reflective writing helps facilitators delve into and explain confusing moments in the dialogue and acknowledge and gain clarity about what went well.

During the next practicum session, Keri and Romina also spent time discussing the episode in detail with their consultant. The primary focus of *consultation sessions* is to debrief the previous dialogue session; talk about the next session; and inquire into any personal, co-facilitation, or group dynamics that may need to be examined. Romina and Keri discussed their facilitation challenges with their consultant, Tanya, before and after every dialogue session and used the next consultation as a forum for exploring the facilitation dynamics that unfolded during the immigration session. Tanya helped Keri and Romina to probe deeper by asking questions about their facilitation, their relationship, and invited them to give attention to their co-facilitation relationship in the dialogue once they finalized their design for the next session. She also took the opportunity to encourage them to examine what had gone well. It was challenging for Tanya to invite Romina and Keri to talk openly about some of the assumptions, perceptions, and emotions that filtered their conflicting understanding of what happened during the immigration session. Due to time constraints and the need to work on planning their next session, the upcoming consultation sessions and practicum class offered the support and the structure for Keri and Romina to continue to make meaning of the experience as they tried to understand and negotiate their roles and relationships as dialogue group facilitators. The instructor of the course (Ximena) also provided guidance and support to Keri and Romina, as well as Tanya, as they struggled to figure out how to respond to the questions and challenges that surfaced during this significant episode.

Microteaching, peer debriefing, log writing, and consultations are complemented by the use of literature in reflective writing throughout the course. In the subsequent weeks, Keri realized she felt unsure about how to use time fairly during a more fluid, and perhaps more messy, dialogue. Through *the use of literature for guidance and further reflection* she was able to see that focusing so much on her fear of making a mistake prevented her from being able to gauge what was going on for and between herself and Romina, and for the group. She was able to identify that her fear of making a mistake was interfering with her ability to surface and work through conflict with her co-facilitator and the group in a constructive way. For her reflective practice assignment, Keri found a very helpful article by Tatum and Ayvazian (2004) that provided a hopeful description of working through conflict in a cross-race collegial relationship. She was able to realize that by communicating and bridging some of their differences in perception and experience across interracial boundaries and realities, she could now trust their ability to work through co-facilitation issues and feel better able to support her co-facilitator if a similar situation arose in the future.

For Romina, the reflective-writing process and relevant readings helped her recognize she had made many assumptions about Keri's feelings and experiences. She assumed that because Keri had the privilege of being a White U.S.-born citizen, it was going to be easier for her to facilitate a dialogue about immigration in the United States. She also recognized that she had made assumptions about the group's ability to handle conflict and emotions. By withholding her thoughts, feelings, and experiences regarding immigration policy and its impact on people's lives, Romina believed she was protecting the relationships she had developed with participants. In questioning these assumptions, she came to realize that by stepping back she might unintentionally have curtailed the quality and depth of the dialogue and, perhaps, the group's ability to explore a broader range of perspectives more fully. Therefore, further reflection led her to the conclusion that she needed to be more open about her feelings, thoughts, and experiences in the group, as well as to work on competencies such as surfacing conflict and asking questions to deepen the conversation. Reading the works of Leas (1982) and Lederach (2003) served as a foundation for Romina to understand conflict as a transformative opportunity for personal growth and group development.

Discussion and Implications for Practice

With support from each other, their peers in the classroom, their consultant, and the instructor, and through the use of relevant literature and reflective writing, Romina and Keri were able to use critical self-reflective practice to gain greater self-awareness about their co-facilitation roles and a greater understanding of how to negotiate roles during the open dialogue. In their own words,

> All in all, this experience taught me the value of surfacing and working through conflict regardless of how unpleasant or uncomfortable it might be. In addition, it helped me to notice the power of viewing one single event through multiple lenses. Furthermore, thanks to the structure critical reflective practice provided, I was able to be vulnerable and open in ways that allowed me to find a deeper meaning in my role as a co-facilitator, particularly as being part of a cross-racial team. (Romina, postdialogue reflection)

> I learned the value of discussing and clarifying expectations of how to support and be supported. Once we clarified what we needed from one another, I was able to focus on connecting to Romina and to the group. I have found that in working in interracial teams, identifying assumptions, honestly communicating expectations, and being aware of how one's own racial identity impacts the ability to feel connected are all behaviors that enable strong co-facilitation. (Keri, postdialogue reflection)

As these postdialogue reflections suggest, using a reflective practice model has its challenges. Reflecting on their perceptions, experiences, and feelings was difficult because Keri and Romina, like most facilitators, wanted to preserve their relationship by remaining focused on positive actions. In addition, they, like most other facilitators, were not always aware of their feelings and needs, especially as they were spending most of their energy focusing on the group's needs. However, Keri and Romina were both willing to look closely at their feelings and actions, open to sharing their perceptions and experiences, and able to use the structured opportunities for discussion and reflection offered by the critical reflective practice model. Having the space and time to reflect allowed Keri and Romina to work through some challenging experiences and learn some valuable lessons about themselves individually and as co-facilitators. Furthermore, going through the reflective process allowed them to contemplate deeply and critically about the episode and, most important, to examine how this experience could be used to strengthen their co-facilitation roles and dialogue facilitation competencies.

This example of critical reflective practice illustrates how this approach may be used to support and enhance the facilitator's knowledge, awareness, and skills in IGD. In order for critical reflective practice to be effective, however, it needs to be implemented in an environment where facilitators can engage in a sustained process of reflection and inquiry that is supported by a learning community. An inclusive learning community is a "safe yet challenging environment composed of people who support each other as they explore their differences . . . in which mistakes are acceptable (and) people support each other and draw on each other's different experiences to expand their own knowledge and capabilities" (Wasserman & Doran, 1999, p. 307). Fostering a learning community helps graduate student facilitators to develop a more nuanced, complex, and holistic understanding of self and others and to identify competencies and actions that may need improvement.

The balance of challenging and supporting is also crucial. Challenging without supporting can hinder self-confidence and cause fatigue. Supporting without challenging prevents facilitators from critically examining what they are doing and limits their ability to enhance the personal and professional development for which they are striving. In the critical reflective practice model, the key components of peer debriefing, consultation, microteaching, reflective writing, and use of relevant literature for guidance and further reflection offer a variety of opportunities for both challenging and supporting intergroup dialogue facilitators. These opportunities, in turn, benefit the dialogue group as a whole. Facilitators who are able to acknowledge and work with their own personal, interpersonal, and social identity–based feelings and reactions are able to better understand what participants are going through and can provide better guidance for the group as it journeys through the dialogue process.

References

Adams, M., Bell, L. A., & Griffin, P. (2007). *Teaching for diversity and social justice* (2nd ed.). New York: Routledge.

Adams, M., & Marchesani, L. S. (1992). Curricular innovations: Social diversity as course content. In M. Adams (Ed.), *Promoting diversity in college classrooms: Innovative responses for the curriculum, faculty, and institutions*, New Directions for Teaching and Learning, no. 52 (pp. 85–98). San Francisco: Jossey-Bass.

Allen, D., & Ryan, K. (1969). *Microteaching*. Reading, MA: Addison-Wesley.

Arnold, R., Burke, B., James, C., Martin, D., & Thomas, B. (1991). Working by design: Putting together a program for change. In *Educating for a change* (pp. 33–67). Toronto: Between the Lines & Doris Marshall Institute for Education and Action.

Beale, R. L., Thompson, M. C., & Chesler, M. (2001). Training peer facilitators for intergroup dialogue leadership. In D. Schoem & S. Hurtado (Eds.), *Intergroup Dialogue: Deliberative democracy in school, college, community, and workplace* (pp. 227–246). Ann Arbor: University of Michigan Press.

Bloom, B. S. (Ed.). (1956). *Taxonomy of educational objectives: Vol. 1. Cognitive domain*. New York: McCay.

Brookfield, S. (1995). *Becoming a critically reflective teacher*. San Francisco: Jossey-Bass.

Cooke, A. L., Brazzel, M., Craig, A. S., & Greig, B. (Eds.). (1999). *Reading book for human relations training* (8th ed.). Alexandria, VA: NTL Institute for Applied Behavioral Sciences.

Ellinor, L., & Girard, G. (1998). *Dialogue: Rediscover the transforming power of conversation*. New York: John Wiley & Sons.

Ghaye, A., & Ghaye, K. (1998). *Teaching and learning through critical reflective practice*. London: David Fulton Publishers.

Goodman, D., & Shapiro, S. (1997). Sexism curriculum design. In M. Adams, L. A. Bell, & P. Griffin (Eds.), *Teaching for diversity and social justice: A sourcebook* (pp. 110–140). New York: Routledge.

Griffin, P., & Ouellette, M. L. (2007). Facilitating social justice education courses. In M. Adams, L. A. Bell, & P. Griffin (Eds.), *Teaching for diversity and social justice: A sourcebook* (pp. 89–116). New York: Routledge.

Hooks, B. (1994). *Teaching to transgress*. New York: Routledge.

Hunter, D., Bailey, A., & Taylor, B. (1995). *The art of facilitation*. MA: Fisher Books.

Jackson, B. W. (n.d.). *PASK: Framework for multicultural competency*. Amherst, MA: New Perspectives. Mimeograph.

Leas, S. (1982). *Leadership and conflict*. Nashville, TN: Abingdon Press.

Lederach, J. P. (1995). *Preparing for peace: Conflict transformation across cultures*. Syracuse, New York: Syracuse University Press.

Lederach, J. P. (2003). *The little book of conflict transformation: Clear articulation of the guiding principles by a pioneer in the field*. Intercourse, PA: Good Books.

Posner, G. (2005). *Field experience: A guide to reflective teaching*. Boston: Allyn & Bacon.

Schon, D. A. (1983). *The reflective practitioner: How professionals think in action*. New York: Basic Books.

Tatum, B. D., & Ayvazian, A. (2004). Women, race and racism: A dialogue in black and white. In J. Jordan, M. Walker, & L. Hartling (Eds.), *The complexity of connection: Writings from the Stone Center's Jean Baker Miller Training Institute* (pp. 147–163). Guilford Press: New York.

Wasserman, I. C., & Doran, R. F. (1999). Creating inclusive learning communities. In A. L. Cooke, M. Brazzel, A. S. Craig, & B. Greig (Eds.), *NTL Reading book for human relations training* (8th ed., pp. 307–310). Alexandria, VA: NTL Institute for Applied Behavioral Sciences.

Zúñiga, X., Nagda, B. A., Chesler, M., & Cytron-Walker, A. (2007). *Intergroup dialogues in higher education: Meaningful learning about social justice*. ASHE Higher Education Report Series, *32*(4). San Francisco: Jossey-Bass.

6

(RE)TRAINING OURSELVES

Professionals Who Facilitate Intergroup Dialogue

Kathleen (Wong) Lau, Joycelyn Landrum-Brown,
and Thomas E. Walker

I ntergroup dialogue as an educational practice is based on a strong assumption that knowledge is constructed through the process of intergroup interactions among participants and facilitators. Intergroup dialogue purposefully resources personal and social group experiences of the participants and the facilitators. Since their inception, intergroup dialogues have had a very particular praxis, where theory and research intersect practice. The curriculum and pedagogy of structured intergroup interaction is developmentally driven based on research and theory from social psychology on intergroup identity and tokenism, social identity development, and social justice education theories (Zúñiga, Nagda, Chesler, & Cytron-Walker, 2007). It is the role of the facilitators to drive, guide, and encourage meaningful interaction among participants within groups and across groups. On university campuses intergroup dialogue facilitators come from a variety of backgrounds including students, graduate students, academic staff, and faculty, all of whom receive varying degrees of formal training and supervision specific to the intergroup dialogue topic.

Whereas other chapters in this book speak to intergroup facilitation in general, or describe programs utilizing peer or near-peer student facilitators, this chapter focuses on the unique challenges and strengths that higher education professionals bring to their role as intergroup dialogue facilitators. Some challenges to professionals-as-facilitators are obvious: generational and socialization differences and experiences related to our social identity group memberships that may be quite different from those of student participants. These natural differences are expected, important, and therefore must be addressed.

Beyond differences based on age, other, less obvious perspectives are also at play among and between facilitators and our student participants. Feminist standpoint theory (Haraway, 1988; Harstock, 1983) assumes that knowledge is multiple and situated because it is rooted in the life experiences of individuals specific to social location based within historical contexts. In particular, Black feminist standpoint theory (Collins, 1991) expands this notion by highlighting the experience of multiple marginalities and contradictory positions of oppression and privilege within marginalized groups. At the same time that we are multiply positioned in terms of race, ethnicity, gender, sexual orientation, and economic class origin, we are positioned as degreed professionals who hold power within university settings. This chapter provides personal insights and conceptual frameworks about the social and institutional positionality of professionals who come to the practice of intergroup dialogue facilitation.

We approach this as three experienced intergroup dialogue facilitators whose personal and social identities and professional backgrounds are traced to various communities, geographic regions, institutions, disciplines, university occupations and educational training. Joycelyn Landrum-Brown is an African American woman who was formally trained as a clinical psychologist and has worked in counseling center settings as well as taught in academic departments on university campuses around the country. Thomas Walker is a White man schooled in intercultural communication and has spent the bulk of his career as a staff member in university intergroup relations offices, working with various campus and community dialogue programs. Kathleen Wong(Lau) is an Asian American woman and an assistant professor and researcher in intercultural communication and has spent part of her career working as a staff member on intergroup relations with faculty and local communities at a public university.

While our diversity is our strength, our professional status provides unique challenges into the informed practice of facilitating intergroup dialogues.[1] In this chapter we speak to the importance of being learners and teachers in the dialogue process. This involves being open to participants as teachers regarding their own experiences and stories.

Teacher–Learner Dichotomy (Unlearning Assumptions About Knowledge Generation: Faculty as Dialogue Facilitators)

Kathleen Wong(Lau): Facilitating a *women of color and White women* intergroup dialogue for the first time was an incredible challenge for me. Being grounded in women's studies, ethnic studies, intercultural communication and gender, and communication literature as an instructor of undergraduate students had not actually prepared me to facilitate rather than teach the course content. Yet, when it came to intergroup dialogues, a dialogic learning practice that places students as sources of knowledge for each other, I was surprised at my reluctance to let go of the role of teacher when I felt the group disagree or misinterpret readings. Instead of focusing on process by highlighting other students who also indicated disagreement with the interpretation and coaching them to ask each other questions, I was focusing on what the author intended in the text. I often found myself suppressing the urge to intervene by providing facts and previously published "expert" interpretations in order to "teach" perspectives. I had to silently redirect myself to focus on facilitating the group through dialogue and mutual discovery of student perspectives. I was ambushed by the energy and vigilance it took to continually unlearn my ingrained teaching practices throughout the eight-week dialogue.

An additional challenge all facilitators face is that students themselves have been rigorously trained in traditional academic ontology. It is easy for both facilitators and students to fall into the comfortable traditional relationships of standard classroom experiences. Typical intergroup dialogues on university campuses take place in classrooms during traditional class meeting times. On most campuses intergroup dialogue participants also receive college credit and a coursework grade. All of these factors can trigger institutionally ingrained communication roles and scripts of what communication scholars have termed *persistence* patterns that interactants jointly construct to resist change (Watzlawick, Weakland, & Fisch, 1974). A facilitator with faculty background needs to be particularly mindful and vigilant to recognize persistent communication and intervene toward dialogue even as students themselves enact the script of calling on the facilitator to be the expert.

As professors we are also trained to look at learning outcomes as the primary measure of curriculum. Even if we focus on pedagogy, it is usually with a general overall goal of being more engaged and interactional—we do not consciously plan or view classroom engagement as a developmental intergroup process shaped by sociocultural history, social identities, and social psychological dynamics such as tokenism and majority/minority relations. The praxis of intergroup dialogues, however, originates in the best research and informed pedagogy on these very processes.

The role of the dialogue facilitator is to be deeply conscious, mindful, and active in driving and allowing developmental dialogue processes to evolve among students who are understood to be rooted in all of these conditions (Beale, Thompson, & Chesler, 2001). It requires trusting that the depth of the learning process will ultimately drive the depth of learning outcomes (Nagda, Gurin, Sorensen, & Zúñiga, 2009). Content is of course important, but knowledge is not exclusive to traditional sources of academic material such as readings, lectures, and exercises. Knowledge is dialogically generated, and the skills and desire for dialogic engagement itself constitute one of the most important "knowledge" outcomes of intergroup dialogues for students (Nagda & Zúñiga, 2003). In intergroup dialogues, knowledge is not found in texts but is produced through the process of sharing and constant self-reflection upon different life experiences and perspectives triggered by texts. The knowledge itself is not merely cognitive and affective, but experienced at an individual and group level. In short, students themselves generate knowledge only if facilitators privilege students as generators of individual and group knowledge, a completely different approach from that of traditional faculty instruction training (Beale & Schoem, 2001).

Most important, being a facilitator requires a genuine trust that students themselves are resources of knowledge and that intergroup-generated knowledge during the dialogue is the most effective transformative knowledge. As a faculty member, this ontological shift is radical. It is a shift that may seem to come easiest intellectually but can be incredibly challenging pedagogically. It is one thing to theorize about student-centered learning and knowledge generation; it is another thing to put it into practice, particularly when one is facilitating on intergroup issues such as discrimination, oppression, and injustice, and developing a sense of common fate and commitment on these issues that are central to our intellectual, personal, and community lives.

Many scholars and practitioners of intergroup dialogue and engaged pedagogy are familiar with Paulo Freire's *Pedagogy of the Oppressed* (1998), in which Freire critiques the traditional teacher–student, teacher–learner dichotomy by using the metaphor of teachers adhering to the "banking method" of learning where all-knowing teachers pour knowledge and content into students' heads so they can accumulate their knowledge. Freire contrasts learning as a knowledge-banking process with dialogic learning whereby teachers and students engage in a two-way dialogue that uses the students' own indigenous experiences of the world as a source of knowledge and means of anchoring learning to the self. Freire's work was innovative at the time and should still serve as a cautionary tale to faculty who want to engage in facilitation of and research on intergroup dialogues. We live and work in institutions built on cultural academic traditions that favor banking of knowledge. And traditionally trained faculty (instructors) who become facilitators must consciously and consistently recognize and engage this different approach with intention and commitment.

Professional–Personal Dichotomy

Thomas E. Walker: Beyond blurring the traditional lines between teacher and learner, intergroup dialogue's mutually shared relationship also involves some dissolution of the traditional professional–personal firewalls between us and colleagues, and especially between us and students. Typically in our professional roles, we are focused on the job content and its connection to the students' development; and we present only those parts of ourselves necessary to those purposes. Our authority and expertise come from credentials such as degrees earned, years worked, and works published. We know that our race, ethnicity, gender expression, and some other identities may be obvious, but especially for those with dominant identities, they may never be discussed. We may occasionally reward "good" colleagues and students with revelations about our earlier years, a dinner at our home, or an introduction to family members—insights into our larger, extraprofessional life. But many of us, most of the time and for several legitimate reasons, maintain a healthy distinction between professional and personal realms.

Intergroup dialogue, meanwhile, asks us not only to share control with a co-facilitator and with participants but also to share ourselves. Our sharing of self adds substance to the dialogue. As professionals we are often older than our participants or, at least, have given considerably more thought to the identities and issues about which we are dialoguing. Therefore, sharing our experience provides insights that otherwise might not be present. The greater quantity of our life and study can add historical perspectives to contemporary experience and can help bust myths or correct misinformation. Our sharing also supports the dialogue process. When the authority figures in the dialogue are willing to share about themselves, participants are more likely to do the same; facilitators' appropriate self-disclosure can model what participants should do. (Dialogues are neither therapy sessions nor awards shows, but we can relate to one another through comparing struggles and successes in our social justice development, experiences, and actions.) We both practice and model the skill of dialoguing.

Yet, for all its benefits, exposing evidence of other aspects of our lives and the emotions around them happens rarely, can seem risky, and therefore can be very uncomfortable for us as professionals. While we are trained to tout our (professional) accomplishments, most of us are not practiced at volunteering publically what we do not know, where we fall short, or where we have struggled or hurt. Such confessions of our fallibility, our insecurity, and ultimately our humanity are not encouraged and may even be punished in our professional contexts. So we must challenge ourselves to practice that constructive discomfort, perhaps discussing it with our co-facilitator, and to push through it if we are truly to be collaborative teacher–learners in dialogue—to open ourselves to the learning we can give and get through sharing our expertise in our experience.

At the same time, we cannot forget that we still carry the institutional authority of our professional roles, in addition to our other social identities and their societal values. As university employees (staff or faculty) in the role of group facilitators, our sharing and other actions carry a power that the participants' do not. Our title and/or apparent age may protect us from some of the authority challenges a peer facilitator can face, but they can also create credibility gaps between us and participants who do not think we can relate. We may be grading participants for the course credit they are receiving for the experience, and that "power over" is not erased by our welcoming invitations and statements of equality within the dialogue.

In race and gender dialogues, for example, my being White and a man carries a social power that my co-facilitators of color or of a different gender typically do not have. As with every facilitator's dominant social identities beyond his or her facilitator/instructor role, I must be mindful of whether, when, and how I wield my stories so as not to privilege them, and must be cognizant of how my experience will differ from the experiences of those in the target/subordinated identity groups. (Though not less valid than others', the privilege inherent in my identities makes my experiences qualitatively different.) I must "sit with" the social justice critiques of my agent identities (and me), and not follow the temptation to "run to" my target identities. Even in dialogues where my target identities are the focus (e.g., sexual orientation or religion), I do not lose the power associated with my professional role or other agent identities.

For example, I will sometimes share an early realization of how my agent identity and experience masked my racialized assumptions about all groups, in this case to my own detriment: how during college I was mugged by a group of other young White men because their skin color did not mark them as threatening to me, despite every other contextual clue shouting "danger." How I, in fact, reacted more hesitantly to the Black passerby who intervened on my behalf because her skin color registered to my socialization as "threatening," despite her clear actions to the contrary.

Each time I consider sharing this story, I first find myself reflecting on whether the particular dialogue participants (and even co-facilitator) will judge me as a weak man (unable to defend himself), whether I think they can see me as more than the racist assumptions obviously operating in me subconsciously, whether they will accept diversity facilitation from someone with that admitted bias, and whether we all can move beyond "poor Thomas, victim of bad individuals" to look at the racial dynamics inherent in the situation. In sharing my vulnerability, I expose myself as an imperfect person, and I make myself available to the group for discussion just as I ask them to do.

At the same time, I must not allow the sharing to recenter my dominant identities, or the discussion to focus on me exclusively. As a facilitator, I must be intentional with my choice, my sharing, and my own focus in facilitating discussion around my own and others' stories, to be sure that this risk and modeling is educational for us all. As a professional, rather than a peer, the offering of self-as-subject can be not only especially uncomfortable, but also powerful, for its rarity.

Thus, as with the teacher position specifically, it is again important for the professional facilitator more generally to be thoughtful and intentional with *how* (not whether!) he or she brings himself or herself into the mutual sharing that, in part, defines intergroup dialogue as a unique learning space and process.

Leveraging and Managing Emotional Engagement

Joycelyn Landrum-Brown: Given the traditional roles and boundaries described above, a particular challenge for many professionals is constructively engaging emotions in intergroup dialogues. In most other professional and educational settings (with therapeutic counseling being the most obvious exception), we are trained and expected to keep emotions "out" of the learning; affect is viewed as irrelevant (to rational learning), uncomfortable (for witnesses), or risky (for fear of committing/allowing emotional trauma). Therefore, academics, in particular, may work hard to keep the dialogue at an intellectual or "in their head" level, whereas trained therapists may be tempted to explore the expressed affect in the service of helping a particular group member resolve identity-based traumas. As an educator trained as a therapist, I believe that an appropriate exploration of affect can be useful, but only in the service of deepening or expanding the dialogue process.

Dialogue without space for participants' emotions becomes just another impersonal, "academic" treatment of a theoretical subject. It has been our experience that the expression of strong feelings accurately reflects the emotional charges that are often part of intergroup history and relations, humanizes the issues, and can act as a catalyst for the group's relationship building and learning. Emotional sharing can deepen the dialogue when the feelings are normalized and considered in light of what a particular perspective means to the speaker and the listeners. When appropriately worked through, affect can move the dialogue participants to a deeper level of sharing, particularly since one fear often expressed is that "people will get offended or hurt" by things shared. When the participants learn that strong emotions can be expressed without things "getting out of control," then the expression of affect is normalized, and its benefits become available to all participants and facilitators.

I recall working with a *race and ethnicity* dialogue where a person of color strongly expressed her anger at a White student who dismissed the impact of racism. As a result, the White students got really quiet and the students of color became more animated. I took that moment to make a process comment and asked the students what they were feeling about the last interaction. When the White students were able to express their fears about making the students of color angry, it opened up the group to talk more honestly about their feelings about not wanting to offend.

This is an example of how a strong expression of affect can be a catalyst for students to then talk about their feelings and how their cultural backgrounds inform their reactions to strong expressions of feelings that, in effect, deepened the dialogue and created an opportunity for students to explore the roles of culture, socialization, and lived experiences in making meaning of affective responses. In addition, it allowed for a teachable moment for the White students, who learned that strong expressions of anger from students of color do not automatically result in violence and physical harm as their stereotypes might have suggested. It provided an opportunity to work through an immediate and pressing conflict and to practice managing their feelings and challenging their assumptions. In a traditional classroom, when strong emotions are expressed and the instructor feels uncomfortable, he or she may silence the speaker by ignoring their comments or by allowing other students to rescue the receiver of the strong emotional expression.

Despite being a facilitator also trained in group therapy techniques, I am clear that the dialogue should not turn into a group therapy session. I feel comfortable allowing the strong expression of emotions in dialogues; at the same time it is important to not lose focus on the goal of the dialogue, which is to provide a safe space for creating understanding and collective meaning making. It is also important to allow participants to have their feelings, to work with others who are feeling uncomfortable, and to manage others' discomfort without attempting to "rescue" them by discounting or diminishing the messages associated with the expression of strong feelings.

While engaging the heart as well as the head in intergroup dialogue is certainly a challenge for every facilitator, helping participants access and engage the often powerful feelings accompanying our life experiences is an important component of IGD facilitation. Professionals-as-facilitators may struggle to balance this approach but may be better able to manage emotions and conflict than younger, less life-experienced peer facilitators.

Walking the Talk

As professionals in educational settings, we regularly challenge students to take the information or skills learned in a particular class or program, and to apply them to other aspects of their studies, work, and larger lives. We are well served to heed our own advice, to incorporate the dialogue process into our repertoire of communication skills, and practice dialogic communications in all of our relationships. In other words, we believe we are more effective as facilitators when dialogic communication becomes our way of relating to others.

We work hard to implement the dialogue methods in everyday relationships with others. This involves an ongoing process of trying to be self-reflective, seek understanding, suspend judgments, listen for the meaning of messages, and actively engage in perspective taking. For example, in staff meetings and research planning meetings I work hard to keep channels of communication clear; to listen to others and encourage their participation; and to be clear about my own baggage, triggers, and perspectives by accounting for them and making them explicit.

The congruence of this communication style in and out of formal dialogue settings makes these practices easier, more natural, and more effective when actually facilitating a group. In the same way, if someone actually incorporate a social justice framework into their life, they will be able to facilitate participants' understanding of the concept more easily.

One example is Deborah Flick's (1998) work in her book *From Debate to Dialogue*. Flick mentions that individuals can affect the (dialogue) "understanding" process, as she calls it, even if the listener has not committed to doing so, reporting that "when one person engages this process, a conversation will shift from debate to dialogue" (p. 43). She goes on to provide examples of how applying the principles of the dialogue process shifts the conversation because it shifts the intention to one of caring about and understanding another.

Doing Our Own Work

A theme implicit in our discussion thus far has been the key willingness of professionals to be vulnerable, to set aside (i.e., to bracket to the extent possible) the perspective and privilege of our professional position in order to engage with participants as a whole person. At the very least, we need to be self-reflective and understand how our professional training has influenced how we experience and relate in dialogues held in academic settings. One who holds a unique process responsibility in the dialogue and has distinct content knowledge to offer remains another human learner nonetheless.

Before and as we ask participants to honestly and holistically reflect on their experience as members of groups in our social structure, we need to do our own work not only know to about the influences and impact of our social identities but also to explore the hurts, wounds, and traumas that we facilitators have experienced in our lives. When individuals have worked through their own wounds and offenses around justice issues, it makes it easier to be aware of triggering statements or arguments and not get distracted by discussions of those trigger-related issues instead of the primary focus of the topic. As discussed earlier, we can also appropriately self-disclose our own stories as models of how to use our own struggles to encourage and challenge participants that this work is an ongoing process and they can do it, too.

It is not appropriate, however, for us to "do" our work with students. As we have discussed, our life experience and responsibilities are quite different from theirs, and centering the dialogue on our developmental needs or desires is unethical. Instead, some people use a variety of resources like in-service training, additional education, personal and professional support groups, or even therapy to work through their personal issues; others utilize dialogue with trusted friends and colleagues. The key is to find the right resource so that student learning and the dialogue process remain central. As with all the suggestions and balances above, doing healing work allows us to be fully present as the participants are working through and exploring their issues.

Resources of Our Professional Fields

One final, unique resource professionals bring to intergroup dialogue participants is that of our colleagues and associations. Unlike most peer and near-peer facilitators whose work experience is largely limited to being a student, we professionals have the formal training, experience, and resources of our career communities. An increasing number of academic disciplines and professional fields are incorporating social justice perspectives and initiatives. It is exciting that disciplines such as education (Brown, 2004; Cambron-McCabe & McCarthy, 2005; Chizhik & Chizhik, 2002; Marshall, 2004; McDonald, 2005; Opfer, 2006; Shields, 2004; Terzi, 2005; Theoharis, 2007), community psychology (Fondacaro & Weinberg, 2002; Prilleltensky, 2001, 2003; White, 2003), social work (Himmelman, 1996; Parker, 2003; Swenson, 1998), and other fields of study (Davis & Wagner, 2005; Sears, 2004; Swan, 2002; Vera & Speight, 2002) have expanded their curricular foci and practices to engage social justice as an important factor for these fields. Being mindful not to utilize these resources as "the expert," more and more of us have field/position-specific professional resources and opportunities to draw upon in our ongoing professional development and action.

As we have described, it can be tempting to engage in intergroup dialogue facilitation as part of our jobs, as "work" we do for *others*, to help *them* learn and grow. Yet, there is a powerful learning dynamic in the dialogue setting when professionals allow the dialogue process to create the environment for learning. Further, sharing important stories and engaging the affect of the dialogue students is a unique challenge that differs from traditional classroom teaching. It is crucial to invest ourselves as whole persons in that effort, both for the strengths that it brings to our relationships with participants, and the benefits the process brings to us as professionals and people.

As our author backgrounds convey, we each bring a long and varied professional experience to our intergroup dialogue facilitation; we have known and worked with one another specifically (and with many other contributors to this book) for the better part of a decade. Over these years, we have shared many stories about our experiences; worked collaboratively on curriculum design; had conversations about educational philosophy and pedagogy; and in fact, become friends through this time and sharing. And yet, through all the work and relationships, until now, we had never (in person or via e-mail) held sustained conversation about what it was like for each of us to be IGD facilitators.

As for other educators, it has been a rare challenge and gift to take the time to focus on the facilitation process for us as professionals and as people. Writing this chapter has allowed us to intentionally dwell on the what, why, and how we bring ourselves to the work of facilitating intergroup dialogue, and to consider both what we offer easily and what we struggle with.

We hope that by sharing our stories, strengths, struggles, and some of ourselves through this chapter, we can invite and encourage other nonstudent facilitators to consider these issues. We suggest that would-be facilitators make the time to articulate their goals, intentions, and experiences relating to dialogue, and to have a focused dialogue with (an)other facilitator(s). In dialogue, we regularly ask our participants to self-reflect on habits, motivations, interactions, and relationships within and across differences. We must remember to heed our own call, to model personally what we ask of others, and to benefit from the wonderful challenges created through introspection and metadialogue.

Note

1. In this chapter, we use the language of U.S. higher education to describe the dialogue context and players. As intergroup dialogues are run in a variety of settings, we invite readers to draw parallels to the facilitators and participants in their own context. (For example, the professionals and students might actually be governmental or nonprofit staff and community members/constituents, respectively.)

References

Beale, R. L., & Schoem, D. (2001). The content/process balance in intergroup dialogue. In D. Schoem, & S. Hurtado (Eds.), *Intergroup Dialogue: Deliberative democracy in school, college, and workplace* (pp. 266–279). Ann Arbor: University of Michigan Press.

Beale, R. L., Thompson, M. C., & Chesler, M. (2001). Training peer facilitators for intergroup dialogue leadership. In D. Schoem, & S. Hurtado (Eds.), *Intergroup Dialogue: Deliberative democracy in school, college, and workplaces* (pp. 227–246). Ann Arbor: University of Michigan Press.

Brown, K. M. (2004). Leadership for social justice and equity: Weaving a transformative framework and pedagogy. *Educational Administration Quarterly, 40*(1), 77–108.

Cambron-McCabe, N., & McCarthy, M. M. (2005). Educating school leaders for social justice. *Educational Policy, 19*(1), 201–222.

Chizhik, E. W., & Chizhik, A. W. (2002). A path to social change: Examining students' responsibility, opportunity, and emotion toward social justice. *Education and Urban Society, 34*(3), 283–297.

Collins, P. H. (1991). *Black feminist thought: Knowledge, consciousness and the politics of empowerment.* New York: Routledg.

Davis, T. L., & Wagner, R. (2005). *Increasing men's development of social justice attitudes and actions* (pp. 29–41). *New directions for student services: Vol. 110.* Amherst, MA: Wiley Periodicals.

Flick, D. L. (1998). *From debate to dialogue: Using the understanding process to transform our conversations.* Boulder, CO: Orchid Publications.

Fondacaro, M. R., & Weinberg, D. (2002). Concepts of social justice in community psychology: Toward a social ecological epistemology. *American Journal of Community Psychology, 30*(4), 473–492.

Freire, P. (1998). *Pedagogy of the oppressed* (M. Bergman Ramos, Trans.). New York: Continuum. (Original work published 1970)

Haraway, D. (1988). Situated knowledges: The science question in feminism and the privilege of partial perspective. *Feminist Studies, 14*(3), 575–600.

Harstock, N. (1983). The feminist standpoint: Developing the ground for a specifically feminist historical materialism. In S. Harding & M. Hintikka (Eds.), *Discovering reality* (pp. 283–311). Dordrecht, Holland: Reidel Publishing Company.

Himmelman, A. T. (1996). On the theory and practice of transformational collaboration: From social service to social justice. In C. Huxham (Ed.), *Creating collaborative advantage* (pp. 19–43). Thousand Oaks, CA: Sage.

Marshall, C. (2004). Social justice challenges to educational administration: Introduction to a special issue. *Educational Administration Quarterly, 40*(1), 3–13.

McDonald, M. A. (2005). The integration of social justice in teacher education: Dimensions of prospective teachers' opportunities to learn. *Journal of Teacher Education, 56*(5), 418–435.

Nagda, B. A., Gurin, P., Sorensen, N., & Zúñiga, X. (2009). Evaluating intergroup dialogue: Engaging diversity for personal and social responsibility. *Diversity & Democracy, 12*(1), 4–6.

Nagda, B. A., & Zúñiga, X. (2003). Fostering meaningful racial engagement through intergroup dialogues. *Group Processes & Intergroup Relations, 6*(1), 111–128.

Opfer, V. D. (2006). Evaluating equity: A framework for understanding action and inaction on social justice issues. *Educational Policy, 20*(1), 271–290.

Parker, L. (2003). A social justice model for clinical social work practice. *Affilia, 18*(3), 272–288.

Prilleltensky, I. (2001). Value-based praxis in community psychology: Moving toward social justice and social action. *American Journal of Community Psychology, 29*(5), 747–778.

Prilleltensky, I. (2003). Understanding, resisting, and overcoming oppression: Toward psychopolitical validity. *American Journal of Community Psychology, 31*(1–2), 195–201.

Sears, D. O. (2004). The psychology of legitimacy: Emerging perspectives on ideology, justice, and intergroup relations. *Political Psychology, 25*(2), 318–328.

Shields, C. M. (2004). Dialogic leadership for social justice: Overcoming pathologies of silence. *Educational Administration Quarterly, 40*(1), 109–132.

Swan, S. (2002). Rhetoric, service, and social justice. *Written Communication, 19*(1), 76–108.

Swenson, C. R. (1998). Clinical social work's contribution to a social justice perspective. *Social Work, 43*(6), 527–528.

Terzi, L. (2005). A capability perspective on impairment, disability and special needs: Towards social justice in education. *Theory and Research in Education, 3*(2), 197–223.

Theoharis, G. (2007). Social justice educational leaders and resistance: Toward a theory of social justice leadership. *Educational Administration Quarterly, 43*(2), 221–258.

Vera, E. M., & Speight, S. L. (2002). Multicultural competence, social justice, and counseling psychology: Expanding our roles. *The Counseling Psychologist, 30*(6), 913–932.

Watzlawick, P., Weakland, J., & Fisch, R. (1974). *Change: Principles of problem formation and problem resolution.* New York: Norton.

White, R. (2003). Communities, conferences and restorative social justice. *Criminal Justice, 3*(2), 139–160.

Zúñiga, X., Nagda, B. A., Chesler, M., & Cytron-Walker, A. (2007). *Intergroup dialogues in higher education: Meaningful learning about social justice.* ASHE Higher Education Report Series, *32*(4). San Francisco: Jossey-Bass.

SECTION TWO

INTERGROUP DIALOGUE FACILITATION TRAINING FOR APPLICATIONS TO CAMPUS AND COMMUNITY SETTINGS

Given the promise and success of intergroup dialogue and its greater exposure in colleges and universities, the practices and processes associated with classroom-based dialogues have been extended and adapted for other campus units and community settings. Chapters in section two provide a unique look at how training in intergroup dialogue facilitation skills enriches a variety of teaching and learning approaches for diversity, multiculturalism, and social justice.

In all the chapters in this section, intergroup dialogue is geared toward building community, broadly defined. Be it in nonacademic campus settings, in online democratic deliberation, or as part of actual community change efforts, intergroup dialogue facilitation is seen to comprise a viable set of skills for both participating in and fostering diverse communities. The chapters reveal three important considerations that are centrally influenced by the context of the learning setting:

- Structure in training facilitators, moderators, or participant–facilitators
- Differential emphasis in training on relationship building, consciousness raising, and social change
- The extent to which "learning by doing" is a significant part of the training

Chapter 7, first in this section, describes the Sustained Dialogue Campus Network and presents a model for training student moderators. Originally developed by Dr. Harold Saunders in international settings to transform communities in conflict through dialogue, Parker, Nemeroff, and Kelleher describe the model that has been adapted to campus communities and has now grown to over a dozen U.S. college campuses. This student-initiated program aims to create stronger communities by initiating collective change through a moderated process of ongoing relationship building, interaction, and action. It seeks to improve campus relationships along lines of race, class, religion, sexual orientation, and other aspects of identity. The role of the moderators, as well as the model for training, is defined.

Unlike all other facilitation training and dialogue models presented in this book that describe extended face-to-face contact and intentional up-front training, chapter 8 presents a unique way of deliberating and facilitating. Author James Knauer describes Democracy Lab, an online learning community that provides forums on public issues for adoption as course requirements by high school and college instructors. In this online space, there are no formal facilitators. Effective facilitation is a shared responsibility of all online members. Knauer describes lessons and assignments built in to the weekly online curriculum that assist participants in creating a safe space, inviting personal sharing, and encouraging deeper inquiry from all. The development and use of these facilitative techniques in the online community reinforces a central goal of Democracy Lab: democratic engagement. It encourages participants to take active responsibility for their online community forum.

Chapter 9 shifts from an emphasis on campus experiences to engagement in community dialogue. Fisher and Checkoway describe Summer Youth Dialogues in Detroit. A dialogue program about race and ethnicity for metropolitan Detroit youth. They emphasize important training techniques for "near-peer" facilitators, that is, undergraduates working with high school youth in a community setting. While much of the intergroup dialogue training issues described in section one apply here, this chapter uniquely addresses training when entering and working in community settings, as well as working with parents. In particular, it addresses the social identity and social justice implications involved in training and supporting facilitators as community change agents who develop relationships with parents; community partners; and, of course, the youth.

Finally, chapter 10 describes a course offered to graduate social work students. Spencer, Martineau, and warren emphasize social work principles of practice that are both ethical and promote diversity and social justice. A central emphasis is for social workers to develop identity awareness and an understanding of social contexts in which they work. The course described seeks to engage students in developing the knowledge and skills to effectively facilitate dialogues with individuals from multiple social identity groups. The authors also describe their reflections as instructors of the course.

7

TRAINING STUDENTS TO CHANGE THEIR OWN CAMPUS CULTURE THROUGH SUSTAINED DIALOGUE

Priya Parker, Teddy Nemeroff, and Christina Kelleher

The Sustained Dialogue Campus Network (SDCN) is a student-led movement on campuses throughout the United States that transforms social tensions by engaging students in dialogue over time to improve their own relationships and develop strategies for strengthening their campus communities (Sustained Dialogue Campus Network, 2009). It was built by campus leaders and young alumni who learned, and adapted to the university setting, a methodology for peace building and conflict transformation called Sustained Dialogue (SD). These beginnings and the assumptions of this methodology have shaped the continuing development of SDCN as an active participant in the growing national intergroup dialogue movement. A key component of this development has been the creation of an approach to training student facilitators, called moderators, in SD.

We begin this chapter by briefly describing SDCN and explaining the training model. First, we provide an overview of SDCN's two-day training workshop that illustrates the way we present SD's core concepts and the role of the moderator in dialogue. We then describe the structures in place to ensure that new moderators continue to develop skills throughout the academic year. Finally, we discuss facilitation dilemmas that moderators of SD face and conclude by sharing lessons learned for the benefit of other practitioners developing training programs for dialogue facilitators.

Formation of the Sustained Dialogue Campus Network

SD is "a systematic, open-ended political process to transform conflictual relationships over time" (Saunders, 1999). SD is a conceptualization of three decades of experience with dialogues among citizens outside government in the Cold War, in the Arab–Israeli peace process, and in Tajikistan. Developed by Dr. Harold Saunders, SD aims to bring people together across lines of difference in a safe space over an extended period of time. The goal is to create the capacity to collectively design change through transforming relationships and building a deeper and more complete understanding of the participants' communities (Chufrin & Saunders, 1993).

The implementation of SD on college campuses began with a few students asking themselves a question: What can I do to improve relationships among diverse students on my campus? At Princeton, student government representatives launched the first SD initiative in 1999 after realizing their previous programmatic efforts to improve campus climate had failed because student leaders did not have a shared understanding of what needed to be addressed. At the University of Virginia, students started SD in 2001 as a way to impact what one founder described as "the most racialized climate I had ever experienced," where "students from different racial backgrounds [did] not interact with one another socially, and when they [did], the interactions [were] awkward at best, and hostile at the extreme" (Parker, 2006). At Colorado College, students turned to SD after the student newspaper printed racist images and articles as an "April Fool's" joke that upset and isolated many students. Different experiences with campus social tension provoked each group of students to implement SD to address campus divisions. However, all were attracted to the SD methodology because, in contrast to diversity events sponsored by campus administrators and onetime forums organized by students, it was a *sustained* and proactive approach to address campus problems that prioritized student ownership (SDCN, 2009).

On each campus where SDCN is present, SD is organized as a campus club. The club leadership selects dialogue "moderators" through an application process that asks applicants to demonstrate their sensitivity and commitment to issues of diversity, and their ability to plan meetings, facilitate difficult conversations, and work effectively with diverse participants. The club leadership forms the dialogue groups, which are composed of 10–15 diverse members of the community who meet throughout the academic year. Dialogue groups are led by teams of two co-moderators who plan activities together but often alternate duties depending on the topic being discussed and their own relative strengths at facilitation. University administrators usually play a support role in helping SD networks get off the ground. Sometimes, administrators participate in the dialogue groups, though a key element of these initiatives is that they are student run. This student activist principle—that the dialogue initiatives are grassroots (student run and initiated) rather than top down (administration run and initiated)—is a common denominator among successful SDCN programs. We believe that students are often best placed to establish and lead dialogue groups that respond to their own experiences of campus social tension.

A project of the International Institute for Sustained Dialogue (IISD), SDCN has grown organically from three campuses to over a dozen since its formation in 2003. Through its link to the IISD in Washington DC, SDCN is also connected globally to organizations that have used or are using SD among students in South Africa, Zimbabwe, Ethiopia, India, and Tajikistan (International Institute for Sustained Dialogue, 2008). SDCN's staff includes alumni of SD who work as program directors to coordinate and provide training, mentorship, and networking opportunities to each SD program within the national network, as well as to student teams initiating new programs. SDCN recently hired its first executive director, who is currently working with SDCN's advisory board to determine the most effective strategy for network development and growth.

SDCN Moderator Training: Learning the Practice of Sustained Dialogue

The goal of the SDCN Moderator Workshop is to equip trainees with the tools to catalyze relationships across lines of difference and implement social action projects that transform community tensions. The workshop focuses on building trainees' understanding of the role of the dialogue moderator and capacity to visualize the progression of the dialogue through the year. The workshops are conducted by SDCN program directors and alumni moderators, usually in pairs of two. Most workshops occur individually on each college campus, though there are some regional workshops. To prepare students to moderate SD, trainers introduce students to a framework of conceptual models, analytical tools, and moderating skills:

- Conceptual models form the organizing foundation on which analytical tools and basic moderating skills are based. SD consists of two basic conceptual models that establish the broad parameters of the dialogue process: (1) the *Five Stages of Sustained Dialogue* and (2) the *Relationship Model*, which describe various dimensions of group and community dynamics that will change over time (Nemeroff, 2006). Both of these will be discussed in further detail later in the chapter.

- Analytical tools are used during the process to monitor group progress and relationships, determine readiness to move toward a later stage, and facilitate deeper discussion among group members (Nemeroff, 2006).
- Moderating skills are the specific techniques a moderator uses to lead a discussion, elicit participation, and resolve moments of tension (Nemeroff, 2006). Examples of skills taught in the two-day Sustained Dialogue Workshop include active listening, asking effective questions, summarizing key points, and reframing ambiguous or contentious statements.

Training workshops begin with a short introduction to SD's conceptual frameworks to provide students with a frame of reference for the purpose, value, and trajectory of the SD process. The workshop features a visioning exercise to enable the team of moderators to develop a collective sense of purpose for SD on their campus. The workshop then focuses on skill-building exercises and activities to help students understand the role of the moderator and the needs of dialogue participants at different stages of the dialogue process. This includes social justice and inclusion language, as well as root-cause analysis to identify actions to take individually and collectively. Finally, because students comment that they learn best from doing, we create as many opportunities as possible during the workshop for new moderators to practice their moderating skills, participate in simulations and role-plays, and apply SD's analytical and conceptual tools. Through structured reflection and coaching by experienced mentors following the workshop and throughout the academic year, trainees develop an understanding of how their moderating skills connect with the larger analytical tools and, ultimately, the broad conceptual models introduced in the training. The goal of the workshop is to simultaneously produce moderators who can independently assess the needs of a dialogue group and to develop a moderator team that encourages ongoing support and collaboration.

SDCN Moderator Training: Day One

The trainers first create a safe space for student trainees by conducting interactive introductions and icebreakers to build trust. Trainers ask the trainees to discuss their reasons for committing to SD and to identify their individual and campus goals for SD. Students share diverse motivations and goals—some are motivated to moderate dialogue out of frustration with the separation of social networks on campus along lines of identity, whereas others are motivated by a desire to increase awareness of issues of diversity and exclusion on campus. Trainers lead students in a visioning exercise to brainstorm the campus dynamics that students seek to improve through SD. Trainers conduct this conversation in order to help moderators identify a sense of purpose for their dialogue initiative and to develop a shared vision among moderators. For schools that participated in SD the previous year, trainers present data from evaluations. Participants' feedback on their SD experience, including the quality of moderators, the topics covered, and the perceived impact of SD, is discussed. Trainers help student leaders and moderators to use the data to inform their campus's vision, focusing on areas for improvement and areas of strength. The trainers close with a brief discussion of the history of the SD process, the potential impact of an SD program on the campus, and how student moderators on other campuses have used SD in their lives after college, in some cases starting SD at their workplaces, and helping younger students launch SD at other institutions.

Trainers elicit the definition of dialogue from the group, in order to help students identify the ways in which dialogue differs from other modes of communication and engagement. Trainers then introduce students to SD founder Hal Saunders's definition of dialogue and the *Five Stages of Sustained Dialogue* (summarized below). The Five Stages describe how SD unfolds over time and help moderators determine the needs of participants and the requirements of a moderator at different points in the process (Saunders, 1999).

The Definition of Dialogue

"Dialogue is a process of genuine interaction through which human beings listen to each other deeply enough to be changed by what they learn. Each makes a serious effort to take others' concerns into her or his own picture, even when disagreement persists. No participant gives up her or his identity, but each recognizes enough of the other's valid human claims that he or she will act differently toward the other" (Saunders, 1999, p. 82).

The Five Stages of Sustained Dialogue

Stage One—Deciding to Engage[1]: Having decided to initiate SD, initiators will

- identify a set of diverse individuals with differing perspectives on campus social tensions to commit to engage in a dialogue process; and
- deliberate over and define the purpose and ground rules of the dialogue with participants.

Stage Two—Experience Exchange: Having convened a dialogue group, moderators will work with participants to

- develop trust among participants;
- share personal stories about backgrounds, identities, and experiences on campus;
- map and explore relationships within both the dialogue group and greater campus community; and
- identify key problems and tensions on campus to probe more deeply in the next stage.

Stage Three—Defining the Problem: With the key issues on the table, the dialogue group

- explores why the problems identified matter to the participants; and
- probes each problem in depth to reveal the underlying relationships that drive it.

Stage Four—Brainstorming Solutions: Having analyzed the dynamics of the community's conflict, participants turn to designing solutions. In order to do this, they

- identify the main obstacles to solving the problem and determine whether they can be overcome;
- consider resources and time restrictions; and
- develop a plan to tackle the issue the group is focusing on, taking into account the obstacles and resources.

Stage Five—Individual and Collective Action: After brainstorming solutions, the group will

- consider whether conditions in the community prevent implementing the action plan;
- divide roles for implementing the steps, taking into consideration the role each group member plays within the larger community;
- make commitments to personal action outside the dialogue and reflect on personal change as a group; and
- execute and evaluate action plans.

Stages One through Five are described in shorthand as "the who," "the what," "the why," "the how," and "the now." Trainers share this shorthand with students to help them understand the progression of group experience the stages describe, and to use the stages as an analytical tool when moderating. (In the second day of the workshop, the trainees practice asking typical "Stage Two," "Stage Three," and "Stage Four" questions to develop a better sense of the distinctive needs of the group during the different stages of dialogue. We describe this exercise in the "Day Two" portion of the chapter.)

Finally, trainers lead the group in a discussion of the difference between the roles of moderator and participant in SD, eliciting from trainees the qualitative differences of the moderator's participation in the SD process as well as the moderator's practical responsibilities. Trainers make clear that while dialogue participants are encouraged to actively share their personal experiences and opinions, moderators must take a more neutral and facilitating posture in the dialogue to create and maintain a safe space for the participants. Trainers also help trainees understand the range of responsibilities a moderator has between meetings—from logistics, to organizing social events for the group between meetings, to debriefing and preparing for the next dialogue with one's co-moderator.

The final major component of the first day of the workshop for new trainees is the modeling of an SD meeting. Trainers highlight certain aspects of facilitating, including encouraging rich dialogue with a thoughtful dialogue prompt and eliciting deep engagement through asking generative questions. Trainers then take on the moderator role in a "mock dialogue" that models a group's opening meeting. After leading the group in identifying ground rules (such as committing to speak from personal experience and to question one's assumptions), trainers typically select a dialogue prompt to encourage a conversation about identity. The trainer might ask participants to each share three words to describe their identity and to explain their selection, or to identify a person, a place, and an event that has shaped the participant's sense of self. A trainee might share his or her experience growing up as an African American in a predominantly White area, practicing Islam on a campus affiliated with another faith, coming out as gay or lesbian to his or her parents, maneuvering campus social networks without the financial resources to join a fraternity or sorority, or arriving at college and becoming aware of social tensions related to identity for the first time. The dialogue helps trainees see the importance of creating a safe space for participants and encouraging personal sharing, before encouraging group analysis of social problems on campus. The trainers use the "mock dialogue" to emphasize the importance of moderators' awareness of their own personal identity. The trainers also use the exercise to model facilitation skills such as sharing personal stories in order to encourage an environment of trust, identifying common themes and connecting participants' contributions, collaborating with one's co-moderator, and debriefing the dialogue.

SDCN Moderator Training: Day Two

The second day of training delves into the *Relationship Model*, the second key conceptual framework in SD. Whereas the Five Stages describe how relationships of individuals in dialogue evolve over time, Saunders (1999) introduces the Relationship Model in his book, *A Public Peace Process*, as a tool to help moderators "get inside" the relationships being examined in dialogue in an analytical way. The model describes five elements of relationship that impact interpersonal and community dynamics:

1. *Identity*: How individuals define their physical, cultural, and human characteristics, such as race, sex, nationality, and occupation; also, the life experiences that brought them where they are
2. *Interests*: What individuals want and care about, in both a substantive context, such as equal education and higher incomes, and a psychological context, such as respect and status
3. *Power*: The capacity of individuals to control not only resources and the actions of others, but also the ability to influence the course of events without material resources
4. *Perceptions, Misperceptions, and Stereotypes*: How individuals and groups view one another and what they assume about the others' identity, interests, and power
5. *Patterns of Interaction*: How individuals and groups interact with one another, whether positively, negatively, or not at all (Saunders, 1999)

Trainers use the popular metaphor of an iceberg to demonstrate the utility of the Relationship Model. The part of the iceberg above water represents what is obvious to a moderator in the dialogue room—a speaker's word choice, how loudly or quickly they are speaking, the quality of their engagement with others, etc. The part of the iceberg below the surface represents what motivates the character of communication that the moderator observes and can be elicited with Saunders's five elements of relationship. As an exercise, the trainer shares a carefully selected personal story about an experience that impacted the trainer's sense of identity. The trainer asks the trainees to listen to the story and the speaker through the lens of the Relationship Model. For example, a trainer might share a story about a conflict with a friend of a different racial background, or a personal experience with subtle discrimination on campus. The moderators-in-training are instructed to ask questions, framed through one or more of the five elements of relationship, to help the storyteller discuss the personal and relational impact of the experience. After the exercise, the trainers debrief with the group, helping trainees see how the five elements of the Relationship Model can be used both as a listening tool—as a lens through which to hear and understand a dialogue participant's story—and as a questioning tool—to help moderators encourage personal exchange in dialogue. The group can do this exercise a number of times with different stories, to practice using the model and to encourage a dialogic environment of respectful listening and trust building within the group.

Trainers also conduct a mapping exercise to demonstrate how the Relationship Model can be used as an analytical tool to help better understand community relationships. The trainers ask the group to identify two communities on campus and, using flip chart paper, have the students describe and compare each community in terms of its identity, interests, power, perceptions, and patterns of interaction. For example, trainees might use the Relationship Model to map the elements of relationship between the Black Student Union and students in a traditionally White fraternity to gain insight into sources of tension and elements of commonality between the two groups. In some cases, trainees might observe limited social interaction, differences in the salience of race in identity, and perceptions of the other characterized by suspicion as sources of tensions between the groups. Using the Relationship Model, trainees might also focus in on shared identity as university students and mutual interest in a harmonious and supportive community as elements of commonality. Trainers debrief the mapping exercise to illustrate the power of the Relationship Model as a tool for moderators to help dialogue participants understand and identify both sources of division and commonality in complex campus relationships. Trainers also expand the mapping exercise to include campus mapping. Here, students identify the major groups on campus from which to recruit dialogue participants and engage in "Pitch Practice" to practice different approaches to soliciting participation in SD.

In the last exercise of the day, trainers set up a two-hour mock dialogue in which pairs of moderators each get 30 minutes to practice moderating a dialogue "through the stages." Each pair is responsible for formally opening and closing the portion of the dialogue they moderate and for practicing their convening and debriefing skills. Each subsequent pair is instructed to facilitate in a manner that simulates a different "stage" of SD. For example, the first moderator pair simulates "Stage One" by facilitating introductions and the generation of ground rules, and the second moderator pair asks "Stage Two" questions focused on encouraging storytelling and trust building in the group.

The third moderator pair asks "Stage Three" questions focused on helping participants define the community problems they are raising, and the fourth moderator pair asks "Stage Four" questions, which encourage participants to identify their own ability to impact the problem in question. At the end of each 30-minute session, the group takes a break to discuss the experience of moderating and to give feedback to one another.

After the Workshop: A "Learn by Doing" Philosophy

SDCN's moderator workshops introduce trainees to the concepts behind SD and to the skills that moderating dialogue requires. SDCN emphasizes a "learn by doing" philosophy and, following the moderator workshop, SDCN's training model shifts from trainer-focused transfers of information to trainee-focused reflective exercises and collective troubleshooting. SDCN program directors work with the trainees to develop a support structure within their dialogue programs to build moderator skills beyond the two-day workshop.

All moderators attend meetings twice a month to address the facilitation dilemmas moderator pairs may be having with their group. Co-moderators share their experiences with the other moderators to receive guidance and troubleshoot with their peers on how to address common issues. In some cases, moderators role-play the specific situation to allow the affected moderator to practice a new technique in a safe environment. Senior student moderators manage this process, with support from SDCN as needed. This transfer of ownership over the training process helps moderators increase their understanding of the SD conceptual model so that they can independently analyze their own needs.

Facilitation Dilemmas for the Sustained Dialogue Campus Network

Every type of social intervention forces practitioners to make trade-offs. SDCN has found that organizers must make a number of difficult decisions when deciding how to run dialogues according to its model. SDCN's student-driven orientation perhaps represents SD's greatest asset as well as its most significant limitation. Initiated, moderated, and developed by students, SD creates a space on the college campus to address identity conflicts and tensions as students experience them. Students examine and learn about the tensions dividing their community without attention to grades, and in a voluntary manner. Accordingly, SD enables an authenticity of response to conflicts and attentiveness to students' communication needs that faculty and administrators struggle to achieve through top-down diversity programming. At the same time, SD programs on campuses compete with many other demands on students' time and energy.

Time Limitations

The college academic year affords SDCN less time to train students in both facilitation and program leadership skills than is desired. SDCN conducts an additional training, called the SDCN Student Leadership Retreat, and provides ongoing mentorship through bimonthly leadership phone calls to develop student leaders' abilities in managing SD initiatives. Looking forward, SDCN is also exploring additional trainings for moderators, focused specifically on developing moderators' abilities beyond the two-day training described herein. In addition, SDCN is currently exploring multiple avenues for mentorship throughout the year, such as live videoconferencing, and better structures for more training time.

Balancing Individual Transformation, Relationship Building, and Collective Action

Managing SD's dual agenda—building relationships and enabling collective action—can be challenging for trainers and students alike. While the individual and interpersonal impact on students of a year in dialogue is highly documented, it is often difficult for dialogue groups to coordinate action projects before the end of an academic year. Trainers and student leaders must carefully manage dialogue participant and moderator expectations so that students do not become frustrated with dialogue if their group does not reach collective action before the end of the school year. Trainers place a high priority on encouraging dialogue groups to spend time at the end of the year reflecting on how the participants have personally changed from their experience in dialogue. This helps participants in groups that have not completed an action project to leave the dialogue with a sense of accomplishment and agency. Moving forward, SDCN is investigating ways to strengthen its training for coordinating action initiatives. In 2010, SDCN partnered with youth action organizations to present at SDCN leadership conferences.

Managing the Role of the Moderator While Maintaining Peer Relations

Not surprisingly, the students who want to be moderators care deeply about the issues discussed in their groups. Since one of the main purposes of the moderator is to provide neutrality and create a safe space, we spend considerable time discussing with trainees the different roles of the moderator and participant. However, participants often want to hear more of the moderators' personal thoughts. SDCN generally encourages moderators to share experiences, not opinions. This distinction usually provides enough guidance to the moderators to allow relationship building among moderators and participants while preserving moderator neutrality. Having two moderators in every dialogue group also allows one moderator to share while the other continues in the facilitator role.

Balancing Participant-Generated Dialogue Content With Outside Information

The SD model does not dictate the content of the dialogue but rather focuses on creating a safe and open space for students to discuss the issues that are affecting them on individual and community levels. Some critics argue that through its focus on participant-generated dialogue content (personal stories and experiences), SD on college campuses does not address the systemic nature of social justice issues (Gorski, 2008). If people in the room learn only from one another's experiences, some argue that participants may not have adequate information to realize that the problems they are discussing occur on a much broader scale in society. SDCN also has received feedback from some students of color and other targeted identity students who express frustration with feeling burdened at times by the need to "teach" their White or privileged counterparts through sharing their own challenging experiences with discrimination. SDCN takes this feedback seriously, as it underscores the importance of adequate preparation for moderators facilitating dialogues about the challenging power dynamics in diverse communities. While continually exploring methods of strengthening its training in this regard, SDCN currently addresses this concern in two ways. First, the *SDCN Moderator Manual* introduces background information, readings, and exercises on systemic issues such as institutional inequity and White privilege to help moderators engage the systemic nature of the problems they are discussing in dialogue. Second, SDCN carefully coaches students in recruiting diverse participants to ensure that dialogue groups reflect key viewpoints in the community and that issues impacting diverse members of the community emerge in dialogue. In addition, SDCN program directors encourage moderators and participants to bring in outside information, articles, movies, and activities to explore issues as they emerge, using the framework of SD to analyze the individual and systemic effect of social inequity.

Depth and Breadth in Dialogue

There are an infinite number of issues to discuss, problems to explore, and relationships to improve on campuses, and student leaders of SD often seek to address a number of different dynamics on campus through SD. While awareness of the broad "map" of a community's dynamics can be helpful for students, it can also limit students' ability to focus indepth on any one issue. The open-ended nature of the SD model complicates this particular dilemma. Trainers describe SD as a process that students can use to address diverse identity conflicts on campus. SDCN has struggled to find the right balance between, on the one hand, training students to understand how to moderate SD with respect to campus identity conflicts generally and, on the other, tailoring trainings to the many specific campus dynamics that trainees are looking to address. SDCN is currently broadening its resources to more effectively support students seeking to use SD to address a broader array of social tensions.

Lessons for Fellow Dialogue and Deliberation Practitioners

Based on our experience training leaders for campus dialogues, we can offer the following lessons:

- *It is challenging for a two-day training curriculum to prepare dialogue moderators to address every possible challenge they are likely to face.* There is a limit to covering in a workshop the number of potential scenarios a moderator might face. Therefore, trainers must emphasize the core concepts and tools that will equip moderators to understand the challenges they are facing, while understanding that new moderators will learn the most when they start leading dialogue. Coaching and peer mentoring to support new facilitators once they begin moderating is also vital to their development. SDCN mentors students through biweekly phone calls and frequent e-mails while advisors support students on campus.
- *The most successful groups are those in which moderators are able to foster group ownership among the participants.* After the training, trainee moderators may become overwhelmed, thinking they will be responsible for making decisions for the group, creating agendas, and diagnosing group problems. While we cover many of these skills in the training, it is important that moderators realize they can and should discuss content and process with their participants. One of the goals of the moderator should be to transfer ownership of the group to the participants. Participants will not reach action if they do not engage with

and take ownership of their group. While moderators should have a strong idea of the direction of the dialogue, they should always ask the group for input and incorporate their ideas and questions. SDCN addresses this dilemma by helping moderators "reflect" questions back to the group, transferring ownership of the group to the participants.

- *The most effective groups are those in which the co-moderators complement each other's abilities, trust one another, and have a strong working relationship.* The pairing of moderators is extremely important. Generally, they should be from different social identity groups and backgrounds to promote a sense among participants that the moderators can relate to their experiences and to ensure that a broader set of perspectives guides the way the discussion is moderated. Co-moderators must build trust with one another, be prepared for meetings, be organized, and share responsibility. They must also take the time to reflect with one another on their own perspectives and experience; build a level of trust and knowledge of one another; know one another's "hot-button" issues; and have a deep level of understanding of one another's backgrounds, opinions, and style of working. The effectiveness and working relationship of the co-moderating pair will directly impact the group.

The expansion of the SD grassroots movement from three campuses in 2003, when the SDCN was formed, to over a dozen campuses today is a testament to the adaptability of SD's conceptual framework, the model's emphasis on student ownership, and its ability to develop students' capacity for meaningful engagement across lines of difference. This rapid growth has relied upon SDCN's development of a training and mentorship model focused on moderator self-sufficiency. The scale of the network's future growth will have significant implications for SDCN's training and mentorship model. As this chapter goes to print, SDCN is preparing to launch a strategic planning process to set new goals for expanding the network and building upon its training model.[2]

Notes

1. The names of the Five Stages have been altered from Saunders's original naming for the SDCN.

2. The authors have been involved in various iterations of the SDCN training model. Still, the SDCN training model is frequently evolving. Contact the current SDCN staff for information about the latest training model.

References

Chufrin, G. I., & Saunders, H. H. (1993). A public peace process. *Negotiation Journal*, *9*(2), 155–177.

Gorski, P. C. (2008). Good intentions are not enough: A decolonizing intercultural education. *Intercultural Education*, *19*(6), 515–525.

International Institute for Sustained Dialogue. (2008). *A guide for moderators—initiating Sustained Dialogue*. Unpublished manual.

Nemeroff, T. (2006). *Sustained Dialogue trainer's manual*. Unpublished manual. Washington, DC: International Institute for Sustained Dialogue and IDASA.

Parker, P. N. (2006). Sustained Dialogue: A student-driven approach to improve student racial climate. *About Campus: Enriching the Student Learning Experience*, *2*(1), 17–23.

Saunders, H. H. (1999). *A public peace process: Sustained Dialogue to transform racial and ethnic conflicts*. New York: St. Martin's Press.

Sustained Dialogue Campus Network. (2009). Retrieved June 12, 2009, from http://www .sdcampusnetwork.org.

8

DEMOCRACY LAB

Online Facilitation Training for Dialogic Teaching and Learning

James T. Knauer

D
emocracy Lab is a web-based dialogic learning community providing forums on public issues for use in high school and college courses across the curriculum. The learning community includes students enrolled in participating courses and their instructors. Most of the students and instructors are new to Democracy Lab and are having their first deliberative dialogue experience. Some students continue with Democracy Lab as civic leadership trainees and interns. New and continuing instructors learn from and contribute to online workshops about dialogic pedagogy. Some instructors go on to conduct research, publish, and lead professional development workshops. The continuing maturation of the project is supported by an expanding, multifaceted network including experienced instructors, student leaders, and research programs in a variety of disciplines.

Democracy Lab originated at Lock Haven University in a collaborative project with the National Collegiate Honors Council. The author, then director of the Lock Haven University Honors Program, continued the program, enlisting courses and instructors outside the honors program, and received a supporting grant from FIPSE in 2004. In 2006, after the author's retirement, Democracy Lab moved to the Institute on the Common Good at Regis University, directed by Paul Alexander who brought a long history of work in community dialogue to the project. Now directed by Malia Crouse, Democracy Lab offers course-based forums and research opportunities for high school and college students at both the undergraduate and graduate levels. Because of fiscal constraints the program has recently been taken off-line until additional resources can be identified.

As a supplement to college and high school courses Democracy Lab is structured, first and foremost, to advance course learning. Providing training in dialogic learning advances the objectives of liberal learning as detailed in *Greater Expectations: A New Vision for Learning as a Nation Goes to College* from the Association of American Colleges and Universities (AAC&U, 2002). In particular, AAC&U calls for educating students to be "purposeful and self-directed" learners who "can adapt to new environments, integrate knowledge from different sources, and continue learning throughout their lives." The pedagogical connection between civic education and liberal learning lies in the fact that the nurturing of strong deliberative citizens with a concern for social justice requires the same kinds of cognitive, ethical, and emotional growth as does the education of AAC&U's "intentional learners" (Barber, 1984; Knauer, 2005). The growing literature on dialogic pedagogy illuminates the central role of dialogue in all learning and the power of dialogic strategies to further liberal learning and civic empowerment (Bohm, 1996; Hess & Posselt, 2002; King, 2002; Knauer, 2005; Knauer & Ross, 2006; Simon, 2003; Vygotsky, 1978; Wells, 1999, 2001).

The dialogue model used in Democracy Lab is based on National Issues Forums (NIF), used successfully for over 25 years by community groups across the country and around the world (National Issues Forums, 2009). These community forums typically focus on specific public issues such as race relations, health care, or the environment, bringing together interested citizens for one to three hours of public deliberation conducted by trained facilitators. The National Issues Forums Network and the Kettering Foundation research public opinion on these issues and publish issue books that provide a shared information framework for the deliberative forums.

The particular type of deliberative dialogue used in NIF and Democracy Lab focuses on specific, complex public problems with prominent moral dimensions. The dialogue process emphasizes giving serious consideration to all points of view, exploring disagreements in order to increase understanding across difference, and searching for underlying common ground for action. Successful deliberative dialogue increases public knowledge—the shared understanding of issue complexities, of different perspectives on the issue, and of shared concerns that could become the basis for civic action.

Deliberative dialogue as implemented on Democracy Lab departs from the NIF model in two important ways. First, because Democracy Lab forums are course based and typically run continuously for 8–10 weeks, course learning supplements the issue materials supplied as part of the forum. Second,

Democracy Lab reduces the role of trained facilitators and emphasizes train-ing all participants to share facilitation responsibilities. This chapter focuses on this second dimension of Democracy Lab and on our unique approach to facilitation training. Unlike most facilitation trainees who have volunteered for training, participants in Democracy Lab training are there simply because they enrolled in a course in which Democracy Lab is being used, usually without knowing that the course would involve online dialogue. Thus, the training challenge in Democracy Lab is quite different from that of more typical facilitation training and, in some ways, much greater. One could say that Democracy Lab trains dialogue groups for *self-facilitation*. By moving the initial training into the dialogues themselves, all participants gain dialogue (and dialogic thinking) skills for the benefit of their future dialogic, civic, and liberal learning.

Facilitation Training Is Embedded in Practice

Democracy Lab forums embed facilitation training in the dialogue process itself using two staples of facilitation training—practice facilitation and re-flective dialogue about the group process. Whereas Democracy Lab provides agenda-setting guidance and assigns specific group tasks and objectives, dia-logue groups are either on their own without the leadership of a designated facilitator (typical at Lock Haven University) or lightly facilitated for model-ing purposes by a facilitator who moves into the background as students pick up the responsibility themselves (introduced at Regis University). While some classroom instructors who happen to have a background in dialogue may sup-plement Democracy Lab facilitation training, most instructors are primarily concerned about the content of the dialogue, have little or no background in dialogue, and do not provide feedback on the dialogue process.

Thus, Democracy Lab provides participants with instructional resources, a schedule of set training exercises and, at most, light facilitation, but otherwise leaves each dialogue group to its own devices for accomplishing the learning. This undoubtedly means that results are much more mixed than for more typical training programs, but Democracy Lab has educational objectives, in addition to the teaching of facilitation skills.

Forum Context

Each Democracy Lab forum addresses an issue such as "Racial and Ethnic Tensions" or "Americans' Role in the World" using a prepared text or "issue framework." In addition to using NIF books, Democracy Lab has successfully originated its own issue frameworks, including one written primarily by student interns. Each issue framework lays out a broad public concern and presents three or four approaches to the issue (see Democracy Lab, 2009). Each approach includes its own value priorities, understanding of the root problem, and prescription for action. Using the issue framework as a starting point, students deliberate, usually for 8–10 weeks, on prethreaded asynchronous bulletin boards. Although hundreds of students participate in a typical forum, they do so in groups of 15–20 so that participants get to know each other and produce public knowledge based on genuine interpersonal understanding. Students in individual participating classes are spread across several online dialogue groups so that each group includes members from several schools. This also means that each dialogue group includes students from classes in several different disciplines, further enriching the dialogue.

Forums begin with introductions that include thoughts, feelings, and experiences related to the issue. About two weeks are devoted to weighing the pros and cons of each approach presented in the issue framework. The middle section of the forum focuses on exploring differences within the group and gathering and discussing additional information that may shed further light on those differences and disagreements. In the concluding two weeks the group task is to identify common ground underlying these differences, and then to propose concrete actions that members would be willing to undertake together. Whereas at Lock Haven this agenda was guided by weekly announcements, at Regis guidance is handled by facilitators.

Facilitation Training

Typically, the dialogue and deliberation community draws facilitators from those who have already participated in the kind of dialogues for which they are being trained to facilitate (Beale, Thompson, & Chesler, 2001; Parker, 2006). It is common practice to include participation in a dialogue, along with some kind of debriefing of that experience, in the facilitator training. What may be unique to Democracy Lab is building the facilitation training into the participant's initial dialogue experience itself.

Six lessons presented weekly constitute the heart of facilitation training. Lessons introduce ideas and strategies for students to practice as their group dialogue continues. With the "light facilitation" model developed at Regis University, the facilitator models the implementation of these lessons.

For the first three weeks lessons focus on creating a shared understanding of the deliberative dialogue process, getting acquainted, and initiating dialogue on the issue. Dialogue tasks during these first weeks include sharing personal experiences and views and a first consideration of the different perspectives presented in the issue framework. Three lessons support this initial facilitation training. (Because of space limits the content of most lessons is abbreviated here. Full text is available at http://www.icgregisonline .org/vle/).

Lesson One—Forum Guidelines

This lesson focuses on acclimating learners to the dialogue process and is designed to help participants weigh the pros and cons of various viewpoints and to come to a better understanding of the issue(s) and representation of different points of view. The first lesson gives some guidelines that will help make the dialogue a success:

Deliberative dialogue, not debate. Although there will often be disagreements, dialogue should not be a debate. Debates tend to be about winning and losing, about knocking down an opponent's arguments. That is not the object here. Participants are not opponents but colleagues pursuing disagreements in order to understand why people see things so differently. It is expected that participants will ask each other questions and reply to questions openly. It even means expressing second thoughts about opinions held.

Exploring agreements and disagreements, not searching for consensus. Engaging in dialogue may be new to some and there can be a tendency to push disagreements into the background in order to reach some sort of consensus. Consensus is not the goal and is highly discouraged in the dialogue process. While there will be areas of agreement to be explored, differences in perspective help everyone learn—if the group works hard at finding the underlying reasons for those differences.

Exploration, not knowing all the answers. In dialogue, no one has all the answers. All opinions are subject to change when faced with new evidence or with new ways of looking at things. Most participants entering the dialogue will feel very unsure about many aspects of the issue. Participants are encouraged not to be defensive about feeling unsure. Instead, it is suggested that they turn to the group for help by explaining why they are unsure, perhaps explaining how it feels to be pulled in different directions.

Open, honest dialogue. Participants are asked to be frank about their concerns and opinions. Disagreements with a colleague should take place openly, honestly, and with respect, even when faced with opinions that shock or anger. Participants are asked to express their shock or anger to the group, then to try to figure out how they have come to such drastically different points of view.

Active and regular participation. The time requirement is that participants try to be online at least three to four days per week—to catch up on messages, to post some questions and comments and to respond to any questions from others. Posting at least two to three messages per week helps the group succeed. We have found that once involved, participants will probably check in almost every day.

Lesson Two—Deliberation and Personal Experience

Introductions and the Issue. Because dialogue is not just about making new friends but about people coming together to deliberate, sharing something about one's relationship to the issue is important. Is the issue one they can relate to or does it seem pretty distant? Does the issue personally affect the participant, their family, or friends?

What Deliberation Is and Isn't. Deliberation is about feelings, beliefs, and experiences, not just about the knowledge of experts. Deliberation consists of exploring and learning from each other, not just learning from books. Deliberation is about listening closely to others, not just about stating one's own opinions.

Getting Acquainted. Getting acquainted is all about asking questions. As participants read what others have to say, they ask follow-up questions much like they might if having just met in a coffee shop. Participants should ask specific questions about feelings and experiences, and questions that facilitate getting to know each other.

The Importance of Disagreements and Differences. Groups are set up as much as possible to bring people with different experiences and opinions together. The point is not to encourage debate but to create opportunities for learning. Differences are important and should not be ignored. Participants should explore differences to learn, not to persuade or debate.

Don't Just Make Nice! Participants are advised to avoid the tendency to say they agree when they are really not sure they do. Even if they really do agree, they should mention things they might disagree about. The goal of learning is much better met by exploring disagreements than by finding things to agree about.

Exploring Differences Respectfully. If someone says something that annoys or upsets a participant, the offended participant must let the speaker know, but in a way that is respectful, explaining why he or she is annoyed or upset. If participants find that an opinion seems a bit ridiculous, they are asked to explain why and ask for help in understanding it from the person who expressed it.

Moving Dialogue Along. Participants are encouraged to use the dialogue to explore different perspectives on the issue, especially focusing on issues they find most different or difficult to understand. Participants work hard at listening and asking questions with the goal of understanding and, of course, of having fun!

Lesson Three—Deliberation Versus Debate

Public issues can be talked about in a number of ways. "Shout radio," as it is sometimes called, is one example of a mode quite familiar to us: debate. Because of its familiarity, it can be easy to jump into debate mode in dialogue groups. But that is not the point of Democracy Lab. Democracy Lab asks participants to perform in another mode: deliberation. As these two modes can sometimes seem similar, it is important to consider the key distinctions between debate and deliberation.

Where debate is competitive, deliberation is cooperative. The goal of deliberation is shared understanding. Participants should seek to understand the views of others, even as they articulate their own.

Where debate is about knowing, deliberation is about learning. The premise of deliberation is that none of us knows everything, and all of us know something. When we admit what we do not know, we can learn from each other, and all emerge knowing more.

Where debate means commitment to a view, deliberation means commitment to each other. Debates are the verbal equivalent to a game of "Red Rover"—if you get the most people on your side, you win. Deliberation is more like a ropes course—no matter what differences we have, we must be careful to respect each other and make sure that we are all working as a team toward our shared goal of learning.

There are several keys to improving deliberation skills:

- Ask questions. It is the best way to get a better understanding of others' views.
- If you tend to be more a talker than a listener, try to be more responsive to others.
- If you tend to be more a listener than a talker, push yourself to be more open with your views.
- Be honest. Say what you think about something, even when you are conflicted. Your mixed feelings might lead your group to recognize underlying tensions with the issue.

Although the material in the first three lessons is typically reviewed briefly in any NIF forum, the coverage provided in the Democracy Lab lessons is much more detailed and focused on using this knowledge in the dialogue process. Whereas in the opening portion of a typical dialogue the facilitator will step in to reinforce these standards, in Democracy Lab, even with light facilitation, all participants are charged to put their new knowledge about dialogue into practice as the first skill-building stage in their self-facilitation training.

While the first three lessons focus on the more general techniques of deliberative dialogue, ensuing lessons distinguish three specific dialogic and intellectual skills: asking questions, initiating further inquiry, and interpreting inquiry results. In addition to their important role in deliberative dialogue, these skills are widely recognized learning skills that might receive attention in any high school or college course. They are as important in texted dialogue as in face-to-face dialogue. For the most part, these skills are not part of NIF facilitator training, primarily because teaching these skills requires an ongoing dialogic inquiry process rather than a single session. These more advanced skills are critical to Democracy Lab because they are central to the process of intellectual inquiry. We believe they are equally important in a strong democracy where citizens need the capacity to dialogue among themselves without reliance on specially trained facilitators (Barber, 1984).

In weeks four through six, groups deliberate the different perspectives on the issue; identify questions for further inquiry; and search for, report, and discuss additional information. Lesson Four addresses the tendency of students to take turns stating their views and to then move on to another topic. The rarity of spontaneous probing questions in student dialogues prompted the creation of a lesson on "digging deeper."

Lesson Four—Digging Deeper

Engaging the process and learning together takes a little digging. Presenting opinions is only the necessary first step of deliberation. Participants need guidance on how to truly engage with each other through probing and digging deeper into each other's views. This lesson is designed to help them take deliberation to the next level. Participants are asked to do the following:

- **Give reasons to support your views.** Try to help people understand why you believe what you do. Sometimes giving reasons means citing facts and figures, but sharing a story about something you experienced can also be a powerful way of giving reasons.
- **Keep asking questions.** Read what other group members have written about each of the approaches and raise questions with them, the kind of questions that will help you better understand where they are coming

from. This is especially important when you are trying to understand someone who seems to see things differently than you do. The point of these questions is not to challenge the person you disagree with, but to begin to understand why the person sees things the way he or she does.

- **Go assumption hunting.** An assumption is a premise; it is a statement that is assumed to be true and from which a conclusion can be drawn. We tend to make assumptions about a host of things—about human nature and motivations, about society, and about the way the world usually works. Generally, our assumptions go unexamined. You can help each other by going assumption hunting. When you think you have identified an assumption someone is making, an assumption that might or might not be valid, ask that person if you are right about his or her assumption: "Are you assuming . . . ? And if so, what makes you think that is a valid assumption?"

- **Be responsive.** When people ask you questions, be as frank and straightforward as you can. But do not feel that you have to have strong and settled opinions about everything. Explaining your strong opinions is important, but it is just as important to discuss things you feel unsure about and explain why you are unsure.

Lesson Five—Creating Inquiry Questions

Inquiry is at the core of dialogue, and the core question is, "What do we need to know more about to better understand and evaluate our disagreements?" There are many types of questions for participants to consider, for example,

Information Questions. "We need to have more facts and figures." "We need to know what happened when . . ." Some information questions will be more complicated than others, but formulating precise information questions will help your group move the deliberations forward. And, of course, facts, figures, and events brought into your deliberations will need to be interpreted.

Questions About Terms. "What exactly does the First Amendment to the U.S. Constitution say?" This question is very straightforward. It can be answered definitively—at least until we ask what the language of the First Amendment means.

"What do people mean by 'equality'?" This kind of question is always tricky. Because different people mean different things when they use the term, the question has no "right" answer. Asking this kind of question is really a way of saying we need to look at the ways people have defined equality and evaluate them.

Questions About Reasons. "Why do people think the First Amendment is so important?" "Why do people care about equality?" These are the most important and most complex questions. They make very good inquiry questions, but recognize there will not be any simple answers.

Formulating Precise Inquiry Questions. As you identify inquiry questions in the forums, help each other make them very clear and precise.

Lesson Six—Using Research to Advance Deliberations

Finding Information. Look for sources in the newsroom and library. Use search engines to find sources on specific topics. Do not forget the materials for the course you are taking.

Evaluating Information Sources. Remember that the Internet will lead you to both reliable, authoritative information and to untrustworthy or false information. Check out the identity and credentials of the website and authors. Compare multiple sources, especially if you are suspicious about a source. Pay attention to the timeliness of the information. When was it posted?

Types of Valuable Information. Use facts and figures, well-argued opinions, reports on events relevant to the issue, reports on past experience with actions and policies, and new perspectives on the issue, other than the approaches in the issue framework.

Reporting Information to Your Group. Summarize the information that you think is important. Provide a link to the source so others can read it. Share your own interpretation of the information, how you think it relates to the issue and the different approaches. Share questions you have about the possible reliability or bias of the website or author.

Deliberating Information and Its Interpretation. When new information is shared, the question is what does it mean? Interpretation is a job for everyone, not just the one reporting the information. If you think the information might be interpreted differently, say so. Often disagreements about what the information means will lead to a search for additional information.

The core of self-facilitation training is complete at this point in the dialogue. Lessons Four through Six cover some of the most critical skills for advancing deliberative learning: asking questions, initiating further inquiry, and interpreting inquiry results. From here on the deliberation agenda and remaining lessons turn to moving from dialogue to action and are less relevant to self-facilitation training.

In addition to the lessons that instruct participants in self-facilitation techniques, at various times a number of supplemental activities have been used to encourage reflective learning through meta-dialogue—dialogue about the dialogue. These reflective activities typically begin with the assignment of a specific group task:

- Propose three "rules for success" that you think should be given to all students starting in Democracy Lab.
- Prepare a report on the most important disagreements within your group over the past two weeks.
- Prepare an evaluation of your group's strengths and weaknesses in accomplishing deliberative learning.
- Contribute to drafting a new perspective on the issue. (This can be a single cross-group activity using wiki software that enables each dialogue group to collaboratively create a document online.)

Generally, reports from each group have been made available to other groups as a means of further enriching and stimulating reflection and meta-dialogue. Because facilitation training is embedded in the dialogue itself, students frequently raise reflective concerns on their own in the course of their dialogue on the issue. Often these discussions start with someone asking others for clarification about the task at hand. Sometimes this leads to both clarification and a proposed plan: "Maybe each of us should . . ." Occasionally, disruptive comments from one participant will lead to a specific proposed guideline for the discussion. As noted, these occurrences led us to incorporate discussion of guidelines as a standard feature. This spontaneous meta-dialogue is a particularly valuable supplement to those that are planned.

The light facilitation approach introduced after Democracy Lab's move to Regis University is a further development that emerged out of experience. Although self-facilitation lessons were adequate for some groups to accomplish real deliberative learning, for many groups these lessons were not enough. Having facilitators model weekly lessons resulted in much more consistent success.

There is no question that teaching self-facilitation skills to hundreds of student "nonvolunteers" online is a challenge. Some will have none of it, which is to be expected. Many will become involved only with appropriate instructor support, which is why faculty development has become an increasingly important part of Democracy Lab activities. On the other hand, some students, not an insignificant number, are so taken by the process of dialogic learning that they arrange to continue with Democracy Lab, honing their self-facilitation skills; organizing forums on their own campuses; and, in some cases, becoming Democracy Lab interns.

The facilitation training described here and the forums within which that training occurs are one piece of the larger dialogic learning community that Democracy Lab is becoming. Each semester is a learning process that includes translating that learning into continual tinkering with the system. One current effort involves structuring the online experience to specifically address state-mandated teaching objectives, an innovation that will facilitate more widespread use in high school classes. Of particular interest for readers of this book is the availability of Democracy Lab online forums for use as a valuable supplement to the face-to-face training programs. Civic groups and concerned citizens are encouraged to inquire about participation possibilities.

References

Association of American Colleges and Universities. (2002). *Greater expectations: A new vision for learning as a nation goes to college.* Retrieved July 31, 2010, from http://www. greaterexpectations.org.

Barber, B. (1984). *Strong democracy: Participatory politics for a new age.* Berkeley: University of California Press.

Beale, R. L., Thompson, M. C., & Chesler, M. (2001). Training peer facilitators for Intergroup Dialogue leadership. In D. Schoem & S. Hurtado (Eds.), *Intergroup Dialogues: Deliberative democracy in school, college, and workplace* (pp. 227–246). Ann Arbor: University of Michigan Press.

Bohm, D. (1996). *On dialogue.* New York: Routledge.

Democracy Lab. (2009). Retrieved July 31, 2010, from www.teachingdemocracyonline.org.

Hess, D., & Posselt, J. (2002). How high school students experience and learn from the discussion of controversial public issues. *Journal of Curriculum and Supervision, 17,* 283–314.

King, A. (2002). Structuring peer interaction to promote high-level cognitive processing. *Theory Into Practice, 41*(1), 33–39.

Knauer, J. (2005). *Democracy Lab: Liberal learning for strong democracy.* LiberalArtsOnline, 5:4. Retrieved July 31, 2010, from http://www.liberalarts.wabash.edu/lao-5-4-democracy-lab-learning/

Knauer, J., & Ross, L. (2006). Citizens talking across the curriculum. In J. Perry, & S. Jones (Eds.), *Quick hits for educating citizens* (pp. 22–24). Bloomington, IN: Indiana University Press.

National Issues Forums. (2009). Retrieved July 31, 2010, from www.nifi.org.

Parker, P. N. (2006). Sustained Dialogue: A student-driven approach to improve student racial climate. *About Campus: Enriching the Student Learning Experience, 2*(1), 17–23.

Simon, K. (2003). *Moral questions in the classroom: How to get kids to think deeply about real life and their schoolwork.* New Haven, CT: Yale University Press.

Vygotsky, L. (1978). *Mind in society: The development of higher psychological processes.* Cambridge, MA: Harvard University Press.

Wells, G. (1999). *Dialogic inquiry: Towards a sociocultural practice and theory of education.* Cambridge, MA: Cambridge University Press.

Wells, G. (2001). *Action, talk, and text: The case for dialogic inquiry.* Retrieved July 31, 2010, from http://people.ucsc.edu/~gwells/Files/Papers_Folder/ATT.theory.pdf. Paper posted online based on selected chapters of Wells, G. (Ed.). (2001). *Action, talk, and text: Learning and teaching through inquiry.* New York: Teachers College Press.

9

INTERGROUP DIALOGUE FACILITATION FOR YOUTH EMPOWERMENT AND COMMUNITY CHANGE

Roger B. Fisher and Barry N. Checkoway

Youth Dialogues stretched me as a facilitator and an agent of social change. . . . I truly felt like a teacher and a learner. . . . (White Jewish man, 2007 Summer Youth Dialogue Facilitator)

Trained college student facilitators are often eager to feel like they are creating positive social change. Opportunities to continue to practice facilitation skills in a community setting present a vehicle for this kind of experience. This chapter will describe and discuss the training and support of college-aged facilitators placed in metropolitan communities to conduct dialogues focusing on race and ethnicity among high school–aged students. This effort began nearly five years ago to address racial isolation and lack of interracial interaction among youth, as assessed in a series of climate surveys conducted by The Skillman Foundation and The University of Michigan (Skillman Foundation, 2003). The surveys found that many young people are open to discussions of race and ethnicity but have few opportunities to communicate with people who are different from themselves. They are aware of the limitations of segregation, appreciate the importance of diversity, and want to increase interaction and build alliances across group boundaries, again with few opportunities to do so (Skillman Foundation, 2003). Without dialogue, the opportunities for positive social contact and intergroup skill development are limited. Therefore, Summer Youth Dialogues on Race and Ethnicity in

Metropolitan Detroit (SYD) was established with support from the Skillman Foundation and the University of Michigan to address these community needs. The SYD Project involves multiple fields of practice: youth civic leadership development, community service-learning, and intergroup dialogue. The dialogues enable the youth to learn more about their identities as well as others who are different from them. The program also engages them in action projects that challenge discrimination and create community change. This chapter will address facilitation of intergroup dialogue for the youth.

Youth Dialogues on Race and Ethnicity in Metropolitan Detroit

Metropolitan Detroit is among the most segregated metropolitan areas in the United States (Kirwan Institute for the Study of Race and Ethnicity, 2008; U.S. Census Bureau, 2010). As some historically White European suburbs increase in Asian, Hispanic, and Middle Eastern, populations, others remain almost exclusively White European. Detroit's population is largely African American with an increasing Latino/a, Middle Eastern, and South Asian population. The regional picture illustrates a metropolitan mosaic. This program features a collaboration of the Skillman Foundation, the University of Michigan, and community-based organizations (CBOs) such as school districts, social agencies, and government-sponsored youth groups. CBOs are chosen to enable young people from diverse racial and ethnic groups to participate in dialogues across their boundaries. They also frequently have the strongest ties to the communities and regularly offer other summer programs and youth advisors who can be drawn upon as resources. Partnership with CBOs is critically important in our work to strengthen the community's commitment to the Summer Youth Dialogue program. The CBOs form small teams of African, Asian, White European, Middle Eastern, and Latin American young people with an adult advisor.

The Summer Youth Dialogue program has three goals: (1) to promote the youths' understanding of their own racial and ethnic identity and that of others; (2) to familiarize youth with the historic and contemporary issues of racial relations, racial inequalities, and social justice in the metropolitan Detroit area; and (3) to strengthen the desire, commitment, and competency to work in groups and coalitions to affect positive community change. These goals inform a process-content curriculum guide developed by The Program on Intergroup Relations at the University of Michigan. The curriculum, while designed specifically for the SYD program, is patterned after the four-stage campus-based intergroup dialogue model (see Zúñiga, Nagda, Chesler, & Cytron-Walker, 2007). Youth dialogues are facilitated by specially trained college students who have experience facilitating campus-based dialogues. These facilitators share the racial/ethnic identity of one of the racial/ethnic groups in the dialogue and, when possible, also come from the same neighborhood, city, or suburb as their participants.

The SYD dialogue groups meet weekly for nine weeks. The first stage includes two sessions that focus on *intra*group concepts and an understanding of the dialogue process. It also introduces elements of identity development. The second stage brings groups together across race in an intergroup setting and includes three sessions that expand understanding of the process of socialization and resulting stereotypes, biases, and prejudices. The third stage involves three sessions where young people examine social justice issues that emphasize multiple interpersonal, institutional, cultural, and societal identities. The investigation of historical and contemporary examples encourages them to become active learners by interviewing family members, interviewing neighborhood and community members, and conducting informal environmental assessments. Finally, in the fourth stage, they consider the benefits and challenges of working together across social identities and segregated communities to plan, implement, and evaluate a community action project. The program also includes a metropolitan area tour, a campus retreat for planning community action projects, and a metropolitan summit for reporting progress on projects and assessing next steps in implementation. In addition, past dialogue participants can become youth leaders who conduct discussions of public policy issues in their home communities.

The Summer Youth Dialogues are distinct from the dialogues conducted among college students during the school year. Specifically, they

- take place in various communities spread across an increasingly racially/ethnically diverse, but segregated, metropolitan area;
- rely heavily on experiential learning with relatively few reading or writing requirements;
- lead to collaboration in action projects at the community level; and
- utilize a modified curriculum to be relevant to the unique developmental stages of high school age adolescents.

Each of these distinctive characteristics has implications for training and supporting facilitators.

Training and Supporting Facilitators for Community-Based Youth Dialogues

The Program on Intergroup Relations staff is responsible for the recruitment, selection, training, and supervision of the college student facilitators, building upon experience and expertise on the University of Michigan campus. College student facilitators are selected from among those with experience in peer facilitation in the classroom, as a result of an extensive recruitment and selection process that includes outreach through campus communications networks, completion of an application, and individual and group interviews with program staff members. These facilitators are carefully selected and have demonstrated advanced facilitation skills conducting intergroup dialogues among their college peers. See chapter 3 in this book for information on the initial training experience.

The Summer Youth Dialogues, like other intergroup dialogue efforts, draw upon intergroup relations theory (Stephan & Stephan, 1996) and social justice education pedagogy (Adams, Bell, & Griffin, 2007). In addition, community organizing and service learning pedagogy (Checkoway, 1996; Checkoway & Gutierrez, 2006) is integral to the curriculum and, thus, to the training and competency of the facilitators. Emphasis on campus-community relationships is critical to the integrity and vitality of the project. Participants, unlike college students, remain in their own or nearby communities and require assistance in developing skills to critically deliberate and deconstruct the realities they face related to inequality and privilege based on race and ethnicity. Similarly, youth participants often look for practical ways to interrupt the discrimination and segregation they face as a part of their everyday existence. In fact, many participants voice feelings of hopelessness with their increasing awareness of the institutional and societal forces related to racism; at the later stages of dialogues they are supported and encouraged to work with others to interrupt this phenomenon. Thus, there are two major foci of specialized training for SYD facilitators beyond that of their typical preparation to facilitate campus-based dialogues: 1, considerations for dialogues among adolescents and 2, considerations for dialogues in community settings. We discuss these below.

Training Considerations for Dialogues Among Adolescents

1. Developmentally appropriate approaches to intergroup facilitation with adolescents

As a part of this intensive training, the facilitators learn about various models of adolescent, human, and social development (Gilligan, 1993; Kohlberg, Levine, & Hewer, 1983). This is important because the cognitive, emotional, and moral decision-making stages of adolescents differ greatly from those of college students. In practice, youth are less likely to respond positively to great amounts of cognitive or emotional dissonance and are less likely to make the sort of separation from their parents and families (or other sources of socialization) that promote moral reasoning and decision making (King & Kitchener, 1994). As a result, youth can often exhibit dualistic notions of social justice. For example, youth often struggle to question the sources of their socialization (particularly parents and other trusted authority figures). They also grapple with the messages they have received about what is "right" or "wrong," or even "good" or "bad" in society.

One goal of dialogue is to increase the participants' understanding of the complexity of issues. The "graying" of issues can be confusing and/or frustrating for youth in these early stages of moral development. Facilitators, then, are challenged to invite youth to critically examine new or complex awareness about social inequality, power, and other social justice concepts while supporting youth as they wrestle with their individual social position and related feelings. Dialogue training includes opportunities for facilitators to practice using the developmental models to assess their own identity development and asks facilitators to consider effective interventions at each developmental stage (Brawarsky, 1996).

2. The blended role of facilitator, "near-peer" mentor, and role model

Facilitators may take mentoring roles with some of the youth participants. In fact, parents often encourage the mentoring relationship for the positive impact it can have on their adolescents. Some youth report greater self-esteem and motivation to attend college as a result of their interaction with their facilitators. This requires discussion about establishing meaningful relationships with youth while maintaining appropriate boundaries. In practice, we discuss how facilitators can leverage their own experiences transitioning from adolescent to young adults and their resulting growing awareness (Brookfield, 1995). Similarly, the facilitators discuss their own commitment to social justice and positive community change, even as a youth dialogue facilitator. Also, because it has been common for participants to disclose very serious issues in the process of dialogue (or privately to their facilitators), facilitators are trained on how to make effective referrals to community resources and/or appropriate adults. Lastly, as "near-peers" (three to seven years older typically), youth dialogue facilitators must manage the balance of being an "authority" in the dialogue space while also maintaining a posture that encourages the youth to relate to them as someone who personally understands their adolescent experiences (Posner, 2005).

> Facilitators are much more inspired by youth leadership. They recognize that there is a delicate balance [with] young leaders who need to be nurtured and guided into [becoming] successful and effective activists. (Latina, 2007 SYD Facilitator)

3. The involvement of parents or other (un)supportive adults

Training includes instruction on how to prepare weekly communications to community agency advisors that build support for participants. In addition, facilitators are trained to reach out to participant families, encouraging them to attend program functions like the Program Orientation, Metropolitan Bus Tour, and Metropolitan Summit. Facilitators work to promote critical thinking about participant experiences and their communities while also acknowledging the reality that these young people will continue to reside in their communities while facilitators themselves will leave at the culmination of the program. This presents facilitators with a challenge because the dialogue experience encourages participants to question their socialization and the institutions they perceive as furthering social inequality. Therefore, facilitators are trained to talk with their participants about developing a "Personal Action Plan" that makes them central participants to change in their own communities. Engaging in this "Cycle of Liberation" (Harro, 2000) where participants take responsibility for their own learning about social inequality in their communities helps them develop strategies for influencing others and build a network of support as they continue to pursue social justice.

Similarly, facilitators often receive questions regarding the pedagogy and curriculum of the program from involved adults. Some parents and other adults resist the emerging awareness or concerns of the young people, or refuse to support the youths' participation (e.g., denying transportation). Facilitators can often speak from their own awakening experience of how their relationships changed with family and community elders. They also learn about respecting the important role of adults and role-play conversations they might have with adults about their adolescent.

> Youth leadership requires elders, more experienced in civic engagement to guide youth and nurture their passions into action, without silencing their growth and idealism. (Black woman, 2006 SYD Facilitator)

Training Considerations for Dialogues in Community Settings

> Most of the facilitators have done extensive community work on campus, but the difference has been learning to work *with* the community. . . . (White woman, 2007 SYD Facilitator)

In addition to the usual intergroup dialogue facilitation skills commonly exercised on campus, youth dialogue facilitators are expected to take leadership roles in site development (preparing the dialogue environment, including the physical space; fostering positive working relationships with site staff; preparing contingency plans for problems at the site; etc.). This includes educating themselves about the communities in which they work (their composition, history, and contemporary issues), establishing positive relationships with adult allies (including youth advisors, agency staff, parents, and teachers), and attending to logistics at the sites as described above.

1. Utilizing community-level information instead of scholarly texts

As part of site development, facilitators are given instruction on how to conduct passive and active community surveys and assessments. They conduct web searches and windshield surveys (taking notes on community characteristics by walking and/or driving through a community or neighborhood) among other techniques. Finally, previous SYD participants introduce new facilitators to their communities and familiarize them with working with youth.

> [I had to gain] a much better understanding of the [local] issues, especially racial segregation and racial tension. (Black man, 2006 SYD Facilitator)

As part of their training, facilitators explore their own stereotypes about each community. In addition, they examine current media portrayals of each community and its surrounding communities and engage in discussions of local narratives about race bounded by geography. Unlike campus-based intergroup dialogues that require weekly readings from both narrative and scholarly academic texts that develop a common basis for discussion, youth dialogue facilitators must use more contemporary, popular media and local sources to catalyze participant interest and participation. YouTube, social networking sites like Facebook, as well as daily, weekly, and monthly local news and periodicals are often used by facilitators to catalyze discussion.

2. Properly negotiating the entering and exiting of communities

Because there is often mistrust from the community toward research universities, facilitators receive training on how to respectfully enter the community; present themselves; discuss roles and relationships; and, ultimately, leave the community. They are sensitized about expressing appropriate attitudes, assessing community strengths, identifying local norms, and respecting resident wisdom. While some facilitators in the program come from and facilitate youth dialogues in their home communities, most do not. During training, facilitators practice mock interviews and meetings meant to simulate their introduction to the designated community advisor, their meeting with other adults in the community, and their first phone call to participants' parents/guardians. In fact, on multiple occasions we have coached facilitators on how to introduce themselves during a meal hosted in the home of one of the families of skeptical parents, or to ask the partnering agency to host a community orientation for the facilitator and his or her assigned participants and families.

> Working with all types of people from so many various backgrounds has been a huge opportunity for growth and development. (Black woman, 2006 SYD Facilitator)

3. Building intergroup capacity and support within communities

As mentioned, facilitators collaborate with participants on the process of determining the social and community issues they would like to address and how they might form community-based coalitions to address those issues through community action projects or public policy education. Thus, facilitators are expected to prepare dialogue participants and supportive adults for their eventual departure, and to prepare youth for leadership roles in their own continuing multicultural education and engagement as citizens. Facilitators are trained and coached on service learning pedagogy and community organizing principles that they then apply to supporting the participants in creating community projects during the dialogues. This often involves the participants getting resources from their communities, soliciting adult support, and promoting the projects locally through media and other venues. At the conclusion of the program, participants have the opportunity to address community leaders at a public policy summit (part of the campus retreat). At the retreat and summit, facilitators coach the participants on how to be collaborators, advocates, and allies with others to work for positive community change.

> This program replaces the current cycle of socialization—that things can't change or that you can't do anything—with the new cycle of civic engagement! (White woman, 2007 SYD Facilitator)

4. Involving community stakeholders (e.g., school districts, religious institutions, local government, local media)

Intergroup dialogues on college campuses rarely involve off-campus stakeholders. The involvement of community stakeholders is not only unique to community-based dialogues *but also central to ongoing program support.* Support from community agencies, school districts, religious organizations, or state and local government units that sponsor youth participants is critical and *must be actively nurtured*. Further, media outlets provide opportunity for publicity and positive public relations for the community and the program. Facilitators, as well as program staff, must play a role in these important relationships.

Facilitators receive training on how to engage community stakeholders in building community capacity for intergroup interaction, promote youth leadership and civic engagement with local stakeholders, and respond to inquiries from local media. For example, in the past, facilitators have been recruited to help a local school district create a dialogue course, and to help a local government-sponsored youth multicultural council develop programming, and they have been interviewed by local print and television media. They are prepared for these roles by learning the language of the community and the primary issues relevant to that community. They receive media training to talk with local print and television audiences in an effective, positive way.

Supporting Facilitators

We have discussed two unique sets of issues—working with adolescents and working in community settings—that we attend to in training facilitators for youth dialogues. Like many other training models discussed in this book, we also provide ongoing support for facilitators while they are facilitating. Facilitators meet regularly, discuss content and process issues in the dialogue, and receive supervision and support from senior staff and other facilitators. During weekly sessions facilitators review the curriculum, prepare for subsequent sessions, and provide opportunities to discuss problems and find solutions.

> Staff meetings were essential to creating this atmosphere of a challenging yet supportive and enjoyable workplace. (White Jewish woman, 2006 SYD Facilitator)

Because of the special nature of youth dialogue projects—including their adolescent participants and campus-community partnerships—project staff members maintain high standards of curriculum and facilitation integrity (a common curriculum is used across all dialogues). Facilitators share difficult situations that may have arisen during previous dialogues (or the anticipation of a difficult upcoming dialogue), and then practice various intervention strategies and facilitation techniques via role-plays in the safety of staff meetings. Weekly dialogue evaluations are completed and shared with project staff and the adult advisors in the community. If problems arise, they are assessed and solutions are implemented as soon as possible. On rare occasions, direct staff intervention may be necessary, and supportive adults (advisors, parents, program coordinators) are involved when appropriate.

These weekly support sessions enhance the transformative experience for facilitators. Facilitators strengthen critical thinking about their own and others' interactions, community organizing, and civic engagement competencies beyond what they did in facilitating the campus dialogues. They not only work with the participants but also involve community members and community resources directed toward a community goal. Facilitators form strong working relationships and social bonds with one another that result in preprofessional educational experiences unavailable elsewhere in the University. Facilitators regularly express their own increasing awareness of institutional and societal forms of oppression and their deepening commitments to participate in social change. The cohesiveness of the facilitator cohort, developed over time in the training and supervised facilitation, is critical to creating a supportive space for facilitators to unpack their experiences in and out of the dialogues.

Evaluation and Outcomes

Evaluation of participant outcomes can shed light on the effectiveness of both the overall program and the facilitators conducting the dialogues (Nagda, Gurin, Sorensen, & Zúñiga, 2009). In the SYD program, facilitators have played a role in the evaluation on multiple levels: as a focus group, as members of the evaluation team, and as recruiters for participant involvement.

Evaluation Design, Findings, and Dissemination

Central to the program is an innovative multilevel evaluation design. First, we enlisted a professional evaluator for formal program evaluations using pre- and postsurvey assessments and social scientific scales related to conflict styles, racial and ethnic identification, self-satisfaction, fairness, discrimination, and racism. Based upon the Multigroup Ethnic Identity Scale (Phinney, 1992), Color-Blind Racial Attitudes Scale (Neville, Duran, & Browne, 2000), Rosenberg Self-Esteem Scale (Rosenberg, 1965), and Global Belief in a Just World Scale (Lipkus, 1991), we have found that young people increase their understanding of their own racial and ethnic identities, their knowledge about others who are racially and ethnically different from themselves, and their knowledge about racism as a force that affects them. Young people also increase their awareness of how to take action against racism and segregation in their community (Richards-Schuster, 2006).

Second, we involve young people in a participatory evaluation process, using age-appropriate methods. An evaluation team of high school students works with youth evaluation liaisons from each community to gather information through weekly journals, interviews, focus groups, and site visits. *Creating a New Beginning: Youth Speak Out on Race and Ethnicity in Metropolitan Detroit* (Richards-Schuster, 2007) describes and analyzes the program through the stories and experiences of the participants themselves. Past facilitators are also featured in that book and have been part of the interview team collecting the qualitative material.

Third, we have utilized many methods of sharing the narratives of the young people and the outcomes of the program. We collaborate with the Mosaic Youth Theatre of Detroit in the dissemination of the outcomes. Mosaic staff members facilitated a workshop of youth dialogues, examined weekly journals and project reports, wrote a script, and prepared a performance that was subsequently titled *Speak for Yourself!* for presentation in schools and community centers. We have partnered with What Kids Can Do, Inc., to publish *My Dreams Are Not a Secret* (Detroit Youth Writers, 2007), a book of poems, essays, and prose describing the experiences of past SYD participants and facilitators. We have partnered with Detroit Public Television to produce *Down Woodward,* a nine-part series documenting the graduates of Summer Youth Dialogues and other young people who have experiences of growing up in the metropolitan Detroit area concerning racial identity, racism, and building positive relationships across race and geography. Facilitators have played integral roles in all of these dissemination vehicles.

Although evaluation is still under way, all these methods indicate that young people recognize racial segregation and social isolation—in addition to racial inequality and social barriers—as problems that need attention. They want more access to intergroup dialogue and are eager to play leadership roles.

Outcomes for Stakeholders

Young people who reside in segregated places share their personal experiences and explore social identities and group memberships, develop communication and dialogue skills, and discuss the structures that perpetuate discrimination. They want to reach out to others, and this program provides opportunities unavailable elsewhere. The involvement of the highly trained facilitators is unquestionably a significant factor in successfully accomplishing this goal.

Participating communities have benefited greatly by the active engagement of their youth who have participated in the Summer Youth Dialogue Program. For example, youth in one community convinced their local school district to create and support a youth leadership course with intergroup dialogue components for their three high schools. The program also contributes to building new leadership capacity in the metropolitan area and to growing a new generation of community change agents.

We observe that *university students* who serve as dialogue facilitators experience significant change in their knowledge and skills. In addition, their attitudes change significantly as a result of this work. Facilitators often describe their experience of working with youth in a community setting as being another growth area for the practice of their skills. They routinely choose academic and career paths that are directly influenced by having been a Summer Youth Dialogue facilitator such as community organizing, working in community-based organizations, public health, and youth development programs. This is consistent with past studies (Vasques-Scalera, 1999) that also found that facilitating intergroup dialogues can be a transformational experience for students (see also chapter 13).

The program enables *the University* to develop durable collaborative partnerships with community-based organizations and civic agencies in the metropolitan area. Such relationships reflect the University's commitment to racial justice and intergroup dialogue and contribute to our core educational mission. The program also enables high school students to learn more about the social commitments of the University. Our retreat features sessions by an admissions officer, and several youth participants have become students at the University of Michigan; some have even trained to become facilitators of campus-based dialogues in The Program on Intergroup Relations!

Many metropolitan areas are becoming both more segregated and more diverse, and there is a growing need for initiatives that challenge segregation, increase intergroup contact and dialogue, and create change. Young people want to reach out to people who are different from themselves; youth dialogues are one approach to bridging the boundaries caused by segregation and developing civic competencies responsive to life in a diverse democracy. As much as the youth become aware of the issues in their communities the SYD program enables college students to become involved in and work with these communities. The facilitators develop and provide strong leadership and a near-peer mentoring relationship that bridges identity groups. These leadership capacities are important both in the specific communities as well as in a larger democratic society that values diversity as an asset. As one 2007 SYD facilitator noted,

> Youth have little opportunity or experience in honing their power for change and so
> it is very inspiring to watch them run with the program's momentum and validation
> of the youth as important individuals of society. (Latina, 2007 SYD Facilitator)

Youth dialogues have the potential to strengthen social justice efforts at the local community level, both by increasing dialogue and by challenging existing norms related to race relations. As is now commonly understood, such efforts, especially in segregated areas, are not onetime events but ongoing processes over time. Racial segregation has been centuries in the making, and the commitment of all parties (participants, practitioners, facilitators, University and community stakeholders) to the process of long-term dialogue and long-term community change must reflect the magnitude of struggle to end racial oppression.

References

Adams, M. B., Bell, L. A., & Griffin, P. (Eds.). (2007). *Teaching for diversity and social justice* (2nd ed). New York: Routledge.

Brawarsky, S. (1996). *Improving intergroup relations among youth.* New York: Carnegie Corporation of New York.

Brookfield, S. (1995). *Becoming a critically reflective teacher.* San Francisco: Jossey-Bass.

Checkoway, B. (1996). Combining service and learning on campus and in the community. *Phi Delta Kappan, 77*(9), 600–602.

Checkoway, B., & Gutierrez, L. (Eds.). (2006). *Youth participation and community change.* New York: Routledge.

Detroit Youth Writers, Abe Louise-Young (Ed.). (2007). *My dreams are not a secret.* Providence, NJ: What Kids Can Do, Inc./Next Generation Press.

Gilligan, C. (1993). *In a different voice.* Cambridge: Harvard University Press.

Harro, B. (2000). The cycle of liberation. In M. Adams, W. J. Blumenfeld, R. Castañeda, H. W. Hackman, M. L. Peters, & X. Zúñiga (Eds.), *Readings for diversity and social justice education* (pp. 463–469). New York: Routledge.

King, P. M., & Kitchener, K. S. (1994). *Developing reflective judgment.* San Francisco: Jossey-Bass.

Kirwan Institute for the Study of Race and Ethnicity. (2008). *Opportunity for all: Inequity, linked fate and social justice in Detroit and Michigan.* Report prepared for the Michigan Roundtable for Diversity and Inclusion. Retrieved August 4, 2010, from http://kirwaninstitute.org/publicationspresentations/publications/index.php.

Kohlberg, L., Levine, C., & Hewer, A. (1983). *Moral stages: A current formulation and a response to critics.* Basel, NY: Karger.

Lipkus, I. (1991). The construction and preliminary validation of a global belief in a just world scale and the exploratory analysis of the multidimensional belief in a just world scale. *Personality and Individual Differences, 12,* 1171–1178.

Nagda, B. A., Gurin, P., Sorensen, N., & Zuniga, X. (2009). Evaluating intergroup dialogue: Engaging diversity for personal and social responsibility. *Diversity & Democracy, 12*(1), 4–6.

Neville, L., Duran, L., & Browne, L. (2000). *Journal of Counseling Psychology, 47*(1), 59.

Phinney, J. S. (1992). The Multi-group Ethnic Identity Measure: A new scale for use with diverse groups. *Journal of Adolescent Research, 7,* 156–176.

Posner, G. (2005). *Field experience: A guide to reflective teaching.* Boston: Allyn & Bacon.

Richards-Schuster, K. (2006). *Creating change with our own two hands.* Summer Youth Dialogues on Race and Ethnicity. Ann Arbor, MI: University of Michigan School of Social Work.

Richards-Schuster, K. (2007). *Creating a new beginning: Youth speak out on race and ethnicity in Metropolitan Detroit.* Summer Youth Dialogues on Race and Ethnicity. Ann Arbor, MI: University of Michigan School of Social Work.

Rosenberg, M. (1965). *Society and the adolescent self-image.* Princeton, NJ: Princeton University Press.

Skillman Foundation. (2003). *Concerning Kids Public Opinion Poll.* Detroit, MI: Skillman Foundation.

Stephan, W., & Stephan, C. (1996). *Intergroup relations.* Madison, NY: Brown & Benchmark.

U.S. Census Bureau. (2010). Retrieved August 4, 2010, from http://factfinder.census.gov/home/saff/main.html?_lang=en.

Vasques Scalera, C. (1999). *Diversity, democracy, dialogue: Education for critical multicultural citizenship.* A dissertation submitted in partial fulfillment of the requirements of the degree of Doctor of Philosophy at the University of Michigan.

Zúñiga, X., Nagda, B. A., Chesler, M., & Cytron-Walker, A. (2007). *Intergroup dialogues in higher education: Meaningful learning about social justice.* ASHE Higher Education Report Series, *32*(4). San Francisco: Jossey-Bass.

10

EXTENDING INTERGROUP DIALOGUE FACILITATION TO MULTICULTURAL SOCIAL WORK PRACTICE

Michael S. Spencer, David J. Martineau, and naomi m. warren

D iversity and social justice are central to the National Association of Social Workers (NASW) Code of Ethics. Social workers are bound to honor "the dignity and worth of the person" and simultaneously "challenge social injustice" (NASW, 1999) as part of ethical practice. Schools of social work and professional development programs must prepare practitioners to engage vulnerable and oppressed individuals and groups in a manner that is respectful of individual differences and cultural and ethnic diversity (NASW, 1999). Advances in social justice education have generated curricular and pedagogical innovations in higher education and schools of social work. One example—intergroup dialogues—provides unique opportunities for social work students to consider how power, unearned privilege, and oppression differentially influence individual experiences and how their social identity group memberships shape their experiences, attitudes, and beliefs as they relate to their practice regardless of concentration.

This course was developed by Michael Spencer, David Martineau, Anna Yeakley, and Julica Hermann, on the basis of examples and models from similar courses offered through the Program on Intergroup Relations (IGR) at the University of Michigan and through the Intergroup Dialogue, Education, and Action (IDEA) Center at the University of Washington School of Social Work directed by Biren (Ratnesh) Nagda. The Center for Research on Learning and Teaching (CRLT) and the Gilbert Whittaker Fund for the Improvement of Teaching provided the funding for developing this course.

Effective facilitation is critical to effective dialogue. Dialogue facilitation requires reflection on our own experiences with oppression and privilege, and leadership around social justice issues that are emotional and controversial. This focus on self-awareness and reflection fosters an important prerequisite skill for ethical social work practice. While models of facilitation have emerged in other fields and professions, a dearth of models for facilitating dialogues on diversity and social justice exists in social work. Although skills and techniques inherent to facilitation and group work are transferable to facilitating dialogues, additional content and skills are necessary. The purpose of this chapter is to describe a model for training social work students in effective dialogue facilitation. We emphasize our own learning through the development and evaluation of this model and hope to present readers with a foundation for developing their own training program to promote intergroup dialogues in schools of social work and the profession.

Since September 2000, Michael Spencer and David Martineau have taught an elective, three-credit Master of Social Work (MSW) course, Training in Intergroup Dialogue Facilitation: Skills for Multicultural Social Work Practice, at three U.S. schools of social work. Since then, naomi warren has been both a student in the course and an instructor. The course addressed a need to more effectively cultivate student learning on unearned privilege, oppression, and social justice—knowledge that is essential for social workers to engage in cross-cultural interactions. Across schools of social work, few courses are dedicated to rigorous learning and application of diversity and social justice, critical consciousness and transformation, and the development of skilled facilitators of multicultural dialogue (see Nagda et al., 1999, for an exception).

Training social work students in intergroup dialogue facilitation is useful in many social worker roles, for example, broker, mediator, community organizer, educator, activist, and group facilitator. Social workers are suited for facilitating dialogues given their professional knowledge, skills, and experience with relationship building, oppression, empowerment, and systemic approaches (Dessel, Rogge, & Garlington, 2006). Because social workers strive to end discrimination, oppression, poverty, and other forms of social injustice, they often find themselves engulfed in social conflict and political discord. Using dialogue as an intervention in intergroup conflict "combines the strengths of micro and macro practice by creating an opportunity for critical self-analysis and relational engagement together with systemic and structural change" (Dessel et al., 2006, p. 305). Intergroup dialogue provides social workers with another avenue for promoting social justice and change in various practice settings.

Overview of Facilitation Training Model for Social Work Practice

Years of teaching the dialogue facilitation course have led us to advance a training model that balances participation in dialogue with presentation of facilitation skills (see Figure 10.1). We find that when students reflectively engage in dialogue, they are able to further their own critical consciousness while practicing skills imparted in lecture.

Curricula for intergroup dialogues typically use a four-stage model (see Nagda et al., 1999):

1. Icebreakers, course overview, and guidelines
2. Learning about commonalities and differences
3. Dialogues on issues and hot topics
4. Action planning and alliance building

FIGURE 10.1
Dialogue facilitation training for social work practice.

This four-stage model is embedded within our facilitation training model, which consists of the following seven components (see Figure 10.1).

1. Getting acquainted and developing guidelines. The first stage focuses on building community among students in preparation for their dialogue experience. In addition to introductions and icebreaker activities useful to group work, we incorporate the Freirian notion of co-learning. For example, on the first day we ask all participants, including the instructors, to introduce themselves to each other as "a teacher and a learner" in the class. This serves to attenuate power hierarchies that exist between and among members of the class. During this phase, participants also develop guidelines for participation to build a sense of psychological safety. Activities facilitated during this phase involve lower levels of risk and self-disclosure. They are designed to introduce social identity groups, concepts of multiple identities and intersectionality, and personal definitions of social justice and social change.

2. Developing skills for dialogue and facilitation. During this phase, we define dialogue—distinguishing it from debate and discussion—and explore listening as a necessary skill for both dialogue participation and facilitation. We use the term "listening with *Ting*," described by Huang-Nissen and Lee (2000). *Ting* is the Chinese character for listen, and it includes the characters for ear, eyes, mind, heart, oneness, and king (although we use the gender-neutral term *royalty*). The combination of characters emphasizes the importance of active listening (using ears and eyes for tone, pitch, and nonverbal cues; using our mind to comprehend the content; and using our hearts to establish empathy for the speaker). The inclusion of royalty and oneness takes this form of listening deeper than active listening, granting the communication the reverence reserved for royalty, and seeking in the message some basis for unity between speaker and listener. Listening with *Ting* searches for opportunities to build bridges and find common ground with the speaker.

Our approach normalizes conflict. In addition to addressing common strategies for dealing with conflict and resistance, we draw on principles of nonviolent communication and action. If practiced, they prepare individuals for dialogue and effective facilitation. The LARA method is a particularly useful technique we use. LARA, an acronym for Listening, Affirming, Responding, and Adding Information, is a dialogic technique developed by the American Friends Service Committee (AFSC) in its community work on heterosexism. The four steps are rooted in a philosophy of nonviolence, exemplified by the Hindu concept of *ahimsa*—Sanskrit for avoidance of injury. Working from *ahimsa,* the speaker communicates "I will not harm you," implicitly conveying trust that "you will not harm me." From this vantage point, the truth of the message will speak for itself if put forth with clarity and compassion; it need not condemn or threaten to be heard. Speech as nonviolent action leaves room for others to share moral ground, and we can come together with our dignity intact (Tinker, 2001).

We have found it useful to walk through an example of using LARA to reply to a personal trigger. A disparaging statement about "Mexican immigrants taking jobs from Americans" is an example of a trigger. Using LARA, we ask students to **L**—Listen with *Ting* to the underlying message in the statement and try to understand where it might come from. Listening with *Ting* prepares us to **A**—Affirm something in the speaker's message. In this example, we might hear the individual's concern about job loss in the United States, and thus affirm that we, too, are concerned with unemployment.

It is only after affirming that we **R**—Respond to the content of the triggering statement. This is generally difficult for students, as they share an intuitive desire to respond directly to what they disagree with in the statement. Doing so cuts short communication and forestalls dialogue. In our working example, we might say, "I am not sure that rising unemployment is meaningfully impacted by immigrants from Mexico, and I worry about the consequences of them being scapegoats for a complex problem." We might then **A**—Add information, such as a personal story, another perspective, or a statistic, that furthers the exchange. For example, "I find that I'm angrier about the corporations that are sending jobs to other countries to maximize their profit." Participants are then asked to practice LARA in pairs around their own triggers with consultation as necessary from the instructors. By understanding others' triggers, we put ourselves in a better position to act as allies within the dialogue.

3. Understanding the dynamics of difference and dominance. Theories of oppression and social justice are discussed in this phase, including the historical, political, and social context of dominant and oppressive policies and outcomes. We assert that social oppression is maintained at the individual, institutional, and societal/cultural levels; is manifested at both the attitudinal and behavioral levels; and may be a conscious or unconscious process for those involved, depending upon one's advocacy, participation, support, or collusion in a system of oppression (Hardiman & Jackson, 2007). We also emphasize social identity developmental stages that people from agent and target groups undergo in their critical consciousness development (Adams, Bell, & Griffin, 2007).

4. Developing critical consciousness and self-awareness. At this point in the training, we expect that participants have begun to internalize the

theoretical concepts and are in the process of considering how their position across social identity groups plays a role in maintaining hegemonic systems of oppression. We challenge participants to make a commitment to social justice, which Freire (1972) describes as a moral and ethical attitude toward equality and a belief in the capacity of people as agents who can act to transform their world. Furthermore, we discuss how a commitment to social justice begins with an examination of the contradiction between our espoused social principles and our lived experience (Freire, 1972). An important goal is to bring these unconscious contradictions into our awareness, which is an important step in critical consciousness development. Furthermore, we define allyship and the characteristics of an ally. We stress the need to be willing to take risks, make mistakes, and try again. We also stress self-care and support systems to nourish our passion for critical consciousness development. Facilitated activities during this phase feature a higher level of risk and self-disclosure among participants and facilitators. When leading reflection on activities, instructors pose critical questions (Freire, 1972), probe comments offered by students, and challenge assumptions and biases that may arise.

5. Demonstrating dialogue facilitation skills. Having laid the foundation for dialogue, participants have the opportunity to practice their new facilitation skills. Working in pairs or small groups (depending on the number of students and time allotted), students develop an agenda for a one-hour dialogue they facilitate in class. We try to balance the social identities of co-facilitators according to the dialogue they will be facilitating. In our course, we use a multi-issue format and include race, ethnicity, gender, class, religion/spirituality, disability, age, and sexual orientation as topics. Although assigned to one topic, we encourage co-facilitators to emphasize the intersectionality of different identities. We encourage the students to meet outside of class—not only to plan the dialogue agenda but also to get to know each other personally and professionally. For example, co-facilitators are expected to discuss their personal histories with the dialogue topic, their triggers, and how their co-facilitator can support them if their triggers arise in the dialogue. We also encourage co-facilitators to discuss their strengths and limitations around the topic area and with facilitation in general, and to design their agenda around their strengths.

Groups deliver a brief encounter activity related to the topic and facilitate a dialogue in the remaining time. The agenda should include the goals and objectives of the dialogue, steps for each activity or component, expected time frame for the components, logistics, facilitation issues, potential questions to initiate dialogue, and anticipated issues. We stress a balance between structure and flexibility; the purpose of the agenda is not to create a rigid structure but to act as a guide for laying out the parameters of the dialogue and to assist in thinking through the issues and triggers that may arise. We review the agendas in advance and provide feedback to the students before they facilitate.

6. Receiving feedback and reflection on one's strengths and areas for improvement in facilitation. Immediately following each group facilitation, an additional 30 minutes is allocated for classmates to provide the group with feedback on their facilitation using a fishbowl strategy (Adams et al., 2007; Schoem, Zúñiga, & Nagda, 1993). During the fishbowl, the co-facilitators sit in an inner circle facing each other to reflect on their experience, whereas the instructors and participants sit silently in an outer circle of chairs and listen. The co-facilitators in the fishbowl are asked to answer three questions: (1) How do they think the facilitation went? (2) What do they think went well? (3) What would they do differently? After about 15 minutes, the fishbowl is opened for others to enter and provide constructive feedback and comments.

This fishbowl format was not part of the original course design. Originally, the instructors would simply open the floor for feedback from classmates following the facilitation. However, this process often led students to be somewhat critical of their facilitators and often around issues that were obvious limitations. Only a few of the comments were positive and supportive. To counteract this effect, we initiated the fishbowl format. A clear difference emerged, as co-facilitators in the fishbowl often noted the obvious limitations of their facilitation and were often harder on themselves than their peers were on them. This provided an opportunity for the participants in the dialogue to provide positive feedback. This process created a far more supportive and nurturing environment for the co-facilitators.

7. Recognizing that learning is continuous. The goal of this phase is to help students develop methods for continuing the lifelong process of recognizing our own biases, learning how to change our oppressive behaviors, and building a more socially just multicultural society. In particular, we try to connect dialogue and the facilitation skills with various roles that social workers play in the field. We accomplish this by engaging students in discussions of how they foresee using dialogue in their field of practice. Recently in one of these discussions, a student mentioned how she is using *Ting* and LARA in her clinical practice and is teaching clients these skills to promote empathy. These skills are useful not only in direct clinical practice but also in contexts in which clients have direct conflict, such as in divorce mediation or family reunification. A strong link also exists between the skills in this course and community organization practice, in which it is important to bring different groups together for dialogue—for example, agency staff and community residents; patients and health/mental health providers; lesbian, gay, bisexual,

and transgender groups and religious leaders; environmentalists and environmental justice advocates; urban planners and social workers. In essence, dialogue is useful as a tool for collaboration and coalition building and can be useful with any groups that have been in conflict and could use common ground to forward their work. This is particularly important during times of scarce resources, competition, and rising demands and costs. It also could be done across agencies that historically have been in conflict or competition.

Students use the skills from this course in other myriad ways. For some students, taking this course has redirected what they want to do with their degrees and their careers. Many students have talked about this course as "transformational"—in terms of both life and career goals. For others, it is simply an added set of skills to use when problems arise in their workplace settings. For example, one student was placed with a city government for practicum and used the skills from this course to facilitate dialogues in relation to sex and race discrimination after an incident occurred among a group of firefighters. Another student now works with juvenile detention, facilitating circles as a form of restorative justice, using skills from the class in circle work and in processing identity-based issues as they come up both for the young people and for the staff who work in the system. For other students, the course impacts how they go about doing their work. For example, one student taught a human diversity course for several years and then moved into teaching policy, infusing the power/privilege/oppression framework into the policy course. Yet another student organized a youth program bringing together Jewish and Muslim high school students, moving it beyond the social component that had characterized it in previous years, to incorporate dialogues through the school year. Table 10.1 provides a brief list of the ways in which students may be able to use their dialogic and facilitation skills in social work across micro and macro practice methods, settings, and roles.

We also incorporate an additional way for students to learn about facilitation. They are asked to attend a facilitated social justice–oriented event as a participant observer. The event does not have to be a dialogue. Students make note of the setting, the facilitation style, their own experience as members of the group, their observation of other group members, things they thought the facilitator did that were useful or not useful, and things the facilitator might have done differently. Students are then asked to distinguish how the group differed from a dialogue or could be improved through dialogic methods.

TABLE 10.1
Using dialogue and facilitation skills in social work practice

Method Area	Settings	Roles	Example
Clinical practice	Schools, mental health centers, child welfare	Counselor, therapist, group worker, case manager	• Listening to client concerns with *Ting* and asking critical questions • Negotiating conflict among clients
Community organizing	Community-based organizations, nongovernmental organizations, social justice advocacy and antibigotry organizations, unions	Community worker, advocate, activist, broker, negotiator, mediator, educator	• Facilitating community dialogues and community forums • Negotiating between clients and social systems • Educating or raising awareness around social injustices • Engaging in coalition building across differences
Social policy and evaluation	Nongovernmental organizations, government and legislative bodies, advocacy organizations	Policy analyst, elected or appointed officials, program evaluator, researcher	• Engaging in perspective taking in understanding ramifications of social policy • Building support for policy and legislation beyond debate • Conducting participatory program evaluations; community-based, participatory research; or action research • Implementing focus groups to assess needs and strengths of individuals and communities
Management of human services	Nonprofit and for-profit organizations, human resources departments	Managers, supervisors, personnel and development officers	• Negotiating conflict among employees • Facilitating individual/group supervision • Conducting diversity training • Communicating with philanthropists, corporate executives, and other potential donors, particularly those with conflicting views

For our final assessment of students, we utilize a capstone assignment for the course—the Taping Project (Garcia & Van Soest, 1997; Millstein, 1997; Tatum, 1992). The Taping Project provides students with the opportunity to take inventory of their learning and instructors with data on the impact of the course on participants. Prior to the beginning of the course, students are asked to tape-record a self-administered interview based on a structured set of questions provided by the instructors. After listening to their recorded interviews at the end of the term, students submit written reflections on their responses in light of their experiences in the class. The data from the Taping Project represent a unique window into the process of self-awareness and social identity development of course participants. The essays help to identify the meaning participants made of the experience and illuminate key areas of learning resulting from the educational opportunity afforded by dialogues. An example from a White female from a privileged class background illustrates how this student shifted her understanding of the concept of allyship during the semester:

> I began to understand why I had felt so awful [in a negative interaction with a Black student the previous year] and what it was that I had to learn: despite any wishes I may have to join with (in this case) people of color, I cannot and should not expect appreciation in return. Whites who want to be allies to people of color can [paraphrasing a course reading] "assume that [their] effort to be a good friend is appreciated," but should not "expect or accept gratitude from people of color" ... We should work on racism for our own sake, not for "their" sake, and to accept making mistakes in the process.

Instructors' Reflections

Our experiences in teaching this facilitation training course have shown us that intergroup dialogue is an important method for social work practice, and facilitating dialogue is a critical skill that has utility across various intergroup contact experiences. We recognize that our growth as instructors and facilitators is ongoing, and we encourage other trainers to take time to process and reflect among themselves regularly and often. Each time we teach the course, we begin by sharing with students how much we learn about ourselves and ways to improve our facilitation skills by teaching the course. The students respond to this expression of humility, and we believe that it has major implications for creating a safe and supportive environment.

We also participate in all of the dialogues that occur within the context of the course, which can feel vulnerable, especially for individuals who are in positions of power within the institution. We recognize that this level of disclosure may be uncomfortable for some instructors, and we are reminded of the importance of establishing safety in order to speak to discomfort. Different institutional and political climates may engender different levels of safety, and we invite instructors to develop their own boundaries with their students.

Also, we recommend that the course be co-taught by experienced individuals who possess differences across social identity groups. Instructors need to be aware of those areas where both hold unearned privilege and make a concerted effort to demonstrate recognition of this privilege. For social identities where both instructors share targeted identities, the concept of no hierarchies of oppression can be incorporated, and instructors can tie examples of their privileged status to those privileged identities they do not possess. Where their identities differ, instructors can act as allies for one another and model this behavior for students. We understand that co-teaching may not be feasible in some institutions or organizations. We have taught this course alone and understand that it is possible to do so, but special effort must be made to address areas where the instructor may or may not hold unearned privilege. If teaching this course alone, we recommend that individuals seek support and/or supervision from an experienced colleague or peer.

Perhaps one of the most important lessons we have learned as instructors, which we try to pass on when training facilitators, is the value of making mistakes. We tell students that this course is the time to make mistakes and that we expect mistakes. Since ours is an academic course, we also tell students that their evaluations will not be penalized for their mistakes. Rather, we tell students that their grades will be based on their ability to reflect on any mistakes they might make through their written assignments. Thus, rather than fearing mistakes, we encourage students to take risks. We find that this tends to alleviate some anxiety that students may have around facilitating, particularly for those who are concerned how their "performance" might affect their grade.

Not only can students make mistakes, but instructors can make mistakes, too, when they are facilitating. Setting a climate where mistakes are allowed sets the stage for instructors to revisit missed opportunities as teaching moments. Instructors may also be confronted on their own blind spots with regard to issues of power and privilege by astute students. We have found through experience that owning our blind spots and embracing our anxieties and fear of exposure is the best way to overcome our defensiveness to being confronted. Again, reflecting on principles of nonviolence can be useful during these stressful moments. For example, we embrace the Gandhian values of truth (*satya*) and self-sacrifice (*tapasya*). When we make mistakes, we acknowledge that admitting error can be embarrassing and painful, but it can give us credibility. We tell ourselves to be courageous. Thus, nonviolence is not an academic exercise—it is a matter of testing theories in practice, asking what went wrong, and trying again. It also models the kind of honesty, humility, and genuineness that is necessary for facilitators.

While it is impossible for us to describe all the elements of the course, its content, and the processes we use to accomplish its goals, we hope that we have been able to provide some building blocks for the development of an effective training program in social work. One element of the course that keeps us motivated to teach the course each year is our own personal growth as facilitators. We look forward each term to a new set of social work students who want to facilitate dialogues and promote social justice through education. We also relish the chance to dialogue ourselves and are honored to be able to engage in the process of our own critical consciousness development with our students. We model that learning is continuous, through our own growth. We model allyship through our support for each other, and we demonstrate genuineness by owning our mistakes. Finally, we model facilitation skills through our own practice and instruction.

References

Adams, M., Bell, L. A., & Griffin, P. (Eds.). (2007). *Teaching for diversity and social justice* (2nd ed.). New York: Routledge.

Dessel, A., Rogge, M. E., & Garlington, S. B. (2006). Using intergroup dialogue to promote social justice and change. *Social Work, 51*, 303–315.

Freire, P. (1972). *Pedagogy of the oppressed*. New York: Seabury Press.

Garcia, B., & Van Soest, D. (1997). Changing perceptions of diversity and oppression: MSW students discuss the effects of a required course. *Journal of Social Work Education, 33*, 119–129.

Hardiman, R., & Jackson, B. W. (2007). Conceptual foundations for social justice education. In M. Adams, L. A. Bell, & P. Griffin (Eds.), *Teaching for diversity and social justice* (2nd ed., pp. 35–66). New York: Routledge.

Huang-Nissen, S., Lin, G., & Lee, C. (2000). *Dialogue groups: A practical guide to facilitate diversity conversations*. Blue Hill, ME: Medicine Bear Publishing.

Millstein, K. H. (1997). The taping project: A method for self-evaluation and "informed consciousness" in racism courses. *Journal of Social Work Education, 33*, 491–506.

Nagda, B. A., Spearmon, M. L., Holley, L. C., Harding, S., Balassone, M. L., Moïse-Swanson, D., et al. (1999). Intergroup dialogues: An innovative approach to teaching about diversity and justice in Social Work programs. *Journal of Social Work Education, 35*(3), 433–449.

National Association of Social Workers. (1999). *Code of ethics for the National Association of Social Workers*. Retrieved June 12, 2006, from http://www.socialworkers.org/pubs/code/code.asp.

Schoem, D., Zúñiga, X., & Nagda, B. A. (1993). Classroom and workshop exercises: Exploring one's group background—the fishbowl exercise. In D. Schoem, L. Frankel, X. Zúñiga, & E. Lewis (Eds.), *Multicultural teaching in the university* (pp. 326–327). Westport, CT: Praeger.

Tatum, B. D. (1992). Talking about race, learning about racism: The application of racial identity development theory in the classroom. *Harvard Educational Review, 62*(1), 1–24.

Tinker, B. (2001). *Speech as non-violent action*. Ann Arbor, MI: American Friends Service Committee LGBT Issues Program.

SECTION THREE

LEARNING FROM AND WITH INTERGROUP DIALOGUE FACILITATORS

Voices on Identity, Alliances, and Career Commitments

Though much has been written recently about the impact of intergroup dialogue practices and learning outcomes for student participants, until now, little has been written about how the preparation and facilitation of intergroup dialogue affects the actual facilitators. We believe that both the training and facilitation have a profound effect on those individuals, particularly when they are undergraduate peers. For them, it is perhaps one of the few opportunities they have had to exercise leadership in a classroom for a sustained period of time, to work across difference intensively, and to learn with fellow facilitators.

This section provides greater insight into the experiences of facilitators themselves: their dilemmas, challenges, and triumphs. Each chapter bridges some part of the theory, research, and practice triangle and

- highlights facilitators' own insights into the critical questions they ask themselves;
- conveys the voices of facilitators by sharing recent qualitative inquiries into the facilitation process and its implications for facilitators; and
- locates the facilitators' voices in theoretical frameworks to help us understand their experiences.

This section seeks to connect the previous chapters that have provided the reader with theoretical, processual, and practical knowledge of the facilitation training process. By listening to the facilitators themselves, readers can understand the important implications that training processes have for those being trained, particularly when they are undergraduate students.

This section begins with Maxwell, Chesler, and Nagda describing an inquiry with recent undergraduate trainees and facilitators of intergroup dialogue. Their chapter examines how dialogue facilitators perceive whether their social identities affect their facilitation processes. It outlines five major themes identified by facilitators themselves related to the significance of their social identities. Through the words of the facilitators, the authors examine the critical lessons about the intersection of social identities and intergroup dialogue facilitation. The chapter concludes with implications for facilitator training and development.

Chapter 12, by Nagda, Timbang, Fulmer, and Tran, draws upon facilitators' learning from the initial preparation and training courses through the actual facilitation experience. They focus on the relational power of intergroup dialogue facilitation. They convey, through prose and poetry, how facilitators come to understand alliance building, and its impact on deepening their relationship as co-facilitators, their own learning about internalized oppression and domination, and their agency as change agents in facilitating the learning of students in their dialogue groups.

In the final chapter Vasques-Scalera examines the longer-term impact of facilitating intergroup dialogues. She describes a study of college graduates, all of whom had been intergroup dialogue facilitators. Through their own words, the author depicts the continuing impact of that facilitation experience on their thinking and actions long after the initial experience. The chapter ends with important training implications for all programs seeking to catalyze change for a lifetime.

11

IDENTITY MATTERS

Facilitators' Struggles and Empowered Use
of Social Identities in Intergroup Dialogue

Kelly E. Maxwell, Mark Chesler,
and Biren (Ratnesh) A. Nagda

The core practices of intergroup dialogue (IGD) involve students exploring their own and others' social identities in the context of broader patterns of systemic inequalities. Exploration of these social identities is critical in building meaningful relationships within and across identity groups and in mobilizing individual and collective agency to promote positive intergroup relationships. We use social identities to refer to group memberships based on physical or social characteristics ascribed by self or others that locate people within societal structures that confer advantage/privilege or disadvantage/oppression. The history of racial/ethnic inequality, sexism, and classism in the United States and around the world makes clear the continuing power of institutional oppression and how these cultural and situational forces affect the daily lives of people (Blauner, 1989; Bonilla-Silva & Forman, 2000; Essed, 1991; Feagin & Sikes, 1994). Social identities thus have internal meaning to us as individuals and also have significance to the rest of the world (Cooley, 1922; Tatum, 2003). Since our social identities shape so much of our internal and external experience, their exploration is crucial to advancing our understanding of ourselves, others, and the social world in which we live.

We are concerned with how IGD facilitators react and respond to this cocreated understanding of their social identities and how it impacts their

We thank Gillian Menaker, Koyonne Mims, Joseph Person, and Monita Thompson for their assistance in the development of this chapter. We alone, however, are responsible for the work and interpretations presented here.

own and others' behavior. In this chapter we share the results of a recent inquiry about how a set of undergraduate peer facilitators perceive their social identities affecting their facilitation processes. Maxwell and Chesler are both White faculty members and, respectively, a woman and man; Nagda is a faculty member and an immigrant man of color. As described below, we analyzed interviews conducted with facilitators of color and White facilitators, with men and women. Just as social identity theory emphasizes the importance of knowing oneself in the context of dialogue, it influences what we see as researchers, the interpretive frames we use, and the sense we make out of the data. As in all works of this sort, it is possible, perhaps likely, that other researchers with different identities, roles, or social and intellectual frames might approach this topic and interpret these data differently.

Social Identities in Intergroup Dialogue Facilitation

Social group identity is relevant not only to the conduct of intergroup dialogues but to the training and practice of facilitation. The training and supervision we provide facilitators is experienced and interpreted through the lens of their locations in the society's structures of race, gender, socioeconomic class, sexual orientation, religion, and other social categories. These identities, locations, and associated experiences provide and reinforce sets of values, talents/skills, and expectations facilitators bring to the dialogic encounter and to their leadership role. Moreover, the responses of students in the dialogue, as well as facilitators' expectations or assessments of these responses, also play a role in their approaches and actions. We can expect, then, that IGD facilitators' social group identities play a role in how they think about acting, plan to act, and do act as they relate with participants and their co-facilitators.

Our interest in these issues comes from our experience training, observing, and supervising facilitators of intergroup dialogues. We have seen, for example, that facilitators from target groups (i.e., identity groups disadvantaged or disenfranchised by a system of oppression that does not favor their group) and co-facilitators from agent groups (i.e., identity groups advantaged or privileged by historic and/or contemporary socioeconomic structures) often view their facilitation experiences differently. Further, the expression of their identities is not simply determined by internal definitions of self and one's membership in social groups; it is also responsive to situational demands and opportunities as well as the responses of dialogue participants (Tappan, 2006). Thus, the relative salience of a particular social identity (or even one's status as an agent or a target group member), and therefore its effect on facilitative behavior, depends on the dialogic context, group composition, and purpose.

Methods of Inquiry

We involved two former facilitators, a White woman and an African American woman, to conduct and tape-record face-to-face individual and small-group interviews with 49 trained facilitators of intergroup dialogues. They asked facilitators whether and how their social identities affected or might affect their dialogue facilitation approaches and behaviors. All of these informants had gone through the training and preparation process, and they either were about to facilitate an intergroup dialogue or already had.

We explored the ways in which facilitators reported they anticipated or experienced their identities playing a role, the issues (either internally or with participants) they wrestled with, and their comfort level in this work and with their co-facilitators. We first read through the transcripts of all the interviews and used open-coding techniques to identify major themes. We then applied these themes systematically to the data set, seeking confirming and disconfirming evidence of their existence and meaning for informants. As a result, this chapter is organized around the five following major themes:

1. Understanding the significance of social identity in the facilitative role
2. Managing the challenges of privilege/dominance and subordination/ oppression in facilitating dialogue groups with both dominant and subordinate group members
3. Establishing and maintaining credibility
4. Establishing relationships with and/or educating members of facilitators' own identity groups, even acting as role models
5. Working with a co-facilitator with different social identities

Not all themes were reported by all facilitators, and some were reported primarily or solely by facilitators acting as members of either dominant or subordinate groups. Since the examination and understanding of dominant-subordinate relations are such substantial elements in the intergroup dialogue programs in which we are involved, we reflect on facilitators' perceptions and experiences largely in terms of their status as dominant/privileged group members or subordinate/oppressed group members in the particular dialogue they would or did facilitate. While we posed the question of social identity broadly in the interviews, most facilitators focused their responses on issues of race and gender. Therefore, we limit the discussion in this chapter to these aspects of identity. In the quotes from informants' interviews we use pseudonyms for their actual names.

Results and Discussion

The Significance of Social Identity in the Facilitative Role

Forty-one of the 49 informants indicated their identities did or would play a role in their work while eight said it did not or would not. Some saw their identities as limiting factors, others saw them as sources of strength, and some saw them as both. Two facilitators, one from dominant racial and gender groups (White and male) and the other from subordinate groups (Asian and female), expressed the views of many as they noted their group's influence on their own approaches to the work.

> Because of the privilege this identity affords me I facilitate with a certain level of ignorance regarding the target group experience. This is evident in the way I respond to language, answer questions and challenge assumptions, and am often unable to notice and challenge comments or words that might be an obvious topic of discussion to those of a target group. I believe some will question what I really know about the issues of race. (Scott, White man)

> Because I am an Asian, passivity and deep listening are reflective of this identity. (Nadia, Asian woman)

The first informant above expressed ignorance and lack of awareness as well as concern about how others will react to his racial group membership. The second informant reported aspects of her group-based style and implied that her cultural attributes of passivity and deep listening influence her behavior. While Nadia suggested that both attributes may impact her facilitative style, it is unclear whether she saw them both as positive contributors or not. Throughout many of these reports we find facilitators expressing both limiting and contributing (negative and positive) influences of their identities on their facilitation and dialogues.

Other members of subordinate racial groups argued that their identity plays out in facilitation, but not in terms of its influence on their own intentions or behaviors as much as in the responses to it from dialogue participants. They noted that this response, or their anticipation of it, might affect their behavior.

> I somewhat expect students to feel uncomfortable with my presence simply because I look different. When others see me they may judge me because of my race identity.... They may feel I do not belong at the university. In addition, others may be frightened by my race identity and these things will change my facilitating style; I would be more conscious about the things that I say. (Vega—Black woman)

Acknowledgment that identity may affect facilitation style is only the beginning of this inquiry. Most facilitators recognized that identity matters, and that as a result there are both challenges and opportunities in their facilitative practice. The overarching challenge is to learn how to work with their own and others' identities in positive ways.

Managing the Challenges of Privilege/Dominance and Subordination/Oppression

Many facilitators, particularly members of agent identity groups, encountered and acknowledged gaps in their own self-awareness and their knowledge of their own group's backgrounds and realities, as well as that of others'. Without knowledge and awareness of the meaning and impact of one's social identity (on oneself, on others in the dialogue, and in the structure and culture of society at large), it would be very difficult to facilitate the consciousness-raising, knowledge development, and relationship-building activities that typically occur in an intergroup dialogue.

Some agent group facilitators acknowledged coming from backgrounds of privilege but indicated they knew little about how it might play out in their own minds or in the participants'. Others recognized clearly that one of the downsides of their privilege was a lack of knowledge about the culture or common experiences of members of oppressed or disadvantaged groups.

> My worst fear is having a conflict arise about something I know nothing about. This is actually quite likely situation in my case as being White has given me the privilege of being unaware of many struggles that occur in everyday life. (Hannah, White woman)

An additional cost of ignorance is the risk that one's behavior might unintentionally offend members of other groups. This concern was expressed by several facilitators with dominant group identities who noted they were cautious or defensive about their privileged status and concerned they might make a mistake or offend members of target groups.

> I had a more difficult time "pushing" participants of color than I had white participants, because I was somewhat more intimidated and worried about offending someone of color than a White person. (Sarah, White woman)

The concern about unintentionally giving racial offense also arises from White facilitators' understanding that some of their attitudes and actions might reflect their implicit or unconscious racism (Bobo, Kluegel, & Smith,

1997; Bonilla-Silva & Forman, 2000; Essed, 1991; Kinder & Sears, 1981; McConahay, 1983; McKinney, 2005). Their internalized privilege and lack of clarity about how to act in ways that reflect a coherent understanding of the implications of such privilege affect both their own behavior and that of target groups. In particular, White students' pervasive ignorance about the reality of lives of people of color, and of their reactions and interactions across racial lines, is typical. Although students of color also often come from segregated backgrounds, they have had to learn about White people and culture in order to succeed and be safe in a White- and male-dominated society. Dominant group members' fear of giving offense is part of the internalization of agent group privilege and reflects the current culture of politeness that characterizes racial conversations and diminishes the possibility of authentic behavior. Target group members rarely mentioned gaps in their knowledge of agent group members' experiences, although several African American facilitators of upper-middle-class origin expressed parallel concern, especially about the degree to which their experience mirrored that of participants of color from less economically advantaged backgrounds.

As some members of dominant groups struggled with the blinders of privilege, some facilitators who were members of socially disadvantaged or oppressed groups struggled with acknowledging and countering internalization of the stereotypes associated with their target group identities. They felt these perceptions could threaten their ability to be authentic and effective in their dialogue leadership roles.

> I hold many characteristics that are consistent with a female stereotype—being kind and caring, sympathetic, sometimes soft-spoken. They may affect how participants in my group view me. I definitely feel that I have been totally socialized to "be a girl," and it is very hard for me to think about many gender issues and speak about them. I feel there will be many blind spots for me in this area. (Trisha—White woman)

> I don't want to fall into the passive female role stereotype. However, I also don't want to be taken as that domineering and angry Black woman that is forever being played out in the media. (Jackie, Black woman)

Many facilitators with subordinate group identities noted that they knew of and needed to deal with the negative stereotypes associated with their group. Some expressed concern about the degree to which they accepted or might conform to such stereotypes (for a discussion of these struggles with the acceptance or rejection of negative stereotypes see Fletcher, 1999; Freire, 1970; Hardiman & Jackson, 1997; Tappan, 2006).

While all comments relating to themes of unclarity and caution about offensiveness were expressed by agent group members (Whites or men), all comments about potential internalization of and coping with negative stereotypes came from women—White women or women of color. Indeed, this is the expected nature of group domination and oppression.

Establishing and Maintaining Credibility

A somewhat unique aspect of the effort to deal with socially constructed patterns of dominance and subordination involves facilitator credibility. Facilitators have immense responsibility in the dialogue, including organizing their dialogue group, setting the agenda, and leading activities and exercises. Their role in the program, and their responsibility for the above tasks, confer upon them leadership status and an aura of credibility and authority on both content and process matters. Such credibility is essential for all instructional leadership, but especially so for peers providing leadership to other undergraduate students.

Several facilitators acknowledged that their group identity status, and how they handled it, also conferred certain credibility and power. They felt they could use their background and knowledge to positively affect their dialogue work. For instance, some facilitators felt they could use their disadvantaged group identities to increase their credibility in the dialogue.

> Since I am of a minority race I can help keep things in balance and I can look at things from an objective point of view. I think my identity as a woman impacts my facilitation style in that I make it a point to dig out the male perspective on things, especially on things that are known as woman topics. (Lian, Asian woman)

Some members of dominant groups indicated their Whiteness was the core of their credibility, especially with other White people, while others stressed the power and privilege associated with their male gender.

> As a male in a patriarchal society I am going to be given the benefit of the doubt. I will be listened to and I will be thought competent until proven otherwise. (Kevin, White man)

While some women and facilitators of color indicated that their membership in disadvantaged groups could or did increase their credibility in the dialogue, most also reported that their status was challenging to their facilitation. In fact, most target group facilitators worried that negative stereotypes might diminish the credibility they had or wished to have in their groups.

> An example of how my Black identity affects how participants may perceive me can be found in discussions of certain topics. I think people have a tendency to disregard to some extent my statements in favor of affirmative action because of my racial identity. (Jada, Black woman)

> Stereotypes of the "typical Asian" who is quiet, timid and not opinionated will definitely prompt others to look at me as a facilitator and think poorly of me. This stereotype of Asians will hurt me in the way that people might not expect a lot of me, which might then lead me to lower my own standards for myself. (Hoshi, Asian woman)

Here Hoshi reflects our earlier discussion of the internalization of negative stereotypes, as she suggests that potential challenges to her credibility might lead her to "lower my own standards for myself."

Another facilitator expressed the complexity that often comes with a target identity. Both positive and negative reactions to her facilitator credibility were articulated.

> I am very passionate about issues pertain[ing] to race and that has been a blessing and a curse. A blessing because it enables me to introduce a different perspective to the students in my dialogues; a curse because I have to constantly check myself. (Pamela, Black woman)

While it is clear facilitators from both agent and target identity groups thought about issues of credibility, they did so in different ways. Agent group members generally recognized and tried to act on the power associated with their group's status, although sometimes they expressed concern about inappropriately utilizing or expressing their power or privilege. Target group members, on the other hand, tended to have more nuanced and complex issues to deal with in establishing or negotiating their credibility. Some found in their target group membership unique aspects of knowledge that gave them power, while others acknowledged the general lack of entitlement or influence normally associated with their disadvantaged group status. This might affect their own inclinations and confidence and could lead them to over anticipate cautious or negative reactions from dialogue participants and also, as we see later, credibility within their own group.

Establishing Relationships With and/or Educating Members of Facilitators' Own Identity Groups

Critical to effective dialogue facilitation is the ability to communicate and establish relationships within and across group differences and identities. Facilitators from both dominant and subordinate groups expressed the importance of using their identity as a tool for relating closely with and educating others of their own identity group. For some, especially for members of subordinate identity groups, like-identity was a pathway to establishing legitimacy and good working relationships with their like-identity participants. Sometimes, these connections led to special opportunities to educate and support students of their own identity group in the dialogue.

> I feel I will be able to relate to some people of color who have had experiences similar to mine. (Camille, Black woman)

> I feel that being a female I would use that authority to allow women to feel more comfortable to speak out. (Vega, Black woman)

Especially for some White facilitators, their privileged identity conveyed a sense of power and authority to act assertively with other White students. Such authority often was reflected in their own and others' assumptions of the legitimacy of their roles and the ways they thought they could be especially useful in relating and effectively working with other White people.

> Being White affects my facilitating in the sense that I want White participants to realize that race is their issue. It is easier for me to understand when White participants have difficulty talking about being an oppressor because I have been there myself. This causes me to push them outside their comfort zones. (Kerry, White woman)

> My White identity provides me with an "excuse" to trigger participants with loaded questions. For example, I can more easily play devil's advocate with Affirmative Action because I can echo the belief that it does not help me as a White person. (Phil, White man)

Several facilitators—members of both dominant groups and subordinate groups—extended this dynamic as they expressed their desire to educate others by being a good role model of their own identity category.

> I believe it is extremely important for me to be a good role model for the other white students in my group. This includes sharing my personal experiences in relation to my whiteness and background and showing that I am open to hearing other people's

experiences. It also means allowing myself to make mistakes so that students can see that this is OK and can be used as a learning experience. (Trisha, White woman)

I always try to present myself as verbally intelligent. I make conscious efforts to speak correct English and to use words properly. I do this because one of the stereotypes of Black people is that we don't know how to speak English correctly. I am aware of that stereotype and I take every opportunity I can to debunk that belief. (Jada, Black woman)

While the White facilitator's comments spoke to being a role model as a way to show or urge other White students that it was okay to explore openly the content of privilege and oppression, the comments by the facilitator of color suggested that her responsibility was connected, in part, to undoing perceived stereotypes of her group. Because there are few women and people of color in positions of academic or public authority, these students felt a particular responsibility that extended beyond that of a typical facilitator. Even among the women in this sample it was primarily African American women who expressed this link between their dialogue facilitation and the desire to counter oppression. Although some White facilitators wanted to demonstrate that not all Whites are prejudiced, and that they could be strong allies, this additional investment in challenging stereotypes was relatively unique to facilitators with subordinate group identities.

Working With a Co-facilitator With Different Social Identities

As noted previously, every dialogue is co-facilitated by two students, one from each of the identity groups that constitute the primary focus of the intergroup dialogue. Since one of these co-facilitators is from an agent identity group and the other is from a target identity group, issues of their relative credibility and power affect them and must be negotiated both in their collaborative working relationship and in their relationships with dialogue participants.

In some instances, facilitators expressed concern about how they would act to achieve and maintain real "co-ness" with their colleague. Indeed, some of these comments from facilitators of target group identities echoed the prior discussion of the struggle with negative target identity stereotypes.

I think that my identification as a female puts me in a position of less power and control. When my co-facilitator speaks I can't help but feel a bit intimidated by him because I want my opinion to count (too). (Malina, Latina woman)

It (my femaleness) could make my co-facilitator feel like he/she has to take the lead because I'm incapable of doing so. (Hannah, White woman)

In at least one instance, a facilitator with an agent group identity acknowledged how he had acted in ways that reflected the internalization of privilege and dominance.

> Because my co-facilitator is a female there have been times where I have accepted gender roles; my co-facilitator did the "busy work" while I asked the questions. (Roger, White man)

Other facilitators expressed concern not about the relationship between themselves and their "co" but about how dialogue participants would read their own and their co's relative credibility and power.

> My identity as a male affords me privilege. Subsequently, normally my participants expect me to be more in control of the class than my female co-facilitator. (Wem, Asian man)

These facilitators' recognition of the potential pressures on and challenges to their own credibility and power, or to that of their co, is an essential part of the feedback and conversation they must invest with one another in order to be an effective team of instructional leaders. It also highlights some of the intricacies of power and privilege in the intergroup dialogue itself, as facilitators deal with participants' socially constructed images of facilitators of different target and agent identities.

Implications for Facilitator Training and Development

Our inquiry about the significance of social identities for intergroup dialogue facilitators clearly shows that the facilitators struggled with their embeddedness in systems of inequalities and the consequent personal impact on their own realities and on the co-facilitation relationship. Facilitators discussed the influence and power they had as facilitators, exploring the way their influence might be constrained or enhanced by whether they and their participants felt they had credibility as sources of knowledge and leadership. Finally, despite the relatively high level of personal insight and knowledge about prejudice and oppression evident in this group of undergraduate students, several acknowledged the degree to which they accepted or struggled with the imposition of stereotypes about their gender and/or racial groups. Throughout all the reports, we see how these concerns and opportunities are different for facilitators from target groups and from privileged groups.

We turn now to the implications of this inquiry for training and supporting facilitators as intergroup and social justice educators/activists. We propose some avenues for strengthening training and support in the areas of social identity development and facilitation.

Critical Self-Reflective Practice

This inquiry emphasizes the importance of facilitators' continual self-reflective practice that extends their personal understanding of identities to working with others on exploring identities. The reports from facilitators indicate the importance of understanding and undoing both internalized oppression and internalized dominance. To the extent students can recognize the deeply rooted nature of racism, sexism, and other forms of oppression, they may be better able to understand and challenge their own behaviors without the immobilizing feelings of anger, guilt, and despair that lead to evasion of conflict and real connection.

For members of target identity groups, especially facilitators of color and women facilitators, it is important to name and explore internalized oppression, the meaning of negative stereotypes regarding their group memberships, and the degree to which they have incorporated these stereotypes into their own sense of self and their facilitative behaviors. For members of agent identity groups, especially White students, identity development means greater self-awareness of the meaning and implications of their own group memberships and those of target groups, including incorporation of a sense of entitlement and privilege. It also means providing an arena where these facilitators can take the risks of expressing their authentic selves, perhaps even giving offense to others in the expression of internalized dominance so that they may gain awareness of their own behaviors and others' potential responses.

In addition to examining and working with internalized dominance and oppression, the facilitators can explore the complexity of their multiple identities and intersecting positionalities. While some identities may be more salient than others, exploring multiple identities can provide facilitators a way to continue their own learning as well as find a constructive avenue for feelings toward self or others that impede effective facilitation and well-being.

Translating Reflection to Relational Work

The critically self-reflective work that supports and deepens facilitators' own learning has direct implications for the relational work they do with their co-facilitators. Working on these identity issues can strengthen facilitators' ability to operate with more knowledge of their own and others' identity processes and styles of communication and interaction. The in-depth identity deliberations can be introduced in facilitator supervision with co- and other facilitators and can serve to build trusting relationships for effective facilitation. Co-facilitator conversations may focus on sharing self-reflections of internalized dominance, internalized oppression, and multiple identities. Such discussions become even more fruitful when there is focused reflection of the identity implications of interpersonal work styles on structural inequality as well as the implications of structural inequality on identity development. The following issues may potentially arise: how the co-facilitation is structured (e.g., who takes the lead in presenting the agenda, who takes notes, who is more time conscious); how the co-facilitators work with participants within their own identity group and across identity groups; and how the focus on personal and interpersonal affective work is balanced with structural analyses, including which co-facilitator tends to do more of the one or the other tasks. Unpacking these issues not only deepens the co-facilitators' self-knowledge and shared understanding, it can also strengthen their co-facilitator relationship and their work with dialogue participants.

Integrating Reflections and Relationships Into Action

Intergroup dialogues are constructed to simultaneously focus on both content and process issues. Thus, facilitators have the opportunity to utilize their identities in their roles to further the learning of participants. Just as facilitators may bring their reflective work on identities and positionalities into the co-facilitation relationship, they also can bring it into their work with dialogue participants. The more the facilitators have worked on understanding multiple and intersecting positionalities and consequent internalized dominance and oppression, the more effective they can be in supporting the learning of all members in their group and not just those with whom they share a particular social identity. Facilitators can draw on their multiple social identities to find points of connections with students, to empathize with the identity development and learning process rather than to impose a prescriptive understanding of identity.

The facilitators' own reflections along with the explorations of the co-facilitation process can help elucidate the personal and group dynamics that arise in dialogue. The collaborative work—in planning the dialogue, debriefing co-facilitation dynamics, and engaging in in-the-moment interventions—can help increase facilitators' awareness of covert intergroup dynamics that underlie the overt conversation. Being aware of and strategizing ways to effectively surface these dynamics can deepen the dialogues. By naming and revealing dynamics, facilitators can show how macrostructural inequality plays out in the dialogue setting. By engaging participants in "dialogues about the dialogue," facilitators can model how to unpack the dialogue process constructively and encourage participants to reflect on other areas of their campus or community lives.

These reports from intergroup dialogue facilitators highlight some of the important roles social identities play in intergroup conversation, exploration, and interaction—both for themselves and for the dialogue participants whose educational efforts they lead. As evidenced in their words, facilitators continue to remain cognizant of how these identities interact within the context of unequal societal power relationships. Their continuing engagement with social identities provides educators and trainers a foundation for deepening the learning about particular social identities as well as expanding this understanding to other identities, interactions with others, and leadership roles.

References

Blauner, R. (1989). *Black lives, White lives: Three decades of race relations in America.* Berkeley: University of California Press.

Bobo, L., Kluegel, J., & Smith, R. (1997). Laissez-faire racism: The crystallization of a kinder, gentler, anti-Black ideology. In S. Tuch & J. Martin (Eds.), *Racial attitudes in the 1990s* (pp. 14–42). Westport, CT: Praeger.

Bonilla-Silva, E., & Forman, T. (2000). "I am not a racist but . . ." Mapping white college students' racial ideologies in the USA. *Discourse & Society, 11,* 50–85.

Cooley, C. (1922). *Human nature and the social order.* New York: Scribner.

Essed, P. (1991). *Understanding everyday racism.* Newbury Park, CA: Sage.

Feagin, J., & Sikes, W. (1994). *Living with racism.* Boston: Beacon Press.

Fletcher, B. (1999). Internalized oppression: The enemy within. In *Reading book for human relations training* (8th ed., pp. 97–102). Arlington, VA: NTL Institute.

Freire, P. (1970). *Pedagogy of the oppressed.* New York: Seabury.

Hardiman, R., & Jackson, B. (1997). Conceptual foundations for social justice courses. In M. Adams, L. Bell, & P. Griffin (Eds.), *Teaching for diversity and social justice* (pp. 16–29). New York: Routledge.

Kinder, D., & Sears, D. (1981). Prejudice and politics: Symbolic racism versus racial threats to the good life. *Journal of Personality and Social Psychology, 40,* 414–431.

McConahay, J. (1983). Modern racism, ambivalence and the modern racism scale. In J. Dovidio & S. Gaertner (Eds.), *Prejudice, discrimination and racism* (pp. 91–126). New York: Academic Press.

McKinney, K. (2005). *Being white: Stories of race and racism.* New York: Routledge.

Tappan, M. (2006). Reframing internalized oppression and internalized domination: From the psychological to the sociocultural. *Teachers College Record, 108*(10), 2115–2144.

Tatum, B. (2003). *"Why are all the Black kids sitting together in the cafeteria?" And other conversations about race.* New York: Basic Books.

12

NOT *FOR* OTHERS, BUT *WITH* OTHERS *FOR ALL OF US*

Weaving Relationships, Co-creating Spaces of Justice

Biren (Ratnesh) A. Nagda, Norma Timbang,
Nichola G. Fulmer, and Thai Hung V. Tran

we come to this space from many places
some continuing a life long journey
others on a journey just begun
some with transformative epiphanies
others despite hurtful experiences
some with hopes of creating the same transformations for others
others out of a sense of social responsibility

we come from many places,
we bring our bodies, minds and hearts
we come with our desires, fears, visions . . .
we all still come
we all still bring what we can
we come together as a gathering

in this place, we make commitments to us
from spaces inside ourselves
to spaces we share together
to spaces outside of ourselves with others not here

from the inner space, i commit to
listening carefully to each of us
sharing myself to deepen, energize, inspire dialogue
taking risks, stepping out of my comfort zone

in the space that we share, we commit to
    making our feelings known to those around us
    being supportive and patient
    cultivating safety by listening, respecting and not expecting
    building inclusion by being patient, encouraging and open
    taking risks by being honest, vulnerable and courageous
    owning this process so that we may together nurture seeds of understanding,
        critical reflection and powerful relating

in joining the inner space to the space that we share, we commit to
    being open to growing and unpacking difficult questions
    viewing individuals not as representatives of their groups
    educating ourselves and learning from others
    engaging ourselves about oppressions occurring in our midst
    confronting conflict over oppressive conditions head on
    opening ourselves to knowledge, growth and change in service to others and
        ourselves

here, we bring our many gifts
    words and poems
    heart and silent connecting
    soul, crystals and clarity
    music, drums, dance
    presence and commitment

now, we share and relish
    the splendor of each others' gifts
    the interweaving of our experiences and lives
    the pregnancy of the space that we share
    the birth of a new wholeness

here, we pursue our commitments and dreams
    to create
    to witness the possibilities of change
    to be the change we wish for others

now, we struggle
    to keep pace with each other
    to pay attention to issues arising among us
    in some places we do well, in others we do not
    yet, even through those we hope to learn

here, we grow the space together
now, we let the questions and answers act as dancing figures
    circling around
    lifting each other to ever more elaborate performance

> moving always in rhythm
> watching the dance with care and attention
> trying not to force the steps or to let them run wild
>
> we enter the dance floor, this space, as a gathering of individuals
> we share this space now as a beloved community
> as we continue on our shared and separate journeys
> we carry this beloved community within each of us, a dance inside of us . . .

"Gathering . . . To Grow a Beloved Community"
—Biren (Ratnesh) A. Nagda

A fundamental and distinguishing quality of intergroup dialogue is that it is a co-facilitated group experience with at least two facilitators representing the focal identities in the dialogue. As other chapters have conveyed, intergroup dialogue facilitators "wear many hats"—establishing an effective climate, choosing appropriate roles, using different engagement methods, organizing discussions, and working with individual and group dynamics (Griffin & Ouellett, 2007). They also "walk the fine lines" between participant–facilitator, co-learner–role model, and guide–change agent (Nagda, Zúñiga, & Sevig, 1995). These are usually conceived of as individual roles and responsibilities. We extend this knowledge base to understanding more about co-facilitation, especially how facilitators conceive of their role and relationships with each other and students in their groups.

In this chapter, we first provide the theoretical context for the ways power may be conceived of in relationships. We focus on the relational engagement of facilitators and what that means for their deepened learning about alliances, and how these alliances manifest in work with their co-facilitators, their students, and themselves. We conclude with an interweaving of two poems, written separately by a pair of co-facilitators, to capture their intertwined journeys and conjoined commitments to social justice.

Engaging the Relational Power in Intergroup Dialogue Facilitation

In the introductory chapter, we emphasized the importance of relationships as a nexus of analysis and a catalyst for change. Beverly Tatum (2007), in writing about cross-racial friendships, shares our emphasis:

> Relationships across lines of difference are essential for the possibility of social transformation. Change is needed. None of us can make change alone. Genuine friendship leads to caring concern. Caring concern leads to action. And we need to take our action from a position of strength that comes from self-knowledge and social awareness. (p. 100)

We have also stressed the importance of both the dialogic relationship building and the critical analysis and action dimensions of a critical-dialogic approach to intergroup dialogue (Nagda & Gurin, 2007). Learners are encouraged to use a power analysis to read structures, policies, and situations with power being understood in terms of relations of domination and subordination (McMahon & Portelli, 2004). Power-over, signifying a hierarchy of advantaged and disadvantaged, characterizes these relationships. Increasing awareness of social identities and social inequalities is understood to motivate learners to engage in changing and challenging these differentials.

While the power-over analysis is important, we also conceive of other forms of power—power-with (Surrey, 1987) and power-within (Starhawk, 1987)—that are geared toward empowerment, equality, and social justice, or what Jean Baker Miller (1982) calls "agency-in-community" as contrasted with "self-separate-from-community." Kreisberg (1992) elaborates,

> Power-with is manifest in relationships of co-agency. These relationships are characterized by people finding ways to satisfy their desires and to fulfill their interests without imposing on one another. The relationship of co-agency is one in which there is equality: situations in which individuals and groups fulfill their desires by acting together. It is jointly developing capacity. The possibility of power-with lies in the reality of human interconnections within communities. (pp. 85–86)

In intergroup dialogue, we attend to strengthening intergroup relationships within the context of identities and inequalities as a catalyst for personal and social change.

The co-facilitation relationship in particular represents the shared space in which to actualize the potential of power-with and power-within. Co-facilitating intergroup dialogues is an avenue to engage in alliance building and action—promoting understanding of identity, inequality, and social justice—by working intensively in intergroup collaboration teams. The co-facilitation relationship involves sustained engagement across different social identities and social positions, harnessing of the different and shared strengths and responsibilities, and commitment to a continual learning process around a specific joint endeavor to advance social justice.

Context and Method of Inquiry

This chapter is based on training senior undergraduate facilitators in a School of Social Work through a two-quarter sequence of courses. The first course focuses on the theory and practice of intergroup dialogue facilitation—dialogic communication and critical analyses integrated with delivery of educational modules and group facilitation skills (Nagda et al., 2001). Students practice facilitation in small (3–5 persons) and larger (10–12) groups. The second course parallels actual facilitation and provides additional skill building and supervision.

The two primary authors—Nagda and Timbang—analyzed papers from one cohort of students who had completed the initial training course and the supervised facilitation practicum. At the beginning of the two-course sequence, all students conducted a "Taping Project," a self-interview using a protocol to audiotape their responses (adapted from Tatum, 1992, and Garcia & Van Soest, 1997). We asked the students to turn in their audio recordings for safekeeping and returned them toward the end of the first quarter. We assured them that we would not listen to these tapes. At the end of the first quarter, the facilitators listened to their tapes to reflect on their learning. At the end of the second quarter, the facilitators wrote a paper reflecting on their overall learning—from the taping assignment and paper at the end of the first quarter, to their actual facilitation experience. Our inquiry was focused on the two papers, not the tapes. The two secondary authors—Fulmer and Tran—were student co-facilitators from a different cohort than the ones whose papers we read. Independently, they each wrote poems as part of their final paper at the end of two quarters. We include their poems to signify the meaning generated for them as part of the dialogue experience that parallels our focus on relationships in intergroup dialogue and co-facilitation.

We paid particular attention to how facilitators wrote about learning in relation to their co-facilitators and students in their dialogue groups. We also looked for ways they talked about the complexity of their own identities, and how that manifested in their relationships with others. The co-facilitation relationship and the collaborative work served as an important crucible for deepened learning. We discuss our findings along the following four major themes.

Re(de)fining Understanding of Alliances

Many social justice educators and practitioners consider alliance building one of the prime outcomes of their efforts and an effective mechanism for social change (Adams, Bell, & Griffin, 2007; Zúñiga, Nagda, Chesler, & Cytron-Walker, 2007). Most of the facilitators' previous learning and consciousness raising had emphasized allies as individuals committed to social justice and speaking out against injustices. Facilitators shared their own nuanced learning about alliances through the deepened relational engagement with the cohort of facilitators, their co-facilitators, and with students.

> I am energized to begin working in a co-facilitator role because of the support built into that relationship. A lot of the speaking out and action for social justice I have taken in my personal and professional life has been by me alone. I look forward to being able to work together with someone who has a similar passion and commitment. . . . too often I am calling out others and do not have anyone calling me out on a consistent basis. As much as I need to challenge myself, I also want to be challenged by others. (White woman)

The facilitator clearly recognizes the significance of the co-facilitation relationship as a place of continued empowerment.

Through the courses, facilitators redefined their understanding of what it meant to be in alliance for social justice. While many facilitators continue to use the language of "being an ally," as will be evident in their quotes throughout the chapter, its meaning changed for them. For example, a facilitator wrote about her shift from seeing an ally as someone who primarily listened to others to someone who is also on a journey of learning about identities with others:

> I would consider changing my response to what it takes to be a good ally in social justice work. I talked a lot about the importance of being a good listener, but I've since realized just how complex being a good ally really is. [It] takes a lot of self-discovery and understanding our own multiple social identities, . . . involves knowing yourself and supporting each other with trust and validation. (Native American White woman)

Another facilitator shared a shift in her understanding from unidimensional concern for equality for all to a multidimensional person who acts toward social change as well as enhances social relations both across and within racial lines:

> In the self-interview, I had difficulty articulating what good allies look like. . . . I had described an ally as someone who is willing to put effort towards creating change for equality of all groups, that's all. Now I feel an ally can be an ally at different levels, such as, an active social-change agent, a person who is willing to speak out against racism and oppression even in the smallest situation (like a racial joke), . . . someone who demonstrates through their own life the value of embracing diversity and teaches others by individual example of how to respect differences. (Latina woman)

Yet another facilitator wrote about the transformation in her understanding of racism, and thus shifting her stance of ally-ship as acting on behalf of others to realizing agency-in-community:

> My story changed dramatically when I realized that I am influenced greatly by racism. My position of dominance doesn't mean that I have been unaffected, or positively affected by racism. I do have societal privilege and power as a White person, but I also have a limited life experience, and my vision of the world is narrowed and incomplete. I have a flawed relationship with myself. These are all parts of being dominant too. By recognizing this, I am no longer fighting racism from a position where I am fighting a problem for someone else, but rather I am fixing it for all people, including myself. Personalizing my experiences as a dominant person in the scope of racism was huge. It changed the entire lens through which I view racism and how I approach fighting it. (White woman)

The theme of collaborative agency and the intertwined nature of personal and social change resonated with others:

> The biggest piece of advice I can offer to future facilitators is to commit yourself fully to this process of personal change and doing anti-racist work with others. This is not just about creating change for others but about changing yourself as you learn about the impact of oppression and privilege on your own life. These two processes are deeply intertwined, and it is because of that union that this will be both incredibly challenging and rewarding. It is also the start, or the continuance, of a life-long journey, and it is helpful to view this experience not as a one-time event but as a piece of a larger puzzle that we all must work together to assemble. (White woman)

With this shifting emphasis on *relations-defining-alliances* in contrast to *actions-defining-allies*, facilitators also became much more in tune with the affective elements of alliances. Reflecting on their original recording, they say,

> The most significant change would be the use of the word "support." I am surprised that I did not use that word even once. . . . Today that is my number one requirement. (White woman)

> In my responses to the ally questions in the interview guide, I never even mentioned the word "trust." I found trust to be a crucial element in alliance building. (Latina woman)

Facilitators redefined allies as individuals taking action against injustices to an emphasis on building relationships of authenticity, mutual support, and challenge in working together for social justice. In essence, they shifted their understanding from *being an ally* to *being in alliance,* and perhaps more fundamentally from facilitating to *co-*facilitating.

Deepening Relations: Care and Conflict in Co-facilitation

The affective reframing of alliances made facilitators aware of the importance of actively building relationships and how easy it may be to take relationships for granted, especially when co-facilitators know each other. One facilitator shared knowing her co-facilitator prior to the course and feeling "so confident that [he] and I would make such a great team, that we really did not talk about the relationship at all." Tatum (2007) titled her essay "What Kind of Friendship Is That?" to grapple specifically with the distinction between superficial acquaintances and genuine cross-racial friendships and, in our case, alliances. She cites authenticity and mutuality as core elements of genuine relationships, much like the facilitators who quickly realized the necessity to strengthen their co-facilitation teams through honesty, support, vulnerability, and trust:

> Being honest and vulnerable with your co-facilitator is very important as it is a great way to model for the group and to move closer to your co-facilitator. (African American woman)

> Another answer that would be different is the importance of supporting and being supported by my co-facilitator ... of being able to trust, and support each other.... The dynamics that go into co-facilitation are hugely important. (White woman)

Engaging and Changing Co-facilitation Dynamics

Developing these caring relationships should not, however, be conceived of as devoid of difficulties. Bernice Johnson Reagon (1995), in her classic essay "Coalition Politics," says that coalitions or alliances are not home spaces; they are not necessarily comfortable or safe. These can be uncomfortable spaces because of both the newness and the challenge to be in relation to others. "Most of the time you feel threatened to the core and if you don't, you're not really doing no coalescing" (p. 541). Thus, authenticity in deeper alliance building across differences must grapple openly with issues of identity and inequality as uncomfortable as it may be (Tatum, 2007). For co-facilitators, some of the strengthening of their alliance came through difficult experiences, both within their teams and in the dialogue groups. One such challenge had to do with a replaying of dominant-subordinate patterns in facilitation with the group:

> [My co-facilitator] was doing more of the calling out and I was the more nurturing one. [She] was focused on the mechanics and I was focused on the emotions. . . . We were playing out internalized domination and internalized oppression within our own team! We need to focus on sharing those roles. I need to do more calling out and she needs to do more connecting to emotions. . . . By mid-quarter, the group was actually noticing the very same thing, as they wrote their comments on their evaluations of our team. This was especially difficult for me to hear because in many of our dialogues, White privilege was playing out. As a person of color, I wanted to be calling out too, especially with *speaking* from my experiences *as* a person of color; I wanted people to hear that and I wasn't sure that they were. . . . I challenged myself to speak from that place, not only for the benefit of the group but for my benefit as well. (African American woman)

> [My co-facilitator] shared with me that she felt herself step into the "touchy feely" role more than she wanted. She felt pressure as the facilitator of color to be the one reaching out emotionally, and we talked about how I felt the pressure to be tough and call out the dynamics. Through mutual support, we helped each other overcome these roles [in] breaking down the typical "White facilitator" and "facilitator of color" roles. (White woman)

These co-facilitators engaged in openly acknowledging and dialoguing about these dynamics to *jointly* problem solve. As is evident, breaking down this dichotomization of roles was important to harness both the collective agency of the co-facilitation team and the individual agency to name oppressive dynamics. While many White facilitators talked about being able to connect with other White participants through their stories, it is important to consider the words of the facilitator of color. In essence, "*speaking* from my experiences *as* a person of color" gives her agency and not to be spoken for or on behalf of. Instead of the intended experience of alliance, she experienced not being able to call out or challenge White privilege as diminishing her agency and thus reproducing White privilege in the co-facilitation work.

Engaging Intersectionality and Multiple Identities

Facilitators also wrote about changing their frames of reference; they moved from recognizing themselves as *only* defined by their positions of dominance *or* subordination to understanding the *intersectionality* of their identities. Owning intersectionality of both positions of privilege *and* subordination appears to have been transformative and directly affected their understanding of productive alliances:

> My own story has changed dramatically. It has been a process of realizing that in order to be an ally to oppressed peoples I must first be an ally to myself and commit to learning about my own oppression. I cannot be truly effective in this work until I can learn to deal with the things that have the power to silence me. I learned this the hard way. When my own oppression got triggered I was left speechless while my co-facilitator waited for me to confront racism. (White woman)

For other facilitation teams, issues emergent in the dialogue groups drove home the lessons of intersectionality. One team, an African American woman and a White woman, talked about how homophobia among their group members challenged them to look at their opposite positionalities:

> Dealing with [blatant homophobia/heterosexism] has been very confusing to me.... One of the most difficult things to work through was dealing with homophobia from the women of color in our group. It was such a struggle for me to think of how I can be an ally to them as a White woman even though I felt attacked by them as a queer woman. This is still an issue that creates a lot of anxiety in me. (White woman)

Through the alliance developing as co-facilitators, her co-facilitator shared this challenge with her:

> There were some very difficult moments.... We were dealing with so much homophobia in our group.... There were many dialogues where the tension between Christianity, which is a very dominant group in our society and a group that I am a part of, and heterosexism and homophobia came up. I had such a struggle internally with these conversations, because I was so disgusted with what I was hearing. It was also hard for me because I didn't want those who were Christians in my group to think that I was denying my faith because I didn't have the same views as them regarding sexual orientation. Even as I tried to call people out in dialogues regarding Christianity being an oppressor in society even today, I got nothing but resistance from many people. This was so disheartening for me because I was not trying to attack anyone, but just bring up some new information to think about, as well as support my co-facilitator. At the same time, I wasn't going to let people off easy, as hard as that was. (African American woman)

While the White co-facilitator experienced homophobia as a direct threat to her being and identity as a queer woman, the African American facilitator found challenging homophobia a potential threat from others to her Christianity. Yet, it pushed her to grapple with the intersectionality of her identities and appreciate her own agency.

> It changed my story. . . . I was speaking from a place of dominance, as I so often speak out of my oppression, failing to see those places of dominance I have as well. It caused me to think about my other places of dominance, like being able-bodied, and how I can become an ally to people in other oppressed groups. It was not that I have never thought about these things before. It was just that I had a chance to actually call out oppression with a pretty tough group, and I felt gratification in doing that. It gave me courage to continue to do this work. (African American woman)

Another facilitator shared his early struggles to confront his own heterosexual socialization into gender roles and gendered hierarchy, and the uncertainties about how he should interact with a White lesbian co-facilitator. Later, he wrote about being angry about the blatant homophobic intolerance in the larger community with anti-gay speakers and engaging in a dialogue with his co-facilitator.

> I became upset by the fact that some guy was coming to my city and getting people angry and riled up about same-sex marriage. . . . As [my co-facilitator] told me about the children that were screaming "You're sinners" and "You're going to hell," I grew so angry that goose bumps rose on my arms. (Latino man)

The growth from uncertainty and anxiety to an empathetic anger was borne out of the close collaboration between them. As she struggled to confront her own Whiteness, he confronted his own maleness, heterosexuality, and homophobia. He acknowledged his own transformation:

> When I was at [my co-facilitator's] wedding ceremony I got goose bumps again. But it was different. I kept on saying to myself, "This is what it is all about." . . . They looked so happy, so in love. . . . Technically they were already married but celebrating their union with family and friends is a big thing. I felt very lucky to have been a part of their big day, to be her friend. (Latino man)

While they were facilitating interracial/interethnic dialogues, the co-facilitators' deeper engagement and meaningful connectivity appears to have helped expand the scope and care of their social justice agency inside and outside the dialogues.

The relational understanding of being in alliance pays special attention to the collective empowerment of all parties, and not a reproduction of power inequalities in striving toward justice. The facilitators' reflections show how their understanding of social justice activism shifted in many ways. They come to appreciate not just being individual or solo activists but being activists in collaboration. They see the value of affective connecting as an important part of alliances as opposed to solely action-based alliances. At the same time, they do not take for granted that affective relations alone are equivalent to alliances, but that actively strengthening and deepening the relations are purposeful toward greater personal and social change.

Deepening Understanding of Self-in-Relation

In structures of domination and subordination, relationships are marred not only by group-based inequalities, intergroup hostilities, and interpersonal distrust, but also by the impact on individuals' sense of self. As articulated by a facilitator earlier, the journey toward social change is intertwined with personal change. Through the preparation courses and actual co-facilitating, facilitators continued to deepen their understanding of self-in-relation to others and the larger society.

Recognizing Internalized Oppression and Internalized Domination

To support the facilitators' continued journey toward change, we empha-sized critical self-reflection of the interconnected nature of structural racism with internalized dominance and internalized oppression. Some students of color wrote about understanding the complexity of racism and the need to understand both the personalized impact of internalized oppression and the diversity of experiences among people of color.

> I became aware of how common the issue of internalized oppression is for people of color ... how embedded it is within us. Before, I attributed my feelings of inferiority to my own personal flaw. To hear from other students of color their feelings of internalized oppression was so emotionally intense for me. (Latina woman)

A White woman facilitator shared her own growing awareness of patri-archy and its impact on her. Her commitment to antiracism was unques-tioned; yet in the class she had shared how she felt stuck in progressing toward redefining herself as an antiracist activist.

> My main challenge was looking at my internalized oppression, it was difficult to realize that it was getting in the way of my being an effective facilitator. There was a strength that came from this, which was the ability to share my strug-gle, and to help others who may be experiencing the same kind of struggle. (White woman)

A White male facilitator revealed how new the experience of sharing in intergroup dialogue was for him, both because of his own life experiences and because he was the only White man in the class:

> I live in a box that has been white male. I could see others around me who were different than me, I just never allowed them into my box and I never ventured out. . . . My willingness to open myself up to others has greatly changed. . . . Communicating in this open space has been huge for me. I don't do this with anyone, and to share like I have done with this group has been a gigantic step for me. I have struggled with being the only White male in our class and trying to keep an open mind and an open heart. I have tried to not personalize any feedback relating to my social identity, but still struggle with that. I realize it is vital that I continue to work on these things. (White man)

Moving Through Internalized Oppression and Internalized Domination

Grappling honestly with internalized domination and internalized oppression enables facilitators to personalize the impact of structural inequalities on themselves and contextualize their previous ways of being in patterns of domination and subordination, including "blocks to openness" or "walls" that hindered deeper relating.

> [I wanted to] bring more heart and feeling into this work. Challenging myself to do this was hard, because of the privilege I have to avoid uncomfortability and express myself with cognition rather than with emotion. In my tape I talked about "not being as open with my feelings as I should be," but I didn't connect this to privilege. I did identify fear as one of the primary blockers to my openness. Sharing my emotions was one of the most significant ways I could encourage other White students in the group to open up. . . . It was critical for me to realize that giving in to my fear of sharing emotion was not only a way for me to act out my privilege, but it was also a way that I would be showing other White students that this is acceptable. . . . [It] was a way that I modeled positive ally behavior. (White woman)

> I was able to [be an effective ally] by being aware of any walls that I was building. I was able to be honest with [my co-facilitator] . . . our partnership became stronger as I knew that she always had my back, and I had hers. (African American woman)

Facilitators' critical self-reflections of internalized oppression and internalized dominance were directly related to how they moved beyond feeling immobilized in the realizations to building deeper relationships with each other and with students in their groups, especially others who were similarly positioned as they were in systems of inequalities.

> I realized that I needed to start with self-examination of how I might be helpful and why I might have the ability to help. . . . I remember this revelation coming to me

> in a personal dialogue [about our internalized oppression] with another member of
> my own ethnic group. . . . I realized how I had not been as full a supporting ally as
> I could be. (Latina woman)

> As I now face my areas of internalized dominance, I feel a new sense of purpose and
> encouragement. . . . Having a fuller understanding has further motivated me to be an
> ally and use my dominant positionalities as a source of commonality in challenging
> others with those same positionalities, especially other White people. . . . As I move
> forward, I challenge myself not to get stuck in feelings of guilt or shame but instead
> to connect with the root of those feelings and use that to spur my energy for personal
> and social change. (White woman)

The facilitators' personal reflections and dialogues with other facilitators appear to destigmatize internalized oppression and internalized domination as personality weaknesses and sources of shame and guilt. At the same time, they see their new realizations not simply as personally liberating, but as socially connecting with others like them and different from them to build more power-within and power-with to affect social injustices.

Deepening Social Justice Practice

Co-facilitators' new and refined understandings of alliances, power-with, and agency-in-community are also influenced by their actual co-facilitation work. We found their learning in facilitating dialogues to resemble their learning in co-facilitation relationships described earlier.

Re(de)fining Leadership

Facilitators' new understanding of *being in alliance* parallels their reconceptualization of their roles as change agents or leaders.

> [I] see my role as creating a climate for change, as opposed to changing the individual.
> When I am faced with the challenge of changing another human being the task seems
> so daunting that all hope of being gentle goes right out the window. However, when
> I am faced with the challenge of creating a "climate" there is no other response than
> to be gentle and loving. (White woman)

> As a leader I am expected to know the answers and lead the group to solutions
> around racism. This is not my job as a facilitator. Rather, it is to help students see
> the issues in different ways to establish better understanding. Then, the student can
> decide for himself/herself what action he/she is prepared to do. (White woman)

For both facilitators, the shift from an authoritarian, power-over leadership to a more connective leadership was profound. Not only was this a conceptual shift, but it was evident in relational ways of being with participants.

> The facilitation experience made me observe as opposed to just seeing, engage in active listening and not just hearing, more consciously validate people's experiences instead of minimizing them. (South Asian woman)

Strengthening Facilitative Agency: Becoming Facilitator-Participants

Facilitators strived to balance their roles as facilitator-participants and discovered ways of participating more authentically. A facilitator shared that being part of the group also meant continuing her learning journey and deepening her engagement:

> I have learned that there are definitely skills involved in being an intergroup dialogue facilitator—validating, probing, making connections—but those skills mean nothing in the absence of a meaningful and challenging personal journey. The times I was most "effective" as a facilitator were the times when I was fully engaged and participating in the dialogue on a personal level, holding myself accountable and examining and acknowledging my White privilege with the group. (White woman)

For another facilitator, the personal journey was coming to understand how his masculinity made it difficult for him to stay present with the emotionality in the dialogues:

> I struggled with sitting in discomfort and not rushing to problem solve, divert topics, or some other tactic to change the feeling in the room (actually in me). It was hard to sit with emotional topics.... This has to do with my social identity. It's not that I can't do it or that I don't want to do it, I just think I was conditioned to not go there, and rather, as a man, to take charge and change it or control it. I can now see how damaging this can be to myself and to others. (Native American man)

Working with the discomfort also involves taking risks and being vulnerable which may challenge prospective facilitators' notion of a leader as *apart* from the group. Rather, they see their own sharing as modeling for participants how to engage in meaningful dialogue through an exchange:

> Taking the risk to share of myself as well as taking risks to probe a participant deeper will enable me to extend my learning from the students in my dialogue group.... Even as a facilitator, I must take responsibility in also sharing in order to learn what others have to say about my thoughts. (Latina woman)

Strengthening Facilitative Agency: Challenging Oneself and Connecting With Others

The theme of working *with* students does not forsake the responsibility that facilitators hold to sustain and deepen the dialogue. Facilitators shared how they came to understand the dilemma of partnering with students, yet challenging students to learn honestly about issues of identity and inequality. The more connective role involved a shift in how facilitators saw the importance of knowledge and storytelling in dialogues, especially bringing their lived experiences as an asset to facilitation.

> Another important aspect of my learning has to do with going with my gut and sharing from my heart. In the beginning of the dialogues, I felt that I thought too much about what I said.... I would think about how what I said was perceived and how especially White students would take it. It really made a difference for me to let go of that as the weeks went on. (African American woman)

In a way, the African American woman facilitator was undoing her own fear connected, as she wrote later, to internalized oppression.

The importance of speaking more heartfully was not only for the facilitators' own learning and growth but directly related to building meaningful relationships with participants through purposeful sharing of stories.

> I was encouraged to talk from my experiences when talking about things like Affirmative Action, internalized oppression and taking action. I was challenged to [share] how I have *come* to learn about privilege, alliances and oppression, and how they are "embodied" in myself [instead of just regurgitating what I had learned].... I feel like there was no better way to share my learning in dialogues.... (African American woman)

> When reading my [first] paper, I feel like I was still "in my head" when trying to own my White experiences. I hadn't pushed myself hard to speak the truth about my own experiences of White privilege.... In order to truly own my experiences as a privileged White person, I had to model sharing my own stories.... I feel like it was [during facilitation] that changed my whole relationship with my stories.... I felt a new sense of responsibility in group as a facilitator. (White woman)

For both these facilitators, owning and embodying their stories fostered greater empowerment in the dialogues.

Another facilitator shared how the co-facilitation partnership provided the context for risk taking; it allowed them as a team to balance the facilitator-participant roles and to "be open and honest about my emotions and experiences." She described a specific incident where she saw her new commitments and risk taking challenge not only the students in her group but her own fears to come to life:

> Hearing the "n" word used so carelessly by a White person [in a story she was telling] struck a very deep emotion inside me. At first I did not know how to respond. In the past I might have just kept quiet and let my feelings stay silent within me. Then I realized that I needed to let my emotions do the talking. I had never before spoken so freely from my heart in a group like that.... Even now thinking about that I have tears in my eyes because it was the first time I think I really let go of both my fear of sharing intense emotion and my privilege to keep silent. (White woman)

The facilitators' shifting conceptions of leadership and commitments to deepened, mindful, heartful, and embodied engagement also show new ways of experiencing social justice agency. Be it through undoing their internalized oppression or internalized domination, giving voice to their own stories to connect with participants, or taking risks to interrupt remarks and dynamics, facilitators availed themselves of power-within to forge power-with for social and personal change.

In conclusion, the facilitators' reflections that we have shared by no means convey an exhaustive picture of what happens in the actuality of co-facilitation. But they do show what is possible in the relational power of co-facilitating intergroup dialogues. The fundamental shift from *being an ally* to *being in alliance* emphasizes relational agency for action: power-with and co-agency to work *with* and not *for* others, power-within to connect personal *and* social change for increased agency, and *productive* power-over to foster environments for deepened learning and relating across differences. Tatum (2007) cites Miller's (1986) work on constructive relational connections: when relationships are marked by authenticity, mutuality, and social transformation, interactants experience five things—increased zest, a greater sense of empowerment, greater self-knowledge, increased self-worth, and a desire for more connection. These are exactly the sentiments that facilitators wrote in concluding their reflections.

> Words can't truly describe how grateful I am for this learning and my personal growth that has made me feel stronger as an African American woman, I feel empowered and more complete.... I have found my voice, a sense of peace and in essence I have found myself. (African American woman)

The relationship that formed between [my co-facilitator] and I had a tremendous impact on my evolution as a co-facilitator, colleague, intern, brother, son, uncle, and friend. . . . I begin to smile because of the person that I am becoming. (Latino man)

I have changed in my [self-]confidence. I no longer wonder about whether or not I will be accepted. I have had several amazing experiences where I felt accepted by people of color on a more intimate level than I have ever experienced. . . . If I am willing to take a long hard look at myself, then perhaps I will be able to see you better. (White woman)

I will continue to look for ways to name things with love, ways that I can continue to educate myself, and ways to connect with others who are active—or want to be—in the work. (Native American man)

The power-with in relationships that the facilitators experienced through intergroup dialogue made an indelible impact on them. In the pursuit of social justice, they see themselves inextricably related to others; their sense of self is intertwined with their relations to others and their *joint* social justice agency. We thus end this chapter with the voices of two co-facilitators, Tran and Fulmer, who each wrote an original poem as part of their final reflections after facilitating intergroup dialogues. We wove the two poems to embrace the truly interconnected nature of their insights, separate yet together, independent yet interdependent.

i (we) have come to know the true reality
not by coincidence
but through deliberate
reflection, engagement, and action
with authenticity, courage, and will power

what do i owe, to myself
to engage in intergroup dialogues?
what comes from the expenditure of:
self-awareness through an increased awareness,
a result of committing to open dialogues
history, truth retold and told
society, unbound and free
personal truths, discovered and redefined

i (we) made my (our) decision!
to change and renew my (our) lens,
to store my (our) blanket(s) of hopelessness and fear,
to search and reach for
hopefulness, empowerment, and compassion

what do i owe?
my entire being
personal truths spoken and held,
yours and mine
my soul of identities
spun undone
woven together
me.
you.
us. together. us, together
supporting our uniqueness, our sameness

i (we) made my (our) decision!
to travel on the road that is less traveled
i am (we are) affected, touched, and appreciative by
those with me (us) and around me (us)
others are moved by me (us)
we are all
traveling together
i (we) made my (our) decision!
not to stop
not to slow down
not to lose direction
not to turn around

what do i owe it to myself?
what do i owe it to you?
our future children, our past parents
what do i owe it to myself?
what do i owe it to you?
to us?
to what was and could have been,
and what we will create

though i (we) may have failed in the past
i (we) will not let myself (ourselves) crumble
instead, i (we) will use it and
turn it into strength
i (we) will rise!
there is an anchor for
my (our) soul and my (our) feelings
there is an anchor for
my (our) actions and battles
i (we) will rise!

i am (we are) the difference!
i am (we are) determined!

what do we *not* owe to intergroup dialogue?
humanity,
yours and mine.
dignity,
yours and mine.
love and compassion,
yours and mine.

Thai Hung V. Tran, 2009   Nichola G. Fulmer, 2009

References

Adams, M., Bell, L. A., & Griffin, P. (2007). *Teaching for diversity and social justice.* New York: Routledge.

Garcia, B., & Van Soest, D. (1997). Changing perceptions of diversity and oppression: MSW students discuss the effects of a required course. *Journal of Social Work Education, 33*(1), 119–129.

Griffin, P., & Ouellett, M. L. (2007). Facilitating social justice education courses. In M. Adams, L. Bell, & P. Griffin (Eds.), *Teaching for diversity and social justice: A sourcebook* (pp. 89–113). New York: Routledge.

Kreisberg, S. (1992). *Transforming power: Domination, empowerment and education.* Albany, NY: SUNY Press.

McMahon, B., & Portelli, J. (2004). Engagement for what? Beyond popular discourses of student engagement. *Leadership and Policy in Schools, 3*(1), 59–76.

Miller, J. B. (1982). *Women and power. Work in progress #82–01.* Wellesley, MA: Stone Center Working Paper Series.

Miller, J. B. (1986). *What do we mean by relationships?* Paper presented at a Stone Center Colloquium, Wellesley College, Massachusetts.

Nagda, B. A., & Gurin, P. (2007). Intergroup Dialogue: A critical-dialogic approach to learning about difference, inequality and social justice. *New Directions for Teaching and Learning,* 111, 35–45.

Nagda, B. A., Harding, S., Moise-Swanson, D., Balassone, M. L., Spearmon, M., & de Mello, S. (2001). Intergroup dialogue, education and action: Innovations at the University of Washington School of Social Work. In D. Schoem & S. Hurtado (Eds.), *Intergroup Dialogue: Deliberative democracy in school, college, community, and workplace* (pp. 115–134). Ann Arbor, MI: University of Michigan Press.

Nagda, B. A., Zúñiga, X., & Sevig, T. D. (1995). Bridging differences through peer-facilitated intergroup dialogues. In S. Hatcher (Ed.), *Peer programs on a college campus: Theory, training and 'voice of the peers'* (pp. 378–414). San Jose, CA: Resources Publications.

Reagon, B. J. (1995). Coalition politics: Turning the century. In M. L. Andersen & P. H. Collins (Eds.), *Race, class and gender: An anthology* (2nd ed., pp. 540–546). Belmont, CA: Wadsworth.

Starhawk. (1987). *Truth or dare*. San Francisco: Harper & Row.

Surrey, J. L. (1987). *Relationship and empowerment. Work in progress*. Wellesley, MA: Stone Center Working Paper Series.

Tatum, B. D. (1992). Talking about race, learning about racism: The application of racial identity development theory in the classroom. *Harvard Educational Review, 62*(1), 1–24.

Tatum, B. D. (2007). *Can we talk about race?: And other conversations in an era of school resegregation*. Boston: Beacon Press.

Zúñiga, X., Nagda, B. A., Chesler, M., & Cytron-Walker, A. (2007). *Intergroup dialogues in higher education: Meaningful learning about social justice*. San Francisco: Jossey-Bass.

13

CHANGING FACILITATORS, FACILITATING CHANGE

The Lives of Intergroup Dialogue Facilitators Post-College

Carolyn Vasques-Scalera

T here is a wealth of research on the positive impact of intergroup dialogues on both the cognitive and social development of student participants as well as on the quality of campus life (Gurin, Dey, Hurtado, & Gurin, 2002; Gurin, Nagda, & Lopez, 2004; Nagda & Zúñiga, 2003; Nagda, Gurin, & Lopez, 2003; Nagda, Kim, & Truelove, 2004; Zúñiga, Nagda, Sevig, Thompson, & Dey, 1995; Zúñiga, Vasques, Nagda, & Sevig, 1997; Zúñiga, Vasques, Sevig, & Nagda, 1996; Zúñiga, Vasques, & Thompson, 1996; Zúñiga, Williams, & Berger, 2005). But until now, little, if any, research has examined either the experiences of peer facilitators (those students trained to co-facilitate intergroup dialogues) or the long-term impacts of intergroup dialogue on students once they leave the university. Beyond the role they play in facilitating learning, facilitators themselves engage in meaningful reflection and learning as part of their training for, and eventual facilitation of, intergroup dialogues. For a fuller description of the role of peer facilitators, see chapter 2 of this volume. This chapter presents findings that speak to the deep and lasting impact of intergroup dialogue facilitation on facilitators by examining the ways in which they draw on their experiences in their post-college lives.

Findings presented here come from questionnaires and interviews with 30 former intergroup dialogue facilitators from the Program on Intergroup Relations (IGR) at the University of Michigan. At the time of the study, the facilitators had been out of the program 1.5 to 4.5 years and were working in a variety of fields including agriculture, business, education, health, information, and politics, and/or were in graduate school (see Vasques-Scalera, 1999 for a more detailed discussion of the theoretical framework and research design of this study). Each described the lasting impact the facilitation experience had on their ways of thinking and their actions. While this chapter focuses on the experiences of student facilitators of intergroup dialogue on a college campus, their experiences and insights have important implications for all facilitation programs aimed at social justice.

Empowering Students to Know, to Care, and to Act

While many courses help students to understand social inequality and issues of oppression, a few also nurture students' senses of agency. But as Tatum (1992) warns, "Heightening students' awareness of racism without also developing an awareness of the possibility of change is a prescription for despair. I consider it unethical to do one without the other" (p. 20). In contrast to other models of diversity education, one of the distinctive features of social justice education is its emphasis on transforming not just individuals but the society in which they live (Adams, 1997; Banks, 1991, 1997, 1999; Bell & Griffin, 1997; Hardiman & Jackson, 1997; Rhoads, 1998; Sleeter, 1996; Sleeter & Grant, 1994). In order to be agents of change, students require "knowledge of their social, political, and economic worlds, the skills to influence their environments, and humane values that will help them to participate in social change to help create a more just society and world" (Banks, 1991, p. 125). In other words, we must empower students "to know, to care, and to act" (Banks, 1999). Others have described the "learning" and "democracy" outcomes (Gurin et al., 2002, 2004) necessary to facilitate such change, including perspective taking, complex thinking, analysis, comfort with conflict, and commitment to action (Bromley, 1989; Harrington, 1994; Houser, 1996; Nagda & Zúñiga, 2003; Nagda et al., 2003, 2004; Sleeter & Grant, 1994; Zúñiga et al., 2005).

In discussions of the impact of their facilitation experience on their investment in and commitment to working on social justice issues, the most recurrent theme in facilitators' discussions was having a *way* to do this work. Whereas many described how they had been on the path of working on these issues, almost all said they felt that the program had "pushed them further," given them "a clue," and provided a way of putting their ideals into practice. Whereas many facilitators described having gained theoretical knowledge prior to or during the program (from coursework in Sociology, Women's Studies, Ethnic Studies and American Culture), IGR provided insight and practice in these issues that was missing from their other courses on campus.

IGR provided students with a vision of what is possible, a model for making it happen, and practice in trying it out. Many facilitators commented that they did not know what the issues were before they participated in IGR or how they were personally impacted by them, which constrained their "ability to do anything about it." Other facilitators described ways in which the competencies and tools involved in this work helped them commit themselves further by giving them concrete ways to make dialogue and change happen. Facilitators cited advancement and important competencies in communication, facilitation, and conflict skills including active listening, recognizing and challenging negative group dynamics, "encouraging people to move outside their comfort zones," "dealing with different people and their different emotions," and "moving the conversation." Having tools to communicate across difference, and practice in doing so, helped them move past feeling "stupid" and scared. Still others described how the compassion and commitment others displayed in IGR provided them with a sense of community. For most, the individual changes they experienced in themselves and others provided hope that change was possible. Having invested so much time and energy in the process and being part of an intensely committed group made it difficult for these former students to "shut off" these issues. This has important implications for how these students live their lives beyond college.

> What it left with me. The desire to further explore and work with the material we struggled with. Oppression, Oppression, Oppression! It's everywhere, everyone is connected to it. IGR helped me get closer to why oppression and injustice is so important to me. IGR has set me off on a drive to fight oppression and seek social justice. (Heterosexual biracial man)

As a result of their facilitation experience, former facilitators describe themselves as being more vocal, more active, and more likely to

- become involved;
- engage in conflict;
- raise issues openly;
- counter people's discriminatory comments;
- seek out information;
- articulate social injustices;
- lobby for a more diverse group in power; and
- challenge corporate authority.

> What I learned through IGR and the way it changed my thinking affects every choice and decision I make at least to some degree. From my conversations and interactions with people at the workplace, to occupation choice, to where I want to

live and settle. I try to be conscious of the way race, sex, sexual identity, etc. play out in situations and then take an active role in fighting "isms," not perpetuating discrimination and stereotypes. Because of IGR I am also more likely to seek out information through TV, books, people, etc. about other groups than my own. (Heterosexual White woman)

First in my personal life—IGR changed me, period. It changed the way I think, approach group situations, it gave me leadership skills in working with diversity. I could go on and on. This then affects how I affect any organization I work for or with, and any community I feel belonging towards. (Heterosexual Asian American woman)

These comments illustrate the impact of facilitation on new thinking and behavior. They also illustrate that former facilitators engage in action at both individual and institutional levels.

Changing Individuals

One of the primary ways former facilitators take action in their personal lives is by challenging individual family members, friends, and coworkers.

It's kind of like the idea of a stone thrown in the lake, you know, it has the ripple effect into everything else I think a lot of it has to do with really what you model, and I think if I can model good behavior to other people, at least if I try, I think that can have an impact on them. (Heterosexual Asian American woman)

I am more likely to speak out and openly support people who are not like me yet experience an injustice. I now challenge others especially of my own race/gender/sexual orientation to examine their actions towards others when exercising their power/privilege or stereotyping. (Heterosexual Black woman)

Many facilitators explained that even if their actions are unlikely to change people's opinions or behaviors, they are "doing their part" by modeling alternative ways of acting. From letting people who say discriminatory things know "Hello, I'm listening, and not everyone agrees with you," to being able to share information and "bring it down to a level of experience" (i.e., share their own experiences working around issues or interacting across difference), facilitators offered many examples of the ways they serve as role models to help others understand social injustice.

I had a friend . . . we were taking this [graduate] class, this cultural competence class, and one of the students in the class . . . was saying some pretty strong things about being African American and some of her anger at White people. And my White friend whom I drove home with afterwards was very upset, because she felt like this person doesn't like me and I'm taking this personally and I don't understand. And I had to explain to her, "Well, what do you do to make things different? Because it's not like this comes from nowhere." . . . I had to explain what racism was, that it's something that is about power as well as prejudice, not just pure prejudice. And I had to explain to her what part did she play in that. And she started crying and I got afraid, but I pushed through, I kept going through the whole dialogue with her, and I think she felt better for having the conversation and she didn't resent me for pushing her. . . . I felt like IGR helped me draw from that source. (Gay White man)

The willingness and ability to hang in there when people are emotional or defensive, and understanding the importance of engaging in dialogue rather than lecture or blaming are important facilitation skills. Being able to connect to larger issues of power also reveals the importance of structural thinking and not just rote skill application.

Changing Institutions

IGR strongly impacted my worldview, my belief system concerning how we should all live together. I work for the government, I want to influence public policy—so I want to be on the frontlines of the movement. But if social institutions and structures are to change, the effort needs to have allies in all corners and I'm fully committed to forging partnerships with the kinds of folks I met through IGR. (Heterosexual White man)

The majority of former facilitators described their work environments as either "moderately" or "greatly" diverse, and many indicated that issues of diversity, intergroup relations, or social justice were a "focal point" of their occupations. However, half the facilitators also described their present work/school environments as only "a little" or "not at all" conducive for working on diversity and/or social justice issues. Yet, they also acknowledged how important it is that institutions work on these issues. Many facilitators explained that they wanted their organizations "to acknowledge that work even needs to be done," including "seeing to it that diversity and social justice education be part of every person's job description," "as an integral part of work" rather than "a problem to be fixed." Facilitators also acknowledged that the "profession has to be more diverse," and "people need to acknowledge their own roles" in issues. They also noted the tendency to focus on a single identity rather than the multiple identity issues that can arise even for those organizations with a social justice mission.

We're so preoccupied with poverty and homelessness that we don't talk as much about our skin color, or sexuality, or things like that. It's just kind of assumed that we're all cool with all those things, that they're not barriers to anything ... and I don't think we draw on all these differences as strength for what we're doing, they're like non-issues, kind of. (Heterosexual White man)

Despite barriers, former facilitators shared examples of ways in which they were able to create institutional change. One woman of color who was working in the corporate world (and very frustrated by the lack of diversity or dialogue there) was able to get a sexist policy changed. A White man who was working at a women's clinic (and felt "fortunate" to be able to do so) was able to push his institution to develop a diversity training program that extended beyond gender issues. A White woman who was working on agricultural and trade issues at a nonprofit organization (and was seen as the "squeaky wheel") refused to accept two different positions within her organization unless people of color were also hired, a tactic she called "using access to the privilege I have, to change things."

Former facilitators also shared many examples of the ways in which they draw on their IGR experiences in their professional lives from challenging individual coworkers and colleagues, to choosing multicultural educational materials, to naming negative group and intergroup dynamics in their board-rooms and classrooms, to creating and facilitating diversity workshops and dialogues. IGR may not have impacted facilitators' choices to enter the career they did (though for many it did), but a resounding theme in their narratives was how IGR impacted their attempts to practice their professions in ways that not only provide better service for clients, but attempt to create more multicultural democratic spaces and a more socially just world.

I guess what IGR has helped me to do and to see as important is putting that stuff on the table, is making that a part of the work, and making that a part of the conversation, you know, systems of oppression, racism, sexism, heterosexism, classism, ageism, ableism, all is part of why we have health problems and we have to make those explicit. (Gay Jewish man pursuing graduate studies in public health)

I feel like there should be more kinds of stakeholders or people that actually come from those communities or at least come from similar communities or have similar backgrounds involved in making those decisions.... (Heterosexual White man, congressional aide)

IGR helped me to be very critical to realize why certain people want to learn or why people are learning and why people aren't learning in my classroom, and to be very sensitive to the people that are in my room ... furthering the questions, furthering the critical thinking skills. . . . I mean, it is ingrained in this culture down here that these kids should only go so far. Like, even though these schools want them to graduate, the culture wants particularly Latinos to not succeed. (Gay Latino, secondary education teacher)

These narratives illustrate the powerful impact that IGR has had on the ways in which these former facilitators approach their work in various fields. The kinds of questions they ask and the forms of actions they advocate in their professional work reveal their understanding of larger structural issues and their willingness and ability to work for social justice. The attempts by facilitators who are engaged in teaching work to help others develop critical thinking skills and an understanding of and commitment for social justice reveals the ripple effect of IGR's transformational pedagogy as they impart facilitation and dialogic skills on future generations.

Changing Society

I have provided examples of the ways in which former facilitators now draw on their IGR training/facilitation experiences in their personal and professional lives. But do their actions constitute social change? When I asked facilitators in interviews if they felt like their work was contributing to social change, most were hesitant to say that it was. Most recognized that social change was a "big humungous thing" that involved individual, institutional, structural, and cultural changes about which they were pessimistic. Their words reveal the important understanding that social justice requires more than just their individual efforts; it requires structural change.

> I know we can make a difference because we've had a lot of victories in the work that we've done, that I've been doing. But not the real change that we want to see happen. You know, we don't want a couple of jobs, we want 40,000 jobs, we want training for people. And I want to see that happen. . . . (Heterosexual biracial man)

> And I started to think about that . . . if I'm against racism, how can I not be against classism and heterosexism and all the other stuff, because they're all related and if one doesn't disappear, the other won't, they all need to disappear together in my opinion. (Heterosexual Latina)

> I mean, at the bottom line it makes me feel like my life has some meaning or that it's worthwhile. . . . I think it makes me feel like I have some direction or purpose in life, but it's also about producing some kind of results so that people don't have to be homeless or that people don't have to suffer racial discrimination or economic discrimination. (Heterosexual White man)

Perhaps the most telling indicator of the empowerment facilitators gained through their experiences is that, despite their pessimism, they were committed to trying and remained hopeful, nonetheless, that their work mattered. Many see their personal and professional lives as an opportunity for continual reflection on their social justice work.

> I see it connected to social justice in that part of social justice is looking at ourselves and our everyday lives and what kind of systems we're perpetuating and involved in and what kind of changes we possibly could make. (Bisexual White woman)

One student fittingly described her post-college experience as planting seeds:

> I see it as a seed.... If you start to make people cognizant, maybe the next time they look at a book, or the next time they talk to somebody they're going to look at it with a little more of a critical eye.... But I also know that it takes a lot of recognizing and unlearning. I think it takes a lot, a lot of effort. So, while I'm very positive that I can plant the seed, I guess in terms of like a world view of changing things, it's hard to really say, OK, I know I can really make that difference on this huge scale ... I can hopefully plant the seed in other people, who will plant the seed in other people. (Heterosexual Asian American woman)

Challenges in the Real World

Although many former facilitators make attempts daily in their personal and professional lives to live and work in socially just ways, it is not easy. Facilitators articulated many challenges that mediate and often subvert both their willingness and ability to take action in their everyday lives.

> I would like to be educating. I would like to be living in an area where I am exposed to people of different identities that challenge me and my assumptions/beliefs daily so that I can grow. I would like not to be bombarded with misinformation and white suburban mentality from family, neighborhood, and co-workers. I would like not to be constantly fighting to maintain and be vocal about the fact that social justice is much needed and that we have a long way to go. The strength of maintained institutions, routine life, and money prevents me. (Heterosexual White woman)

> I think I could always do more. Ultimately part of it is that taking time out as we did with the IGR facilitator group, to reflect constantly made me think about almost every action I did, and how it related to diversity. I wish I still had that forum and support to help me truly stay focused. (Heterosexual Asian American woman)

Many of these students have found opportunities to act, and support for acting, on their social justice commitments and characterize themselves as "lucky," "fortunate," and even "privileged" to be able to do so. Many more, however, find themselves struggling to balance work, family, and other commitments with fighting for social justice in the face of a reality that "after you leave the University of Michigan you realize that many people don't give a damn about multicultural issues."

The two biggest challenges that former facilitators repeatedly described were lack of opportunity, and lack of support to do this work "in the real world." Many describe feeling "much more on my own," like "a lone voice" or "an aberration" in their current social and occupational environments, and being labeled as "P.C.," "agitator," or "radical" by family, friends, and colleagues. The recurring theme in these accounts was the ways in which college in general, and IGR in particular, were unlike "the real world" where people lack experience and knowledge, or need a model of how to do this work. In the "real world," facilitators face, on the one hand, "others' disinterest, ignorance of, or intentional unwillingness to discuss and/or understand situations in terms of identity dynamics," and, on the other, the fact that "many of [their] coworkers feel they know everything about racial and other diversity issues and are not open to reflecting on their biases." In general, facilitators are facing the reality that outside the university environment, "it often doesn't seem appropriate to raise questions with people about attitudes involving race, class, gender, etc. People seem to think there's something naïve or hopeless about trying to confront these issues in their lives and the greater world around them." Perhaps the most telling indicator of facilitators' understanding and commitment to social justice is their willingness to continue the work despite the challenges.

Practice Implications

It is important to emphasize the role the intergroup dialogue facilitation program has played and could play in preparing these students for the challenges they face. When I asked facilitators if there were any things the program could have done to better prepare them to continue this work, most described a need for a better transition into the realities of life outside of IGR and academe, such as more experience with people who are not as committed to the issues; more contacts and networks in other groups, organizations, and community action groups; more job listings; and more information on how to facilitate on your own (without a co-facilitator). Their responses indicate the difficulty in finding opportunities to engage in social justice work in the real world.

Intergroup dialogue programs must take these needs and realities seriously if they are to truly empower facilitators to engage in action on the outside. Some ways in which programs could do this include exposing facilitators to more resistant voices (many facilitators felt that the voluntary nature of the intergroup dialogue program often precludes highly resistant students from joining), establishing social justice networks, and providing help with identifying possible careers in which to apply facilitation skills.

While in more recent years the IGR program has moved forward on the issue of action, in the years researched, facilitators often felt at a loss for ways to take action and felt ambiguous over what constituted action. Many facilitators felt "sucky" about what they perceived was a lack of action or "dinky activism." While it is critical to instill in students a sense of the importance of large-scale structural and coalitional action in order to effect change, students who emerge feeling that this is the only type of relevant or useful action are likely to feel disempowered, hopeless, and helpless to effect change.

Another important practice implication concerns the need for providing frameworks for facilitators to understand intergroup relationships in a larger context. Although it is important for students to have an opportunity to talk with one another, if they cannot get beyond the immediacy of the dialogue and their relationships with one another to larger issues of intergroup relationships and social injustice, then these programs will not help facilitators translate what they learn to life outside the dialogues. These programs must nurture facilitators' conceptual competencies as well as their facilitation skills, or else they must recruit facilitators who already have the conceptual understanding of issues. An important theme throughout the quotes in this chapter is facilitators' complex thinking about identity and inequality. They recognize the need to take individual action, but also that true social justice requires addressing complex issues across multiple identities and involves changing institutions and social structures.

Findings presented in this chapter provide evidence of the long-term impact of intergroup dialogue facilitation on facilitators' ability "to know, to care, and to act" (Banks, 1999). Former facilitators continue to draw on their facilitation experiences in both their personal and professional lives in multiple and varied ways. In doing so, they have been able to both act upon their own individual change, and to do so in ways that contribute to the change of other individuals and institutions. While many are skeptical or pessimistic about the likelihood of swift structural change, they are, nevertheless, committed to making social change a reality, personally and professionally. Their narratives illustrate not only the ways in which former facilitators analyze and comprehend social injustice, but how they share those interpretations with others and act on those interpretations to demand more diverse democratic practices in their personal and professional lives.

> Through my dialogue I realized that there's a space for people who, say, come from a similar background as me and want to figure out how to talk about these issues. And then there's also a space for people who consider themselves in the know, or at least socially conscious but still unaware of outside themselves and outside their immediate groups. So I feel like I can fill in some of those spaces . . . unlike when I entered [the university] when I felt like I didn't have a voice and there wasn't a space for me to be able to talk about whatever my issues might be. . . . Now I feel like not only do I have a space, but I could actually even create that space if I needed to, for other people, or for myself whenever I have to. . . . I feel like now I have maybe the confidence, the ability . . . to do it on my own. (Heterosexual Biracial woman)

Programs such as IGR provide a model for education that is individually and socially transformative. Yet helping facilitators create change requires a long-term commitment to nurture and support them after they leave the university and enter a new setting.

References

Adams, M. (1997). Pedagogical frameworks for social justice education. In M. Adams, L. Bell, & P. Griffin (Eds.), *Teaching for diversity and social justice: A sourcebook* (pp. 30–43). New York: Routledge.

Banks, J. (1991). A curriculum for empowerment, action, and change. In C. Sleeter (Ed.), *Empowerment through multicultural education* (pp. 125–142). New York: State University of New York Press.

Banks, J. (1997). *Educating citizens in a multicultural society.* New York: Teachers College Press.

Banks, J. (1999). *An introduction to multicultural education* (2nd ed.). Boston: Allyn & Bacon.

Bell, L., & Griffin, P. (1997). Designing social justice education courses. In M. Adams, L. Bell, & P. Griffin (Eds.), *Teaching for diversity and social justice: A sourcebook* (pp. 44–58). New York: Routledge.

Bromley, H. (1989). Identity politics and critical pedagogy. *Educational Theory, 39*(3), 207–223.

Gurin, P., Dey, E., Hurtado, S., & Gurin, G. (2002). Diversity and higher education: Theory and impact on educational outcomes. *Harvard Educational Review, 72*(3), 330–366.

Gurin, P., Nagda, B., & Lopez, G. (2004). The benefits of diversity in education for democratic citizenship. *Journal of Social Issues, 60*(1), 17–34.

Hardiman, R., & Jackson, B. (1997). Conceptual foundations for social justice courses. In M. Adams, L. Bell, & P. Griffin (Eds.), *Teaching for diversity and social justice: A sourcebook* (pp. 16–29). New York: Routledge.

Harrington, H. (1994). Teaching and knowing. *Journal of Teacher Education, 45*(3), 190–198.

Houser, N. O. (1996). Multicultural education for the dominant culture: Toward the development of a multicultural sense of self. *Urban Education*, (2), 125–148.

Nagda, B., Gurin, P., & Lopez, G. (2003). Transformative pedagogy for democracy and social justice. *Race Ethnicity and Education*, *6*(2), 165–191.

Nagda, B., Kim, C., & Truelove, Y. (2004). Learning about difference, learning with others, learning to transgress. *Journal of Social Issues*, *60*(1), 194–214.

Nagda, B., & Zúñiga, X. (2003). Fostering meaningful racial engagement through intergroup dialogues. *Group Process and Intergroup Relations*, *6*(1), 111–128.

Rhoads, R. (1998). Critical multiculturalism and service learning. *New Directions for Teaching and Learning*, *73*, 39–46.

Sleeter, C. (1996). *Multicultural education as social activism*. Albany: State University of New York Press.

Sleeter, C., & Grant, C. (1994). *Making choices for multicultural education: Five approaches to race, class and gender* (2nd ed.). Upper Saddle River, NJ: Prentice-Hall.

Tatum, B. (1992, Spring). Talking about race, learning about racism: The application of racial identity development theory in the classroom. *Harvard Educational Review*, *62*(1), 1–24.

Vasques-Scalera, C. (1999). *Diversity, democracy, dialogue: Education for critical multicultural citizenship*. Unpublished doctoral dissertation, University of Michigan.

Zúñiga, X., Nagda, B., Sevig, T., Thompson, M., & Dey, E. (1995, November). *Speaking the unspeakable: Student learning outcomes in intergroup dialogues on a college campus*. Paper presented at the Annual Meeting of the Association for the Study of Higher Education, Orlando, FL.

Zúñiga, X., Vasques, C., Nagda, B., & Sevig, T. (1997, March). *Imagining what is possible: Learning processes in inter-race/ethnic dialogues*. Paper presented at the Conference of the American Educational Research Association, Chicago.

Zúñiga, X., Vasques, C., Sevig, T., & Nagda, B. (1996, April). *Tearing down the walls: Peer-facilitated intergroup dialogue processes and experiences*. Paper presented at the Conference of the American Educational Research Association, New York.

Zúñiga, X., Vasques, C., & Thompson, M. (1996, January). *Voices and experiences of diversity: Women of color at the University of Michigan*. Paper presented at the Women of Color in the University and the Community It Serves Conference, Ann Arbor, MI.

Zúñiga, X., Williams, E., & Berger, J. (2005). Action-oriented democratic outcomes: The impact of student involvement with campus diversity. *Journal of College Student Development*, *46*(6), 660–678.

CONTRIBUTOR BIOGRAPHIES

About the Editors

Kelly E. Maxwell, PhD, is a faculty member and codirector of The Program on Intergroup Relations (IGR) at the University of Michigan. She teaches courses on intergroup issues including social identity, privilege, oppression, and power. She also trains students to facilitate intergroup dialogues on campus. Her PhD is from Arizona State University, where she coordinated the university's intergroup dialogues program. Her research interests include dialogue and intergroup relations issues in higher education, particularly related to the critical examination of White privilege and its role in maintaining systems of inequity in education. She regularly presents workshops and consults nationally on intergroup dialogue, facilitation, and social justice issues.

Biren (Ratnesh) A. Nagda, PhD, MSW, MA, is associate professor of social work and director of the Intergroup Dialogue, Education and Action (IDEA) Center at the University of Washington. He received his PhD in social work and psychology from the University of Michigan, Ann Arbor, where he developed the intergroup dialogue model with colleagues. He has received numerous departmental and university-wide teaching awards, including the 2001 University of Washington Distinguished Teaching Award. His recent publications include a book, *Intergroup Dialogue in Higher Education: Meaningful Learning About Social Justice*, and a special issue of the *Journal of Social Issue*, "Reducing Prejudice and Promoting Social Inclusion: Integrating Research, Theory and Practice on Intergroup Relations." He is also a Co-Principal Investigator on the Multi-university Intergroup Dialogue Research Project investigating the effectiveness of intergroup dialogues.

Monita C. Thompson is assistant dean of students and codirector of The Program on Intergroup Relations (IGR) at the University of Michigan. Her work focuses on the training, development, and support of peer educators in skills and techniques of intergroup dialogue facilitation, community building in residence halls, conflict management, and students becoming social change agents. She has published in the areas of intergroup education and social justice in student conduct administration and has presented workshops on intergroup dialogue, social identity awareness, and social justice education.

About the Contributing Authors

Charles Behling, PhD, co-director emeritus of The Program on Intergroup Relations (IGR) at the University of Michigan, was chair of the Psychology Department at Lake Forest College and director of undergraduates, SUNY Buffalo, where he received awards for outstanding teaching. Lake Forest's Award for Promotion of Cultural Diversity is named for him, and he is a recipient of Buffalo's Award for Services to Underrepresented Students.

Barry Checkoway is professor of social work and urban planning, and founding director of the Ginsberg Center for Community Service and Learning at the University of Michigan. With Roger Fisher, he directs the Summer Youth Dialogues on Race and Ethnicity in Metropolitan Detroit.

Mark Chesler is professor emeritus of sociology at the University of Michigan and executive director of Community Resources Limited. He is an activist researcher with primary interests in scholarship and action related to organizational and social change, especially focusing on issues of institutional discrimination and privilege. His most recent work is *Intergroup Dialogue in Higher Education: Meaningful Learning About Social Justice* (with Zúñiga, Nagda and Cytron-Walker).

Keri DeJong, MEd, a doctoral student in Social Justice Education at the University of Massachusetts, Amherst, is an experienced dialogue facilitator, facilitator trainer, consultant, and social justice educator. She organizes, designs, and facilitates workshops and dialogues using a liberatory framework. Her primary research is focused on adultism and youth oppression, critical liberation theory, and intergroup dialogue.

Roger Fisher is an associate director of The Program on Intergroup Relations (IGR) at the University of Michigan. He is a student affairs professional with experience in student activities, leadership education, multiethnic student affairs, and intergroup relations. He is a co-director of the Summer Youth Dialogues on Race and Ethnicity in Metropolitan Detroit and an executive producer of the PBS series *Down Woodward,* based on those dialogues.

Nichola G. Fulmer graduated from the University of Washington, School of Social Work in 2009 with a bachelor of arts in social welfare. Taking her skills and tools from intergroup dialogue, Nichola is looking forward to continuing to support equality for all people.

Patricia Gurin is the Nancy Cantor Distinguished University Professor and Thurnau Professor, Emerita, of Psychology and Women's Studies and Faculty Associate of the Center for African and Afro-American Studies at the University of Michigan. She received her PhD in the Joint Program in Social Psychology at the University of Michigan in 1964. She was the expert witness on the value of diversity for the University of Michigan's defense of its admission policies in *Grutter v. Bollinger* and *Gratz v. Bollinger*. Her work, using both survey and field experiments, has focused on the role of social identity in political behavior and intergroup relations. She is also the PI on the Multi-university Intergroup Dialogue Research Project that investigates the effectiveness of intergroup dialogues.

Tanya Kachwaha, an experienced educator and group facilitator with a Certificate of Advanced Graduate Study in feminist studies and an MEd in social justice education, regularly consults at colleges and universities on issues of oppression and intergroup dialogue facilitation. She writes in the areas of gender and sexism, IGD curriculum and facilitation, and working with youth.

Christina Kelleher became involved with the intergroup dialogue movement as an undergraduate student leader of Sustained Dialogue at the University of Virginia. After graduating in 2006, Christina led the development of the Sustained Dialogue Campus Network, an initiative that supports student-led dialogue programs on campuses nationally, until 2010. As this text goes to print, Christina is preparing to start her MBA at the MIT Sloan School of Management, where she plans to study the use of business tools for social impact.

Ariel Kirkland received her BA in sociology from Occidental College and is a Masters of Human Development candidate at Pacific Oaks College. She is currently researching ways to increase cultural sensitivity and responsibility in pre-service teachers. Ariel serves on the Human Services Commission for the city of Pasadena.

James Knauer, professor emeritus of political science at Lock Haven University of Pennsylvania, had long taught dialogue-based courses when he first encountered National Issues Forum community dialogues in State College, Pennsylvania. After work with the Kettering Foundation, he developed an experimental Internet-based dialogue program with the National Collegiate Honors Council that led to the creation of Democracy Lab.

Joycelyn Landrum-Brown earned her PhD in clinical psychology from Michigan State University. She teaches in educational psychology and is a dialogue facilitator and trainer and the program coordinator overseeing the intergroup dialogue courses offered through Diversity & Social Justice Programs at the University of Illinois at Urbana-Champaign.

Shaquanda D. Lindsey teaches at New Village Leadership Academy in Calabasas, California. Her work emphasizes process-based education that heightens critical consciousness and dynamic thinking. She earned a master's in human development from Pacific Oaks College and holds a California Clear Teaching Credential. She is the founder of Distinguished Learning Group, a progressive educational company.

David J. Martineau, MSW, is a doctoral student in social work at Washington University in St. Louis. He is researching interventions to promote cultural competence and social justice. He conducts antioppression training programs for health-care providers, educators, and young people as program manager of the National Conference of Community and Justice of Metropolitan St. Louis. He and his partner are grateful for the opportunity to parent their preschool son.

Teddy Nemeroff cofounded the first campus Sustained Dialogue initiative as an undergraduate at Princeton University. After graduating in 2001, Teddy worked in management consulting and spent three years in southern Africa, establishing a Sustained Dialogue program to address political and economic conflict. He has a JD from Columbia Law School.

Romina Pacheco, born and raised in Venezuela, is a doctoral student of Curriculum and Instruction with a specialization in critical pedagogies at New Mexico State University. Romina has an MEd in social justice education from the University of Massachusetts, Amherst. Her research interests include critical race theory, liberation theory, feminist theory, and intergroup dialogue.

Priya Parker is a founding member of the Sustained Dialogue Campus Network. She has conducted sustained dialogue workshops in the United

States, India, South Africa, and Zambia. Priya received her BA from the University of Virginia, master's in public policy at the Harvard Kennedy School, and MBA from MIT Sloan.

Jaclyn Rodríguez is professor of psychology and director of Occidental's Intergroup Dialogue Program. Prior to founding the program, she served as the College's associate dean for the social sciences and faculty associate to the Intercultural Community Center. Her intellectual interests in social identity, intergroup relations, and socially just communities form a natural link to intergroup dialogue pedagogy and practice.

Andréa C. Rodríguez-Scheel is a graduate student in the Social Science and Comparative Education PhD program at UCLA. She has served as an intergroup dialogue facilitator as well as research associate for the Intergroup Dialogue Program at Occidental College. Her intellectual interests include diversity in education, the creation of social identities through critical pedagogies, language, peer culture, and Chicana/o schooling experiences.

Michael Spencer is associate dean for educational programs and associate professor of social work at the University of Michigan. His research interests include the well-being of populations of color. He has been a social justice educator for over 18 years and has facilitated dialogues in schools of social work and in community settings since 1997.

Norma Timbang, MSW, is a 2010 graduate of the University of Washington School of Social Work, where she also worked as a Program Associate for the Intergroup Dialogue, Education, and Action (IDEA) Center. She is an organizational development consultant, supporting organizational wellness and sustainable movements toward social justice and social change. She is a queer Filipina activist, life partner, mother, and grandmother.

Thai Hung V. Tran earned his bachelor of arts in social welfare from the University of Washington School of Social Work in 2009. He is planning to become an elementary school teacher and apply his social work lens to promote social justice in the field of public education.

Carolyn Vasques-Scalera, PhD, began her intergroup dialogue work with the Program on Intergroup Relations and Conflict at the University of Michigan. She has worked at both the local and national level on issues of diversity and education. She is currently working with public schools in the Washington, D.C. area to use dialogue to help close the achievement gap.

Thomas E. Walker, PhD, is the associate director of the Center for Multicultural Excellence at the University of Denver. His academic background is in intercultural communication. He has been involved in campus and community dialogue-based diversity and intergroup relations programs for 20 years.

naomi m. warren is a research assistant at the Program on Intergroup Relations at the University of Michigan and program coordinator for Intergroup, a high school–based intergroup dialogue project. naomi has a master's degree in social work and a law degree. Her passion is in facilitating conversations about diversity and social justice.

Kathleen (Wong) Lau, PhD, is an assistant professor in the School of Communication at Western Michigan University specializing in intercultural and gendered communication. She is a professional consultant and trainer on diversity issues in higher education. She is an executive board member of Campus Women Lead, a multicultural women's leadership initiative of the Association of American Colleges and Universities.

Anna M. Yeakley is a consultant, trainer, and professor teaching intergroup dialogue, social justice education, and facilitation training courses to college students in southern California. She earned her doctorate in social work and social psychology from the University of Michigan, with a dissertation focused on intergroup dialogue outcomes and processes.

Ximena Zúñiga is associate professor of education at the University of Massachusetts, Amherst in the social justice concentration. Her background is in social philosophy, critical pedagogy, participatory education, and action research. Before joining the faculty at UMASS Amherst, she directed the Program on Intergroup Relations and Conflict at the University of Michigan, where she participated in developing the intergroup dialogue educational model in higher education. Her current activities include a multi-institutional action research effort aimed at studying the impact of race and gender intergroup dialogues on college students.

INDEX

Multiculturalism on Campus
http://stylus.styluspub.com/Books/BookDetail.aspx?productID=239786
Theory, Models, and Practices for Understanding Diversity and Creating Inclusion
Edited by Michael Cuyjet, Mary F. Howard-Hamilton and Diane L. Cooper

This book presents a comprehensive set of resources to guide students, faculty, and higher education administrators in creating an inclusive environment for under-represented groups on campus. It is intended as a guide to gaining a deeper understanding of the various multicultural groups on college campuses and is intended to be useful to faculty and students in the classroom, as well as to professional staff who desire to increase their understanding of the complexity of the students they serve.

The contributors introduce the reader to the relevant theory, models, practices, and assessment methods to prepare for, and implement, a genuinely multicultural environment. Recognizing that cultural identity is more than a matter of ethnicity and race, they equally address factors such as gender, age, religion, and sexual orientation. In the process, they ask the reader to assess his or her own levels of multicultural sensitivity, awareness, and competence.

Exposing the "Culture of Arrogance" in the Academy
http://stylus.styluspub.com/Books/BookDetail.aspx?productID=92621
A Blueprint for Increasing Black Faculty Satisfaction in Higher Education
Gail L. Thompson and Angela C. Louque

There generally remains a gulf between the way most Black faculty perceive the racial climate at their institutions and the recognition by non-Black faculty and administrators that there are problems and that these perceptions have merit. This book is intended to promote a productive dialogue.

22883 Quicksilver Drive
Sterling, VA 20166-2102

Subscribe to our e-mail alerts: www.Styluspub.com

Also available from Stylus

Journal Keeping
http://stylus.styluspub.com/Books/BookDetail.aspx?productID=
138778
How to Use Reflective Writing for Learning, Teaching, Professional Insight and Positive Change
Dannelle D. Stevens and Joanne E. Cooper

One of the most powerful ways to learn, reflect, and make sense of our lives is through journal keeping.

This book presents the potential uses and benefits of journals for personal and professional development—particularly for those in academic life; and demonstrates journals' potential to foster college students' learning, fluency and voice, and creative thinking.

"An impressively complete and well organized exploration of the uses of journal writing. It provides rich backing for John Dewey's key insight, namely that it's not experience that makes us learn, it's reflection on experience."—**Peter Elbow**, *author of* Writing with Power, *and* Everyone Can Write, *and Professor Emeritus, University of Massachusetts, Amherst*

Ethnicity in College
http://stylus.styluspub.com/Books/BookDetail.aspx?productID=
208207
Advancing Theory and Improving Diversity Practices on Campus
Anna M. Ortiz and Silvia J. Santos

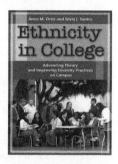

"By studying the experiences of 120 Southern California college students, researchers Ortiz and Santos take an in-depth look at the role college plays in ethnic identity development. Their book provides a close look at the divergent developmental paths traversed by students of different ethnicities, and the effect college has on students' understanding of their ethnicity. With smart analysis and helpful suggestions for maximizing the positive effects of campus diversity, the volume is a significant contribution to the literature on identity, diversity, and education." —**Diversity & Democracy** *(AAC&U)*

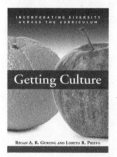

Getting Culture
http://stylus.styluspub.com/Books/BookDetail.aspx?productID=
171940
Incorporating Diversity Across the Curriculum
Edited by Regan A. R. Gurung and Loreto R. Prieto

"Provides a set of 'best practices' for approaching the pedagogical challenges of teaching diversity . . . Recommended."—**Choice**

"This volume's editors have compiled a set of wide-ranging tools for teaching about diversity among diverse student populations. Articles cover an array of topics, including general approaches to diversity education, specific exercises within and across disciplines, and strategies for coping with the stresses of teaching controversial topics. The collection offers guidance that is particularly valuable for those just beginning to incorporate diversity in the classroom – and is pertinent to veteran teachers as well."—**Diversity & Democracy** *(AAC&U)*